UNLOCKING THE RED CLOSET

Unlocking the Red Closet

Gay Male Sex Workers in China

Eileen Yuk-ha Tsang

NEW YORK UNIVERSITY PRESS
New York

NEW YORK UNIVERSITY PRESS
New York
www.nyupress.org

© 2025 by New York University
All rights reserved

Library of Congress Cataloging-in-Publication Data
Names: Tsang, Eileen Yuk-Ha, author.
Title: Unlocking the red closet : gay male sex workers in China / Eileen Yuk-ha Tsang.
Description: New York : New York University Press, [2025] | Includes bibliographical
 references and index.
Identifiers: LCCN 2024040436 (print) | LCCN 2024040437 (ebook) | ISBN 9781479821174
 (hardback ; alk. paper) | ISBN 9781479821228 (paperback ; alk. paper) |
 ISBN 9781479821235 (ebook) | ISBN 9781479821242 (ebook other)
Subjects: LCSH: Male prostitutes–China. | Homophobia–China. | Gay people–China.
Classification: LCC HQ119.4.C6 T73 2025 (print) | LCC HQ119.4.C6 (ebook) | DDC
 306.740811/0951–dc23/eng/20250210
LC record available at https://lccn.loc.gov/2024040436
LC ebook record available at https://lccn.loc.gov/2024040437

This book is printed on acid-free paper, and its binding materials are chosen for strength and durability. We strive to use environmentally responsible suppliers and materials to the greatest extent possible in publishing our books.

The manufacturer's authorized representative in the EU for product safety is Mare Nostrum Group B.V., Mauritskade 21D, 1091 GC Amsterdam, The Netherlands.
Email: gpsr@mare-nostrum.co.uk.

Manufactured in the United States of America

10 9 8 7 6 5 4 3 2 1

Also available as an ebook

CONTENTS

Introduction: Conceptualizing Necropolitics of Social Death   1

1. Welcome to Pistachio: An Ethnographic Journey of Sex Work in North China   29

2. China's Male Commercial Sex Industry: Rural-to-Urban Migration   49

3. "I Don't Want to Hurt an Innocent Country Girl, So I'll Marry a Lesbian": Male Sex Workers, Parents' Expectations, and Face   74

4. A Phoenix Rising from the Ashes: China's *Tongqi*, Marriage Fraud, and Resistance   99

5. "Buying Sex Makes Me Sky-High": Relationship between Male Sex Workers and Male/Female Clients   119

6. Male Sex Workers and Stigma: The Queer Body, Necropolitics, and the Medical System   143

7. A Sisterhood of Hope: How China's Transgender Sex Workers Cope with Intimate Partner Violence   167

Conclusion: Life after Sex Work   189

Acknowledgments   205

Bibliography   207

Index   221

About the Author   233

Introduction

Conceptualizing Necropolitics of Social Death

China's Historical Relationship with Lesbian and Gay Culture

With its rich history spanning several millennia, Chinese culture has seen attitudes to sexuality fluctuate over time. The narrative of the LGBTQ+ community in China is both intricate and multifaceted, extending back thousands of years. Unlike European and European-ruled societies where Christianity formed the basis of staunch anti-LGBTQ+ laws until recent times, LGBTQ+ identities were historically met with less hostility in Chinese societies. LGBTQ+ communities have been documented in China since ancient times, with their acceptance varying among different social classes and sexes. Several early Chinese emperors are speculated to have had homosexual relationships alongside heterosexual ones.

During the Zhou dynasty (1046 BCE–256 BCE), LGBTQ+ communities openly thrived across every social stratum, from nobility and the upper classes to the middle and working classes. A well-known anecdote from this era tells of Duke Ling of Wei and his court official Mi Zixia sharing a peach. This story illuminates the history of same-sex relationships in ancient China. The Han Dynasty (206 BCE–220 CE) was known for its bisexual emperors. Historical records indicate several accounts of homosexual activity practiced by many princes and members of the royal family who broke from heteronormative values. One notable story involves Emperor Ai and his male staff member Dong Xian, who were sleeping together on a couch. When Emperor Ai rose early one morning for a meeting, he found that his sleeve had become caught beneath Dong Xian, still asleep beside him. Rather than disturb his partner, the emperor severed his sleeve before slipping out of bed.

This act of consideration and intimacy between the two men intrigued many and shed light on the history of same-sex relationships in ancient China.

In modern China, the establishment of the People's Republic of China (PRC) in 1949 under Mao Zedong marked some of the darkest periods for queer sexuality in China. During Mao's rule, non-heteronormative sexuality was considered a form of Western "spiritual pollution," and those identified as LGBTQ+ faced criticism, marginalization, and violence. Some were even beaten to death. Admitting to being gay resulted in forced trips to re-education camps and intense interrogation. During the decade-long disaster known as the Cultural Revolution (1966–76), the LGBTQ+ community was portrayed as a threat to China's progress, and gay men were depicted as weights dragging China backward. The law classified gays as "black enemies" (*heiwulei* 黑五类). It wasn't until 1997 that LGBTQ+ communities were decriminalized, and the Chinese government gradually loosened its control and policing of same-sex relationships after 2000. Thus, understanding the historical context of LGBTQ+ communities in China provides a crucial backdrop for examining the contemporary experiences of gay sex workers and *tongqi* (cisgender heterosexual women married to gay men). This historical perspective illuminates the deep-seated societal norms and legal biases that these marginalized groups continue to navigate in present-day China.

Opposition to queers did not become firmly entrenched in China until the nineteenth and twentieth centuries, mainly due to the Westernization efforts of the late Qing Dynasty and the early Republic of China. Transitioning to the topic of sex work in China, it is noteworthy that China was once colloquially referred to as the "brothel of Asia" due to the widespread prevalence of prostitution in the nineteenth and twentieth centuries. The rapid expansion of factories, migration, and refugees in Shanghai led to a swift proliferation of gangs and prostitution throughout the city. This resulted in the exploitation of young women and children, sex trafficking, and imperialist policies. Despite the Chinese Communist Party's efforts to eradicate prostitution from mainland China by the early 1960s, prostitution has now developed to such an extent that it constitutes an industry involving a significant number of people and producing a substantial economic output.

Despite the decriminalization of the LGBTQ+ community, they continue to face numerous issues like stigma, discrimination, and even violence. For male sex workers (hereafter, MSWs or MSW), there are significant risks due to their proximity to organized crime members, illicit drugs, and violence. There are also substantial public health issues, particularly about risks associated with the transmission and infection of sexually transmitted diseases such as HIV. A lesser-known but significant area of concern arises when an MSW marries a heterosexual woman to produce a child and alleviate familial and social pressures. These women, commonly referred to as *tongqi* (a term perceived to be more neutral than the English literal translation of "homowives"), face a host of severe social and psychological issues, including physical domestic violence. Thus, understanding the historical context of the LGBTQ+ community and sex work in China provides a crucial backdrop for examining the contemporary experiences of gay sex workers and *tongqi*. This historical perspective illuminates the deep-seated societal norms and legal biases that these marginalized groups continue to navigate in present-day China (Tsang 2021a).

Since the early 2000s, MSWs have gained significant attention from sociologists. In the Chinese context, they are called "money boys," "technicians" (*jishi* 技师), or "little boys" (*xiaodi* 小弟) (Kong 2017). The MSW engages in sexual activity primarily with other men for a fee. It is sex work for a living. As a sociological public health issue, MSWs have attracted considerable attention from policymakers, public health workers, and law enforcement professionals (Kong 2009, 2012b).

The term *queer* is multifaceted, having evolved over time and carrying various connotations within the context of gender, sexuality, and identity. This scholarly examination delves into its nuanced dimensions from a sociological perspective, particularly emphasizing its significance for the LGBTQ+ community. *Queer* serves as an encompassing term for those who deviate from heterosexual norms or cisgender identities. From a sociological perspective, queer contests the dominant binary framework of sexuality and gender. It disrupts conventional understandings of sexual orientation and identity, emphasizing fluidity, diversity, and nonconformity (Jagose 1996). Rather than adhering to fixed categories, queer invites exploration and celebration of difference (Butler 1990). It encompasses a broad spectrum of experiences, including same-sex attraction, nonbinary gender identities, and alternative sexual practices. As an identity category, queer provides a space for individuals to resist normative labels. It rejects the constraints of rigid definitions and allows for self-determination. Some individuals proudly identify as queer, finding empowerment in its inclusivity. Sociologist Jane Ward (2015) challenged the long-held assumption that sexual orientation is inherent and unavoidable for males. While this assumption was long used to discourage same-sex experimentation, Ward argued that for straight white men, same-sex activity is a part of male sexuality regardless of orientation. Ward noted that "straightness" primarily reflects the dominant culture, particularly the valuing of heteronormativity and a celebration of what is labeled as normal. By challenging these cultural boundaries, Ward's work opens up new possibilities for understanding and exploring diverse sexualities, including those of gay migrant sex workers in China.

LGBTQ+ communities in China often face systemic discrimination, which is particularly severe within families and social services. The Chinese government's increasing push for conformity and traditional values has further marginalized LGBTQ+ communities. Advocates have been arrested and questioned by police, and queer groups have faced closure. LGBTQ+ nongovernmental organizations (NGOs), activists, and scholars continue to work to promote acceptance and awareness, provide social services, and conduct queer studies in higher education institutions. Therefore, in this book, queer transcends its status as a mere adjective; it embodies a complex interplay of identity, resistance, and theoretical inquiry. From a sociological perspective, understanding queer involves acknowledging its historical context, respecting individual preferences, and recognizing its potential for transformative change within the LGBTQ+ community.

It is essential to decouple queer from sex work. Sex work is illegal and associated with human trafficking and violence. Queer is more complicated and involves stigmatization by families and friends, particularly in rural areas. The government has decriminalized being gay, but the Chinese government openly considers being gay inappropriate and a destabilizing threat to Chinese society. Combining queer with sex work is like adding stigmas together. In terms of the illegality of sex work, it is important to remember that the Chinese legal system is opaque by Western standards. Trials are not open to the public, and law enforcement regarding sex work is, at best, arbitrary. Female sex workers are routinely arrested on the street or in clubs, but rarely does anyone go before a judge. More commonly, they will pay a fine and spend a night in jail. Female sex workers say it is common for police to extort bribes or demand free sex before releasing them (Tsang 2019a). For MSWs, the story is different. Paying bribes is still the norm, but beatings by police are far more common than demands for free sex. This disparity between the treatment of females and the treatment of male sex workers by police underscores the complexity of being queer in China.

Although same-sex relationships now appear to be gaining acceptance, if not outright support, in many urban areas in China, LGBTQ+ communities continue to face obstacles when reporting intimate partner violence (IPV) to law enforcement. These challenges include a lack of trust, stereotyping, inadequate training, and fear of humiliation. Instances of humiliation may involve misgendering, insensitive remarks, and public shaming. That thinking persists in many places, particularly in rural areas and among older populations. Younger demographic groups have shown more openness and acceptance about being queer. Every year, on December 1, the Chinese government releases an updated report on population demographics. While the number of people identifying as gay men and lesbian women continually increases, there are still numerous accounts of violence and discrimination against them (Kong 2012a). Improving cultural competency, creating safe reporting spaces, and fostering community partnerships are essential for better support and equitable treatment of IPV survivors. There is still a long way to go.

An Ethnographers Journey Begins in Birmingham

My interest in the growing number of stakeholder groups involved with MSWs—*tongqi*, medical doctors, NGO directors, and even staff workers in gay bars—began with my graduate experiences at the University of Birmingham in England. There, I first learned that research is primarily about discovering new knowledge (Gilbert 1993, 33) and that qualitative research involves peeling away layers of judgments and stereotyping so one can know each informant as a unique individual. I evolved through the research process as ideas emerged to take the work in unexpected directions. For example, one afternoon, I observed one informant briefly interact with another man from across the bar where I was working. From the outside, the conversation appeared to be cordial and formal. However, after the interaction, he sat at the bar before me and wept because that polite conversation had marked the end of their relationship. On the first leg of my research journey in Tianjin, North China, in May 2015, I had crude ideas about what my research would involve. My friend Lennon helped me begin to learn more about MSWs through direct and sincere interactions. My interactions with stakeholder groups allowed me to gain a better understanding of the complex social and cultural dynamics surrounding MSWs in China. Although I did not know it at the time, my two best friends in Birmingham were gay men. I had recently ended a relationship in Hong Kong and moved to England to start my sociology doctoral studies. I went to a local bar to meet some classmates, and that is where I met Peter. He caught my attention right away because he was tall, muscular, and strikingly handsome. After talking to him, I discovered that he was also intelligent and had a wonderful sense of humor. Peter was a doctoral candidate majoring in law at the University of Oxford, and I felt we had remarkable chemistry. Peter and I both lived in Harborne, a small town near the University of Birmingham, but he often had to stay in Oxford to work on his PhD. One night, he suggested I move into his spare room and stay rent free. I was not sure of the intentions at first, but he reassured me that it was a sincere offer to help. Not long after I moved in, he confided to me that he was gay, clarifying our relationship once and for all. The time I stayed with him was wonderfully positive. We had lots of good times, and I would often cook for his parents, who loved authentic Chinese food.

Peter's lived experiences as a gay man piqued my academic curiosity about the LGBTQ+ community. His stories gave me valuable knowledge and understanding of life in the LGBTQ+ community, laying the foundation for my three-year-long research in North China. I dedicate this book to Peter for his generosity and for being a key influence in my research. Without his kindness, my journey would have been much more difficult.

My Introduction to Gay Bar Culture in Tianjin

Over the last thirty years, China has undergone significant changes, moving from an agricultural society to rapidly becoming the world's second-largest economy. However, along with the economic, political, and ideological changes during these turbulent years, there have been fundamental transformations in Chinese values, morals, and worldviews. Consequently, these transformations have engendered a degree of comprehension and cognizance regarding the mental and physical health of LGBTQ+ communities. Despite these changes, China has maintained a heteronormative gender order where non-normative sexuality is viewed as immoral "hooliganism." China has publicly upheld this perspective from the twentieth century into the twenty-first.

Negative views toward non-normative sexuality are prevalent throughout China. Therefore, pseudonyms are used for the individuals mentioned in this book. For example, during my first trip to Tianjin, Lennon (pseudonym) took me to a sauna club to visit some MSWs. I felt some concern that we might encounter the police, which could lead to detainment or worse. In the context of ethnographic fieldwork, Paul Rabinow (2007) has addressed the ethics of, for example, his visiting a prostitute during his research in Morocco. However, face-to-face interactions provide valuable insights into the complexities of cultural practices and power dynamics. Limiting my interactions to conversations and what I might observe in public spaces would remove me from being directly complicit in the illegal activities that might be going on around me. Acknowledging these nuances is essential for scholarly discourse and understanding the challenges inherent in ethnographic research. Therefore, in this book, I complied with ethical review procedures, safety and ethical issues, and the boundaries of participant observation. Still, many questions ran through my mind as we slowly drove through the city streets in Lennon's car. How would these men respond to me? Would they be hostile or ignore me? How would I react to them—would I be distant and cold—or would we feel an immediate bond and enjoy each other's company? I was open to the outcome and hoped to gain something helpful for my research.

When we arrived at the spa and parked, I noticed that the grounds were well maintained and the building was in good condition. Since it was early afternoon, we did not see any patrons and encountered only one or two staff as we entered through the front door and walked down a hallway to an open area in the center of the spa. There, I was surprised to see four naked men playing mahjong. I tried to mask my surprise and behaved like they were fully clothed, focusing on maintaining eye contact and studying their faces. Lennon introduced me to the men, and we pulled up chairs to sit, talk, and observe while they played.

The youngest looked to be around twenty years old and had striking, model-like features. His body was hairless except for the stylish boyband haircut, which made him appear dangerously young. Seated to his left was a slightly older man puffing on an e-cigarette. His thin mustache made his large ears even more pronounced. He was not conventionally handsome, but he was thin and sculpted. I noticed that his legs were uncomfortably apart, and I wondered if it was to feed his ego or shock me with his nudity. Next to him, the older, forty-ish man was of average build with thinning hair but a surprisingly muscular body. The rings on his hand conveyed success and a touch of vanity. However, all the attention was on the most prominent player, a loud thirty-something, short and stocky with thinning hair dyed jet black. The other three referred to him affectionately as Fatty. He seemed to be the leader, regaling the others with stories and setting the pace for each round of mahjong.

Lennon did most of the talking, engaging in light barter and keeping the mood casual. He talked the most with Fatty, asking about the latest news or gossip he had missed. I mostly sat quietly and observed. Between rounds, the players touched and sometimes kissed each other. Perhaps it was because they felt they were in a safe space to show physical affection openly. Or maybe it was done for shock value to see how I would react. Even though Fatty seemed to win most of the rounds, they were passing the time and waiting for their clients to arrive for sex services. This was confirmed when the first client came, and the game suddenly ended. We abruptly said our goodbyes and went our separate ways.

As Lennon and I walked toward the entrance, we passed the private room area covered and semi-hidden by a gigantic Guan Gong poster. Guan Gong (關公) is the traditional hero-looking warlord who symbolizes justice and integrity and is known for destroying ghosts and all forms of evil. A Guan Gong statue is believed to protect an establishment from corruption and to bring prosperity. Large posters of Mao Zedong, known as the Great Helmsman and symbolizing justice and integrity, are similarly used as a public facade to hide the true nature of a business and to conceal private rooms. It is common to see posters of Guan Gong and Chairman Mao (毛主席) in gay bars around Tianjin.

In China, LGBTQ+ communities are both shunned and admired. They are discouraged in official circles, but among younger crowds, and especially in the underground dance clubs throughout China, being gay is bold and assertive. However, this dynamic makes it difficult for outsiders to gain access to the community, as one must prove that one is not a spy or an infiltrator or working on behalf of the government. Under President Xi Jinping, the government has launched campaigns to crack down on gay-friendly social media and to generally discourage LGBTQ+ communities from becoming more visible.

The core issue addressed in this book is the marginalization of LGBTQ+ individuals from rural backgrounds in China. The government views these populations as unnatural or dangerous, requiring biopolitical surveillance and management. Biopolitics is a concept that originated with the French philosopher Michel Foucault to explain how liberal democracies control populations by regulating their biological and social lives. Foucault argued that power was diffused throughout all social strata, from the bottom up as much as from the top down. However, governments are the ultimate deciders of which social policies are to be implemented, and invariably, some groups are favored over others. Biopolitical measures that control specific at-risk populations are commonly justified by emphasizing the need to protect the majority's values and way of life. In Xi Jinping's China, biopolitical measures are used to police homosexuals—especially effeminate gay men—who are seen as corrupting the moral culture of China. This governing view is where the line between biopolitics and necropolitics becomes blurred. Through government eyes, viewing gay and bisexual men simply as potential HIV carriers justifies efforts to marginalize and control them.

In China, when an individual contracts HIV, the hospital will demand information on how the person contracted it. If the transmission occurred through same-sex relationships and activity, the particular person would face an extension of biopolitical control termed *necropolitics*. According to Achille Mbembe (2003), necropolitics is the collective stigma that creates an environment in which an individual or community is marginalized, shunned, and made to feel less than human. Necropolitics initially referred to individuals desperately seeking political asylum to escape the imminent threat of physical death. This concept deals with matters of life and death in the context of political power wielded against marginalized groups. But a recontextualization of necropolitics, the necropolitics of social death, allows for a more nuanced understanding of the experiences of the *tongqi* and MSWs. The necropolitics of social death acknowledges their struggles and accurately captures the crucial issue for forming effective policies and interventions. China's population has considerable racial differences and significant ethnic diversity. This diversity can lead to different experiences and forms of oppression, even within the same overarching Chinese identity. For instance, MSWs and *tongqi* from minority ethnic groups may face additional challenges due to their ethnicity, further compounding their struggles.

Therefore, the necropolitics of social death in this context reflects the struggles of being an MSW or a *tongqi* and how they navigate these identities within a society that does not fully accept them. This intersectionality of oppression—being queer, potentially from a minority ethnic group, in a heteronormative society—adds another layer to their experiences of social death.

My introduction to and awareness of the biopolitical apparatuses that feed gay stigma in China began with my friend Lennon. Lennon is a fifty-something Hong Kong Chinese man I met years ago through a college classmate. We have maintained contact over the years, and he has become a leader in gay issues in China. Despite his openness about his sexuality, he is so well-connected that no one, not even the police, harasses him about his sexual orientation. Lennon has worked with NGOs in China for over a decade and has extensive connections throughout the country, likely numbering in the hundreds. He is well known in the north but enjoys high status in large southern cities like Hong Kong. Lennon introduced me to other contacts who in turn allowed me to work and meet several additional contacts. Lennon exemplifies the urban gay elite in China, raising the issue of homonormativity. Duggan (2002) noted that the terms *homonormative* and *heteronormative* operate in complementary ways. Heteronormativity is an ideology often mentioned in gender and women's studies that describes the dominant culture and the pressure on individuals to conform to the norms of that culture. In most societies, heterosexual populations are dominant over homosexual populations, and institutions and social structures reinforce this dominance. Rather than challenge the status quo, homonormativity can instead demobilize gay culture, anchoring it in domesticity and consumption and reinforcing traditional norms and values (Duggan 2002). In academic writing, heteronormativity suggests a gender binary that follows conventional and cultural norms in society; heteronormativity aligns people with biological sex, sexuality, gender identity, and gender roles. But heteronormativity is also linked to heterosexism and homophobia (Rich 1980), which involves the preference for opposite-sex relationships and the aversion to same-sex relationships. As such, heteronormative men and women hold class standing and represent socially sanctioned examples of proper model citizens.

Similarly, particular sets of gay men and women may become LGBTQ+ communities and be deemed models for others to follow. In China, upper-middle-class LGBTQ+ communities are perceived as homonormative. Several interviewees from rural areas described experiences where homonormative urban gay elites looked down on them.

After completing my studies and embarking on my research career, I had the chance to meet Lennon again at an NGO conference in Hong Kong. After a session, I met him in a hallway and agreed to have tea at a nearby café. Our conversation flowed naturally as we caught up on recent developments and shared old memories. He was effusive, as usual. Part of his charm is his open affection—he loves to hug and greet friends with a kiss on the cheek. We talked about my research interests, and I shared my thoughts about sex workers and marginalized communities. He sat silent for a moment and then asked me some probing questions about my thoughts regarding LGBTQ+ communities in Hong Kong. As Lennon began describing the differences between Hong Kong and mainland China, I realized how interested I was in discovering more. A plan quickly took shape, and we agreed that he would take me to a bar in China catering to the gay community. We arrived in Tianjin one week later and immediately took a taxi to the club. Upon arriving, I took the next step and asked Lennon if I could work as a bartender to observe and get to know people there. Lennon nodded, smiled, and said, "Be careful."

Pistachio Bar

Although there are some low-end and middle-class gay clubs, I chose to spend most of my time in the high-end bars during my fieldwork.

Pistachio (a pseudonym) is located near the Haihe River in downtown Tianjin, situated between traditional old Chinese-style buildings, modern skyscrapers, and luxurious boutiques. It embodies the typical fusion of Eastern and Western styles, with Chinese pagodas flanked by the bar street, which lies in the heart of Tianjin. It is a high-end bar that revels in its glorious stereotype: high ceilings, plush carpet, gaudy drapes, overstuffed furniture, and erotic artwork tastefully displayed. The decor is reminiscent of luxury hotels in Paris, London, or New York. But the carefree atmosphere makes it distinctly unique.

My first visit to Pistachio was in May 2015, and during that first week, I was walking around on the second floor when I ducked into a washroom. As I exited and headed toward a nearby elevator, I stumbled upon two young men in an alcove off the hallway, presumably a sex worker and a client in the middle of a transaction. I was so startled that I just stopped and stared, unsure how to react. What does one say in this situation? I decided to nod and shuffled off to the elevator quietly.

Club Pistachio is typically open from around 3 p.m. until 7 a.m., with nightly shows from 9 p.m. to midnight. These shows can range from drag performances, striptease, simulated sex, and even Chinese opera. The club has a regular group of clients, but it also attracts new customers through advertising and word of mouth. It has a good reputation and rarely runs into trouble with the police. During my four-month stint, I became acquainted with several men who worked there. Some even became good friends with whom I still correspond.

Tianjin, like many metropolises throughout China, is a wonderland of modern skyscrapers and has put many counterpart cities around the world to shame. Pistachio reflects this blend of modern and historic architecture. The exterior might feature sleek lines and glass facades characteristic of contemporary design, while the interior could pay homage to the city's rich history with intricate woodwork, antique furnishings, and traditional Chinese motifs. The bar area would likely be a focal point, with high ceilings and strategically placed lighting to create a sense of spaciousness and luxury. Plush seating, rich draperies, and high-end finishes would add to the opulent feel of the space. There was a backlit wall showcasing an array of premium liquors. Art installations, perhaps by local artists, could adorn the walls, adding a touch of cultural relevance and interest. State-of-the-art sound and lighting systems would ensure a vibrant atmosphere for patrons to enjoy their evening.

The author's hand-written notes from that first night convey the excitement and allure of the club experience:

The Pistachio is alive with a pulsating rhythm that reverberates through the room, a seductive beat that invites patrons to lose themselves in the music. Amidst this, the MSWs move with effortless grace, their bodies swaying in time with the rhythm, a dance that is as much a part of their job as the expertly crafted drinks. Pistachio is electric, charged with anticipation and excitement. The soft glow of the lights, the clink of glasses, the murmur of conversation, and the occasional burst of laughter create a symphony of sound that is both comforting and exhilarating. The air is filled with a mix of enticing aromas—the tang of citrus, the sweetness of fruit, the warmth of whiskey, and the rich scent of coffee.

The grand ballroom is a huge, high-ceilinged space where a few hundred at a time gather to sit, saunter, or stare at the patrons congregating along the performing stage area. A high-definition video wall backs the stage, darkened to encourage dancing as the loud stereo speakers thump incessantly while laser lights and flashing strobes set the mood. The MSWs present a captivating spectacle. They are standing tall at over six feet with well-defined muscles that hint at countless hours spent in the gym. For example, Mamasan Yang greets regular patrons by name, remembering their favorite drinks and personal anecdotes they have shared. His smile is genuine, and his demeanor is warm and inviting. Newcomers are welcomed with the same open-hearted friendliness, quickly feeling part of the bar's community. As he dances behind the bar, his movements are fluid, a captivating performance that draws the eyes of the patrons. He flips bottles with an acrobat's precision, pours drinks with a dancer's grace, and presents each cocktail with a flourish that is met with appreciative applause.

Jinmin (twenty-three) is especially charming. He dressed in a crisp, white button-down shirt, the top two buttons undone, revealing a hint of his toned chest. The shirt is tucked into a pair of sleek, black trousers that fit him like a glove, highlighting his strong, muscular legs. A thin, black leather belt encircles his narrow waist, and polished black shoes complete the ensemble, reflecting the soft glow of the bar lights. His costume, a nod to the bar's upscale ambiance, is a classic black vest worn over the shirt. The vest fits snugly, further emphasizing his muscular torso. A silver pocket watch is attached to the vest, symbolizing his punctuality and attention to detail. His biceps, visible as he expertly mixes cocktails, are impressive, a result of both his physical training and the demands of his job. His muscular forearms moved with a grace and precision that spoke volumes about his expertise.

Mamasan Yang is more than just a figure behind the counter. He is a performer, a confidant, and a papa to all the MSWs. His presence contributes to the vibrant atmosphere, making each night at the bar an unforgettable experience. His charm, skill, and charisma make him a beloved figure among the patrons, a shining star in the constellation of Pistachio's charm.

At 9 p.m., a voice echoes through the dimly lit club, announcing that the show is about to begin. There is a smattering of applause as the music gets noticeably louder. A fog machine kicks in, adding to the ambiance as the first performer struts to the edge of the stage. He is tall, dark, and well built, with a full head of hair and youthful features marked by perfect teeth. He smiles broadly and waves before getting into character. The show is an elaborately choreographed striptease perfectly synced with the pulsating soundtrack. The performer removes his shirt, revealing a tight stomach, broad shoulders, and biceps, then removes his tear-away pants to reveal his red G-string.

Around the fourth performer, I felt I had reached my limit. As a handsome young man stripped completely naked and got on all fours while another man came up behind him and mimicked a sexual act, I found myself growing increasingly bored. Thankfully, Lennon sensed my restlessness and said, "Come with me; I want to show you something." I was curious but also unsure of what he had planned. We walked toward the right side of the stage and passed through a side door into a reasonably well-lit corridor. "This way," he pointed, "are the VIP rooms." Suddenly, he stopped and turned to the door to his left. He pushed it open and turned on the light.

As we stepped into the VIP room, I was taken aback by its ostentatiousness. The reddish lighting gave it a seedy vibe, but it was nonetheless impressive. There was a bar, refrigerator, big screen TV for karaoke, a carpeted sitting area, and a parquet-floor dance area. The sitting-area furniture was faux-fur and modular. Lennon interrupted my thoughts by touching my shoulder. "This is the most important part of the tour," he said as we exited the room. He turned left again and continued down the corridor. A dim red sign read "NO EXIT 不准进入". Lennon walked directly under the sign and reached behind a black drape. He turned to me and smiled proudly. "In an emergency, VIPs are taken care of first." Whatever he pushed—a button, latch, or key—a narrow door opened to a darkened alley no more than thirty meters from the main road. "If there was a raid, the VIPs could get out in less than a minute. Over there are food stalls and noodle shops. It's easy to blend in, get lost, and not be found by anyone!"

In the context of Pistachio, the behaviors and appearances of MSWs are shaped by a complex interplay of cultural and societal factors. For instance, pressures to adhere to specific beauty standards, the aspiration to articulate one's identity, or the necessity to navigate societal norms and expectations can all contribute in China. The behaviors exhibited by individuals in these settings are not merely for shock value. Instead, they can be interpreted as a form of self-expression, a means to negotiate their identities within a society that may not fully acknowledge them. It is also a response to the dynamics of the spaces they inhabit, where specific behaviors might be encouraged or expected. The social and cultural factors influencing the behavior and appearance of gay and queer individuals in high-end bars in Tianjin, are multifaceted and intricate. The prevailing culture does not support queer identities and upholds heteronormativity. This can lead to a unique form of self-expression within these spaces, where LGBTQ+ communities may feel more liberated to express their identities. The ambiance of the bar, typically designed to be relaxed, liberal, and fashionable, contributes to this sense of freedom. This is one reason why patrons may feel more uninhibited in these establishments.

Queer Theories in Post-reform China

This book examines queer communities, gay sex workers and their clients, and expressions of queerness in China, drawing from a range of literature, including Western scholarship and the emerging field called queer Sinophone studies, which examines queerness from a Chinese perspective. While much of this literature focuses on the diaspora of

Chinese gay men and lesbians, bisexuals, and transgender who live, work, and thrive outside of their birth nation, studies of queerness inside China have also emerged.

This book seeks to contribute to this emerging field by examining how queerness is expressed and experienced in China and exploring the social, cultural, and political factors shaping these experiences. Another factor to consider is the assumption that economic freedom automatically leads to greater social freedom, which is a core belief of neoliberalism. In the case of China, the country's economic growth and prosperity may be expected to lead to greater acceptance of nonbinary identities and same-sex relationships. However, this seems to be happening at a glacial pace in China. An important counterpoint to neoliberalism was noted by Messerschmidt et al. (2018), who warned that hegemonic masculinity perpetuates traditional male-oriented and male-dominated social orders and values. Recent public pronouncements by President Xi Jinping reflect the pushback from the state against such challenges and have reinforced traditional male roles or values.

Sexual identity and orientation do not exist in a vacuum. Connell and Messerschmidt (2005) advocated for intersectional analysis to understand how domination by the economically and militarily robust Global North helps maintain race and class inequalities and shape feminist perspectives and social movements. Hegemonic masculinity refers to a socially constructed archetype that legitimizes the dominant position of men in society. This concept justifies the subordination of women and other marginalized forms of masculinity. Cultural norms and power dynamics shape it (Connell 1998; Connell and Messerschmidt 2005).

In China, traditional gender norms often bolster hegemonic masculinity, emphasizing patriarchy, dominance, and the role of the primary earner. However, shifting social attitudes and movements advocating gender equality challenge these norms, leading to a more diverse range of masculinity expressions. Intersectional analysis is a method that scrutinizes how various factors, such as gender, ethnicity, and class, intersect to shape an individual's experiences. This approach transcends isolated categories to comprehend the unique, combined effects. In the Chinese context, intersectional analysis can shed light on the disparities faced by marginalized groups. Applying intersectional analysis to queer studies addresses how gender inequalities vary and are perpetuated among people of different races, ethnicities, classes, and nationalities. For example, Angela Jones's fieldwork (2020) provided supporting evidence for both Messerschmidt et al. (2018) and Ward (2015), who proposed a model of intersectional analysis exploring how gender, race, and sexuality work together to shape same-sex sexual practices among straight white men.

Queer Sinophone studies addresses issues of queer identity outside of Western conceptualizations. In their introduction to queer Sinophone studies, Chiang and Wong (2020) offered a framework that emphasizes the diversity of Chinese-speaking communities around the world and sought to move beyond a binary model of China and the West. Tan (2013) showed how generations of subjects reconstruct and articulate their memories, desires, dreams, hopes, and longings when they reinvent their ethnic culture in different stages of migration. The Sinophone identity is always transitional and open for construction and reconstruction. This provides a starting point for discussing the Sinophone identities that have emerged in Sino-queer studies. For example, Liu examined queer theory and Marxism, the art and literary works emerging in Taiwan. Through analytical comparisons with mainland China, Liu argued that historical geopolitical tensions resulted in Taiwan embracing a Euro-American variant of queer theory.

Brainer's (2019) research in Taiwan drew attention to family and kinship systems in China, challenging Western assumptions about the importance of independence and individualism in queer research. Taiwan is more open than the mainland in terms of acceptance and visibility of people identifying as LGBTQ+. Brainer noted the various ways that queer kin—aunts, uncles, nieces, nephews, cousins—changed and adapted to harmonize family structures and reduced conflict while non-LGBTQ+ family members reoriented themselves. Brainer analyzed queerness within patrilineal communities and how LGBTQ+ kin in Taiwan have reshaped and continue to co-create their role in the family and everyday life.

Brainer (2019, 84) observed that queer communities often engage in marriages that align with heteronormative practices. They perceive heterosexual marriage to be a social contract and an economic arrangement. This institution unites not only two individuals but also their families and financial circumstances. Brainer marked an important milestone in studying queer families in East Asia by avoiding the pitfalls of merely transplanting Western coming-out narratives. She situated Taiwanese queer experiences within the evolving Taiwanese society, which has undergone rapid change since the late twentieth century. Her research has explored the transformation of family structures (from extended to nuclear), parenting styles—especially among the middle class—and the emerging tensions between gender and sexual movements from the West and traditional family values rooted in Confucian culture.

Another area of queer studies focuses on queer migrant sexual minorities in Western countries (Minichiello and Scott 2014; Minichiello, Scott, and Callander 2013). In China, recent scholarship sought to contextualize queer theory within political economy (Kong 2012b, 2017; Liu 2013) as many rural gay male migrants turned to sex work to earn money in urban China (Kong 2012b). These migrants face a range of discriminatory practices, from the passive coercion of the institutionalized *hukou* system to being actively blamed for sexually transmitted diseases by the middle-class gay communities they seek to join (Kong 2012b, 2017).

The *hukou* system in China is especially problematic. *Hukou* is the household registration system that identifies where one was born. An individual with a rural *hukou* must go to their birth village for services like affordable housing, health care, and educational opportunities. But services are typically better in urban locations, and cities are more accepting of gay communities. Thus, the *hukou* system constitutes institutionalized exclusion, creating second-class citizenship for those born in rural areas. It is a critical structural factor facilitating the marginalization of MSWs (Gong and Liu 2022; Kong 2012a; Xie and Wu 2008). For instance, Liu (2013) observed that Chinese lesbians who migrate from rural to urban areas do so to escape "patriarchal and homophobic family relations" and achieve economic independence. Gong and Liu (2022) found that Chinese gay migrants survived by "lying flat" to maintain a productive life, assuming multiple identities to resist heteronormativity and actively adopting transient and transactional relationships for mutual support. In other words, they keep low visibility, maintain various personas to suit different situations, and form distant allyships.

More conceptual development is needed regarding queer studies and male migrants who move to the city and become sex workers. Key questions remain unanswered regarding their upbringing in rural towns and villages. When did they know they were gay? What were they taught about sexual orientation and same-sex relationships? What type of roles did the parents play? As young adults, gay migrant sex workers encounter a host of dilemmas. They go to the city with few skills or opportunities for success and face family pressure to marry heterosexual women. They experience emotional or physical abuse from clients and partners as well as discrimination from the state, including police, government services, and health professionals. To cope with these difficulties, many turn to drug abuse and high-risk sexual behavior.

A helpful framework for understanding the dilemma and difficulties across various life situations faced by the MSWs and *tongqi* comes from scholarship on necropolitics. The different stigmas and pressures experienced by MSWs create enormous stress, eroding their self-esteem and confidence (Scambler 2018). The toll on their physical body and social relationships becomes especially acute for those who contract HIV. The possible silver lining is that amid social death, these individuals exhibit resistance and agency to overcome their circumstances. As such, the necropolitics of social death remains the central conceptual framework for this book, pulling together the disparate parts into a coherent whole.

Necropolitics and Queer Studies

The Chinese government will likely continue to exercise its power to isolate and marginalize MSWs until major social reforms are put in place. The question is whether gay bars can be viewed as oases where queer individuals can thrive or necropolises, where they exist and wait to die. The 151 MSWs who participated in this research are neither victims nor perpetrators of human trafficking, but they typically have little control over how they are treated. The MSWs try to make a living by embracing the "desiring and enterprising China" to become an individualized self (Kleinman et al. 2011). In this context, the "individualized self" refers to the notion of the "divided self," which suggests that ordinary people in contemporary China take dual actions of resistance and accommodation simultaneously while negotiating with China's social reality.

The fact that numerous MSWs have opted for this profession complicates their situation. However, their choice becomes more comprehensible when viewed through necropolitics. Jones (2020) found that the physical pleasure of sex work is a powerful motivator. Jones examined webcam models in the sex work industry and proposed a "sociology of pleasure." The models whom Jones studied derived several benefits from their work, including intimacy, empowerment, pleasure, and fair wages. The pleasure of work was a way of resisting and "cracking" capitalist alienation. Based on these findings, Jones challenged the assumption that sex work cannot be pleasurable for workers and must, therefore, be controlled both legally and socially. Jones suggested instead that pleasure is a motivator for peoples' work choices. This perspective helps shed light on the complex motivation and experiences of male migrant sex workers in China.

Current research on sex work disproportionally focuses on female sex workers (Bernstein 2007; Hoang 2015; Tsang 2017, 2019; Tsang et al. 2019; Zheng 2008), but the male-to-male commercial sex industry in China is equally significantly evolving. The spaces of the male sex work industry now include niche markets, informal organizations, and cyber settings through different online apps. Since the 1980s, several studies have examined the issues surrounding the estimated eight million MSWs in China (Chou 2001, 2003; Ho 2009; Kong 2012b, 2017; Zheng 2015). Researchers have extensively articulated the critical issues regarding Chinese same-sex identity (Li 2006; Pan 2006; Pan and Wang 2004; Pan and Yang 2004).

Recent research has suggested that a collective identity has been forged by MSWs based on labels commonly assigned to queer individuals, such as abnormal, deviant, and derogatory (Zheng 2015, 15). However, it is essential to understand how these men use different mechanisms to externalize their internal selves in the face of stigma and disapproval. Lisa Rofel (2007) explained that the changes in sexual norms are part of a larger project of a neoliberal, modernizing China, which she framed as "desiring China." Rofel also warned that promoting the queer self through cosmopolitanism might run the risk of classed exclusion as cosmopolitanism is a technique that is facilitated through materiality or capital accumulation, so only the resourceful and privileged can harness this to legitimize themselves. Cosmopolitanism reflects materialism, economic capital, and how people upgrade their lives to appear successful and upwardly mobile. Rofel (2007) has posited cosmopolitanism as the core value for understanding the queer Chinese self. She proposed that neoliberal developments in China are fueled by people's desire to broaden their knowledge and understanding of LGBTQ+ across nation-state boundaries. With the growth of cosmopolitan identity, queerness has emerged as a more open avenue. With more people understanding and knowing more about the LGBTQ+ communities, China can enable individual citizens to freely cultivate, pursue, and fulfill sexual, material, and affective desires.

Sociologists have linked detraditionalization (Ho 2009; Kleinman et al. 2011; Wang 2014; Yan 2010; Zheng et al. 2011) with freeing male migrants from traditional Chinese values and norms. Kong (2012, 285) argued that neoliberalism is a mode of governance rather than a political philosophy or economic ideology. To produce a desirable citizenry "at a distance," Arthur Kleinman and his research team (2011, 30) noted the emergence of a "new Chinese self," which involves the reshaping of governance by the "divided self." China's gay culture is said to combine globalized gay culture with local Indigenous perspectives (Chou 2001; Ho 2009; Kleinman et al. 2011; Rofel 2007). These gay spaces are easily found online and reflect a culture described as liberal, individualized, and open, yet still conforming to family, self, and state control (Ho 2009, 138). Despite this, many MSWs are still bound by filial piety obligations to their parents and opt to marry to procreate and make their parents grandparents (Chen and Ghaill 2015; Lin 2014). This book addresses how global interconnectedness has facilitated a blending of Western notions of gay identity in a non-Western society like China.

MSWs often adopt Western modes of queerness while also embracing "authentic" Chinese values rooted in Confucianism, leading to questions about how the individualized self is defined and situated amid Chinese values that reflect conflicting ethical values and moral practices. Existing theories of the new Chinese self fail to recognize how the new market has produced this self, nor has sufficient effort been made to note the conditionality of these newly emerging MSW communities. The foundational issue continues to be China's anxiety about balancing Western influence and modernity. How can China appear modern without appearing to be overly Western? How does same-sex eroticism animate Chinese society's varied and conflicted imaginations regarding modernity and the West?

A Holistic Approach to Necropolitics and Social Death

The application of necropolitics to MSWs can help identify problems and offer solutions to the complex situation involving MSWs and their wives (*tongqi*) (Tsang 2021b). For MSWs, this could include examining how societal norms, laws, and policies impact their lives, often in harmful ways. For example, in extreme cases, MSWs have committed suicide after discovering they have contracted HIV from clients. The risk to public health is further exacerbated when MSWs transmit HIV to their wives, who often are ignorant of their husbands' lifestyles and sexual orientations. Despite the challenges of social stigma and HIV risk, MSWs remain resolute in finding ways to resist, cope, survive, and eventually achieve a new "normal" life. The accounts presented here reveal that they are not merely passive victims of unfair social and cultural policies in China, but instead, their efforts to escape the slow violence of queer necropolitics represent a brave reclamation of their identity. Therefore, necropolitics of social death can apply to any of the MSWs, *tongqi*, MSWs living with HIV, and transgender sex workers (TSWs). Their situation is not defined by physical death, despair, and desperation but by endurance in the face of constant stigma and marginalization.

For *tongqi*, the application of necropolitics could involve exploring how societal expectations and the stigmatization of LGBTQ+ communities in China have led to the emergence of this group. *Tongqi* often suffer severe mental, physical, and health-related harm due to their husbands' hidden sexual orientation. However, many of them are also working together to effect social change. In both cases, applying necropolitics of social death can help identify the systemic issues that contribute to the problems these groups face and could offer insights for them to find a solution. This might involve advocating for policy changes, raising public awareness, or providing support and resources to these marginalized populations.

The concept of necropolitics highlights and critiques the systemic injustices faced by these groups. This death, from Mbembe's framework, typically refers to physical death, as these underprivileged groups have been denied legal, biomedical, and cultural recognition and their fundamental human rights (Mayblin et al 2019; Mbembe 2003; Threadcraft 2017; Wright 2011). Necropolitics is thus a "concept-metaphor that illuminates and connects a range of spectacular and mundane forms of killing and of 'letting die,' throwing the interplay between life and death into relief" (Haritaworn et al. 2014, 4). The term typically fails to account for how nation-states exercise necropolitical power over different populations. Even in liberal democracies, the state manages people and either overtly or covertly earmarks certain bodies for death. Biopolitics refers to the management and regulation of life worlds as a mechanism of state power. Necropolitics succinctly describes how a society can attack marginalized groups, forcing them into isolated communities shunned by outsiders (death worlds). These individuals become ostracized, ignored, and emotionally numb in what they perceive to be a society that is unfeeling and uncaring; it confers on them the status of the living dead.

Haritaworn et al. (2014) have argued that necropolitics gives rise to queer necropolises in the West, where marginalized communities face precarious living conditions and pressure from government, family, and peers. They advocate a reimagining of the meanings of queerness and regimes that attribute "liveliness and deadliness of subjects, bodies, communities and populations and their instantiation through performatives of gender, sexuality, and kinship, as well as through processes of confinement, removal, and exhaustion" (Haritaworn et al. 2014, 4). This reimagination suggests a pathway to resist and challenge necropolitical practices that profoundly impact underprivileged groups' well-being and survival.

The mechanisms faced by underprivileged groups can bring isolation and death and have been extended to those labeled queer (McKinnon 2016). Jasbir Puar's (2007) core argument about queerness is not about being lesbian or gay but about pursuing activities that counter the state's ambitions and norms. In coining the term *queer necropolitics*, Puar argued that non-heteronormative bodies are marked for death, supporting the state's hegemony and nationalism. Debrix (2016, 85) noted the horror of relegating people to conditions where they are left to die, which results in human beings becoming "unrecognizable, unidentifiable and sometimes indistinguishable from non-human matter." Jasbir Puar (2007) and Debrix (2016) suggested that when the state neglects marginalized groups, it can lead to a state of "living death" whereby the quality of life is so poor that it resembles living in a state of death. An example given is permanent expulsion from the country, when individuals are forced to leave their country immediately and without any opportunity for legal appeal, further exacerbating their marginalization and hardship. This social and political abandonment pushes them into a state of "living death" (Puar 2013).

Migration and Male Sex Workers: A Snapshot

In China, rural migrants are a significant population impacted by necropolitics. Government statistics estimate that there are more than 288 million rural migrants in China, approximately 172 million of whom are male (National Bureau of Statistics 2019). While most studies focus on female migrants who perform precarious labor in the manufacturing and service industries, there is an urgent need to study male migrants beyond their economic and family reasons for moving to the city. These migrants are often unprepared—insufficiently skilled or credentialed—to secure stable employment. As reported by the *Economist* (2019), a considerable number—an estimated eight million—engage in sex work in the urban centers' gay sex industry to make ends meet. One of the central themes in this book is how these rural male migrants escape poverty and reconcile their queer urban life with their heterosexual rural family life. These migrants did not receive financial or social support from traditional institutions like the government or labor market groups. They had to rely on themselves to achieve their goals of individualized self, freedom, and autonomy.

Hukou *and the Urban versus Rural Binary*

Rural masses are labeled by the neoliberal state as "low *suzhi*" (quality, 素质), "uncouth," and "desperate." Rural gay men who fail to conform to societal expectations are often shunned (Kong 2012a; Rofel 2010) and stigmatized for displaying markers of their rural origins and rural queer masculinity. In addition, the urban gay community sets and maintains normative expectations for physical appearance, behavior, and speech. Within this context, male rural migrants attempt to become cosmopolitan in an urban environment (Song and Lee 2012), with some turning to cosmetic surgery to attain a "softer" facial look, which signifies youth and thus carries with it a degree of erotic power (Symons 1979). This emphasis on male beauty and soft masculinity prompts male rural migrants to engage in strategies to make consumer choices that position themselves as modern, which is equated with success (Song and Hird 2014). Rather than being "simple farm boys from the subtropical south," these men seek to present themselves as successful cosmopolites. Such strategies help them survive in a high-risk, competitive service industry.

Objectives and Aims of the Book

Much of the literature on male rural migrants has focused on their migration to cities for economic and family reasons, portraying them as victims in a global capitalist system. Due to the lack of skills or credentials, rural migrants typically face job insecurity, low pay and benefits, and little opportunity for upward mobility (Swider 2015). Urban attitudes to rural male migrants can often be overtly discriminatory, reinforcing the stereotype of rural life being inferior to the metropolitan. These attitudes invariably impact migrants' sense of self-worth, masculinity, and potential for success when they arrive in the city.

The book has four primary objectives. First, it aims to improve knowledge of the sociology of sex work by exploring how necropolitics of social death interact with coping strategies such as emotional labor and technologies of embodiment to enable these peasant male migrants to attain self-defined notions of success in urban China. Second, it explores the broader implications of self-help strategies to facilitate internal migration among China's peasant male migrants and how they employ effective labor to improve their social mobility. Third, it examines how a self-prescribed program and strategy used by male migrants are regarded as more effective than migrants' educational attainment, marketable skills, and government policies to assist rural male migrants. Finally, it uses the necropolitics of social death to conceptualize and interpret the challenges faced by MSWs and *tongqi* in contemporary China. These four broad yet interconnected concepts provide a nuanced understanding of the political and economic complexity that shapes the experience of MSWs in China's commercial sexscapes (Zheng 2008, 2015).

In this book, several critical research questions concerning the experiences of marginalized communities in China are examined. First,

I explore the applicability of necropolitics to MSWs within the Chinese context. By examining the extent to which necropolitics can shed light on the precarious existence of MSWs, the intricate dynamics of power, vulnerability, and survival may be revealed. Second, I investigate the impact of being gay in China, specifically focusing on the stigma that exposes individuals to necropolitical death conditions. This exploration delves into the intersection of sexual identity, societal norms, and the state's role in shaping life and death. Third, I scrutinize the phenomenon of *tongqi*—the wives of gay men—and the implications for China's marriage law. By identifying gaps in the legal framework, I seek to propose potential revisions that address the unique challenges faced by these women (Liu 2013). Fourth, I analyze how the socialist state's health-care system treats MSWs as nonliving entities or "the living dead." This examination sheds light on the dehumanization and neglect faced by this vulnerable population. Fifth, I investigate the intricate interplay of gender, sexuality, and state-led stigma, which collectively contribute to the creation of gay communities as "living dead" in China. Finally, at the social policy level, I explore the intersections between MSWs, *tongqi*, medical professionals, and male clients. By addressing issues such as marriage law and the HIV pandemic, comprehensive solutions that promote equity, dignity, and well-being in contemporary China can be proposed.

Chapter Summaries

This book is a compilation of interviews conducted over four years, from May 2015 to August 2019, with a follow-up visit to Tianjin in January 2020 before the outbreak of COVID-19. The data was collected during semester and summer breaks. A series of interviews are combined with various documents and personal records involving anecdotes and accounts of life among gay men in China over the past several years. During the first excursion of data collection—from May 2015 to Dec 2016—I spent time in a high-end bar called Pistachio (a pseudonym) as an unpaid bartender to collect data through interactions with the MSWs. The second phase involved data collection through a series of in-depth interviews in North China with 151 MSWs, 25 MSWs living with HIV, 59 *tongqi*, 25 TSWs who experienced IPV, 15 HIV doctors, 12 NGO directors, 57 male clients (bisexual/gay men), and 27 female clients (heterosexual, single, married) buying commercial sex from January 2017 to August 2019.

Chapter 1 presents the background and discusses how the necropolitics of social death is a foundational theme throughout each chapter. It covers the inspiration behind the book, the methodology and design of the research, the qualitative perspective, and how the ethnographic data was collected and analyzed with particular emphasis on the high-end bar Pistachio in North China.

Chapter 2 delves into the transformative emotional labor and cosmetic surgery in China's male sex industry. It explores how migrant rural-to-urban MSWs adopt embodiments of emotional labor to enhance their economic survival in China's urban gay commercial sex industry by transforming their physical appearance through cosmetic surgeries to conform to the soft-masculine urban standards of maleness deemed most attractive and appealing (Bridges and Pascoe 2014).

Chapter 3 explores the concept of marriage of convenience from the perspective of MSWs. These men often succumb to family pressure and marry heterosexual women (*tongqi*) or lesbians (in the Chinese context, *lala*) to fulfill their role as filial sons. Although these men may initially keep their true sexual desires secret, their wives invariably discover the truth and realize they are in a sham marriage. In some cases, *tongqi* contract HIV from their husbands. In an increasingly commercialized Chinese society, the marriage of convenience is a transactional practice for MSWs married to *tongqi* or *lala*.

Chapter 4 examines the experiences of the *tongqi* upon discovering their husbands' queer and MSW identities in Tianjin. The debilitating impact of necropower on their own lives is examined, highlighting the devastating effects of societal stigma and discrimination. This chapter also highlights how *tongqi* choose to stay with their husbands and maintain the status quo because marriage law does not recognize men-with-men relationships as constituting adultery.

Chapter 5 presents the accounts of fifty-seven male clients (bisexual/gay men) and twenty-seven female clients (heterosexual, single, married) who purchase commercial sex at Pistachio and other bars in China. This chapter argues that the relationships between MSWs and their clients are transactional, driven by the pursuit of sexual thrills and excitement. The twenty-seven female clients reported deriving the same sexual pleasure as their male counterparts when buying commercial sex. The chapter offers insight into the complex and multifaceted nature of commercial sex work in China and challenges societal stereotypes and expectations surrounding gender and sexuality.

Chapter 6 examines the close connection between sex work and drug addiction and even drug smuggling among MSWs who try to cope with the harsh realities of exposure to death. It also explores aspects of the social death of twenty-five MSWs living with HIV and the discrimination they face in China. These men reported instances when they were denied basic health care due to technicalities related to China's birth registration and identification system. Because they lack the urban *hukou*, they are not eligible for free treatment in the city and must return to their hometowns, where they face questions and stigma from the medical community.

Chapter 7 explores the struggles of some of the TSWs, particularly those who experience IPV. This chapter introduces a new approach to queer criminology and self-help programs to help TSWs who experience IPV. TSWs face considerable challenges that affect their mental health and make them more vulnerable to abuse. The chapter offers insight into the complex and multifaceted nature of commercial sex work in China and challenges societal stereotypes and expectations surrounding gender and sexuality.

The eighth and final chapter recaps our conceptualization of the necropolitics of social death. It is estimated that more than half of the MSWs interviewed during this study have since changed to other professions, as careers in sex work are notoriously brief. Some MSWs capitalize on their emotional labor, attractive physical appearance, and masculine body to enter other service industries, as in the case of one internet celebrity (livestreamer网红) who uses his charm to market products online. Final insights are presented, arguing for a fresh approach to unlock the red closet by rethinking biopolitics, necropolitics, *tongqi*, drug addiction, and the male commercial sex industry as necropolitical sexscapes.

The book explores the broader implications of self-help initiated by MSWs and *tongqi* on the internal migration of China's peasant male migrants and how they employ affective labor to improve their social mobility. It seeks to analyze how self-help programs and strategies used by male migrants are regarded as more effective than migrants' educational attainment, marketable skills, and government policies aimed at assisting educated rural male migrants.

1

Welcome to Pistachio

An Ethnographic Journey of Sex Work in North China

One night, I was standing at a bus stop in Tianjin, wondering if I should get a bowl of noodles when a middle-aged man approached me and asked for directions. We chatted a bit, and he introduced himself as Fang. He said he came from another one of the big cities in North China. He asked me why a single woman like me walked alone at night in the red-light district. I told him I had just finished my bartending shift and was finishing up a project researching female sex workers and wanted to enjoy the night air. I could see the surprise on his face, but he surprised me even more with his reply. He straightaway asked in Putonghua (the standard national language of the PRC), "Why limit your research to women? Why not also interview MSWs?" At that time, I was focused exclusively on interviewing female sex workers, research that had started in Dongguan. MSWs were not on my radar at that time, but Fang made me stop and think. After talking to Lennon and making some calls, I discovered that an old college friend had a bar nearby. Soon after, the new project began.

This work is based on ethnographic field notes taken during more than four years of ethnographic research, from May 2015 to August 2019. The data collection came from two excursions to North China using ethnography and in-depth interviews. The first excursion was from May 2015 to December 2016.

Sex work, as a multifaceted phenomenon, intersects with a variety of sociocultural, economic, and individual factors. The sexual identities of MSWs have been a subject of scholarly exploration, albeit within a complex and nuanced context. Research indicates that a significant proportion of MSWs already identify with non-heteronormative sexual orientations before entering the sex industry. Economic circumstances indeed play a pivotal role in shaping individuals' choices, including their involvement in sex work. Financial necessity can drive individuals to sex work, irrespective of their preexisting sexual identity. MSWs, particularly those facing economic hardship, may exhibit a degree of sexual flexibility. This adaptability arises from pragmatic considerations, such as securing income and subsistence. Consequently, some MSWs may privilege economic incentives over their natural sexual inclination and engage in acts that diverge from their intrinsic sexual preferences. This pragmatic approach underscores the complex interplay between economic exigency and sexual behavior. Once ensconced in sex work, MSWs navigate a dynamic landscape where their sexual identities intersect with client expectations, societal stigma, and economic imperatives. The negotiation of sexual identity within this context is multifaceted. Some MSWs may compartmentalize their sexual identity from their professional persona, adopting a pragmatic stance to meet client demands. Others may experience a fluidity of sexual expression, adapting to diverse client preferences while maintaining a core sense of self.

Paradoxically, sex work can serve as a crucible for identity exploration. Some MSWs report discovering facets of their sexual selves during their professional engagements. The transactional nature of sex work provides a unique space for experimentation, self-discovery, and boundary negotiation. This process may lead to shifts in sexual identity over time. As we engage in scholarly discourse, we must remain attuned to the nuances and complexities inherent in this domain (Tsang 2019a).

The second excursion of data collection in North China involved conducting in-depth interviews with MSWs, MSWs living with HIV, *tongqi*, TSWs, clinical HIV doctors, and directors of gay-oriented NGOs from 2017 to 2019. The interviews were held in cafés, saunas, clubhouses, and NGO offices. My friend Lennon referred me to people he was connected with who were working in gay NGOs in North China. The in-depth interviews were conducted from January 2017 to August 2019. All informants were compensated for their time with cash coupons, meals, or both. Recorded interviews, in situ note-taking, post-event field notes, and less conventional methods such as QQ/WeChat interviews and photo-elicitation were also used.

Finding Male Sex Workers in Tianjin

After my short conversation with Fang, I called my good friend Lennon for advice on how to proceed. He had worked with gay NGOs in Hong

Kong and China for several years. Lennon agreed that the phenomenon of the MSWs had so far escaped notice in post-reform China and offered his network of connections to help gather the experiences and stories of MSWs, which are both dramatic and complex. My academic instincts told me that a book about MSWs could make a significant contribution by sharing the individual stories of MSWs within the context of the layers of overt discrimination and stigma faced by LGBTQ+ communities in China.

This book focuses on the stories of MSWs in the context of a globalized China, where they must also cope with traditional Chinese cultural values. Single males are under social pressure to marry and have children. To escape that pressure, gay men will enter heterosexual marriage relationships. The voices of the heterosexual women who have married the MSWs are also rarely found in the existing literature. These stories—which come from MSWs, their *tongqi*, the clinical doctors, and the HIV patients—need to be heard. The situations are complex, dangerous, and often sad. There are very few happy endings. However, by understanding the context and background of their lives, one can better appreciate their humanity, feelings, and pain. Perhaps we can one day begin a global dialogue on fixing these impossible dilemmas and improving the human condition.

I began this new journey by reestablishing important personal and professional contacts. As with my friend Lennon, all names used throughout are pseudonyms. I was given access to Pistachio, the high-end gay bar in Tianjin, because the owner, Herman, was a college classmate in Hong Kong. I asked if I could work in his bar as an unpaid bartender, as I did for a different study in Dongguan (Tsang 2019a). Herman agreed, so I made the proper arrangements and preparations. I found a cheap but safe apartment to live in and brought clothes that I thought would be appropriate, neither too flashy nor too conservative.

The Local Center for Disease Control (CDC)

In August 2015, I wanted to work with the local Center for Disease Control (CDC) and local government-owned nongovernmental organizations (GONGOs) to widen the pool of participants for this research. I wanted to bring in different voices to provide a comprehensive snapshot of MSWs, *tongqi*, and HIV issues. However, obtaining help from the CDC or the GONGOs was arduous. With the help of Lennon and others, I was allowed to conduct some interviews in January 2016 at one CDC in Tianjin. I met with a group of doctors, directors, and staff. Before I went to the center, I emailed them a list of specific questions. The actual meeting was hospitable, and the delegates from the CDC were friendly and accommodating. They gave me excellent Chinese tea, coffee, dim sum, and Western snacks like cookies and cupcakes. They also bought me lunch in an upscale Chinese seafood restaurant. However, I did not receive answers to any of the questions I sent in advance. I began to realize then how political correctness and general sensitivity to anything HIV-related are stumbling blocks when trying to get help from the CDC and the GONGOs. Understandably, they had no idea how I would use the sensitive data. They may have thought that since I am not a local mainlander, I might be a spy from Hong Kong or the United States who would manipulate the data and write something negative about China that would hurt China's reputation. There were more than enough reasons for the CDC director to dismiss my request.

The NGOs

Fortunately, Lennon stepped in and passed his network on to me so I could conduct pilot interviews with MSWs from different NGOs in North China. He did it for friendship, and the only way I could return the favor was by treating him to dinner. That second incursion of data collection began when I returned to North China in March 2017. Lennon helped me look for additional NGOs in that region. He had worked at one NGO in Hong Kong for over fifteen years and knew several people working in similar NGOs throughout North China. He made the initial contact with each of the directors, explaining who I was and my purpose in talking to them. I then followed up and interviewed each of the twelve directors individually. In those meetings, each director also introduced me to one or two sex workers for further interviews. Afterward, I was introduced to additional MSWs in saunas, private clubhouses, public parks, on the street, and via the internet. With this snowball sample, I completed several formal, informal, and group interviews with around fifty MSWs and some of their *tongqi*.

During the meetings, I could probe further on points raised in the initial group of interviews. These interviews primarily focused on gaining information about NGOs, their role, helpfulness in advocacy, and educational initiatives and outreach. The officially recognized duty of these NGOs is to disseminate information to alert the gay community about preventing the transmission of HIV. The NGOs are the first line of defense to help at-risk groups like sex workers and the gay community educate themselves to prevent the spread of sexually transmitted diseases. The NGOs help with confidential screening and testing for diseases like HIV.

Interviews with Male Sex Workers

I met with the MSWs individually and often spoke with them in a nearby café. The MSWs were aged eighteen to fifty-nine, and the mean age was twenty-five. But the golden years for a sex worker are roughly between eighteen and twenty-five, depending on several factors. Clients prefer younger MSWs because they have less life experience and more enthusiasm and sexual stamina. Another general preference expressed was tan skin and toned bodies rather than pale skin and gentler, effeminate personas, although most of the MSWs interviewed fit into the latter category.

Therefore, many of the MSWs inside the club—even the older ones—often wore tight tops and too-tight, too-short pants. Depending on the outfit, the footwear may be, for example, Chloe male boots with silver metallic decorations. When dressed in drag (women's clothing), they wear high heels or clogs. When dressed for adventure (S&M), they may wear tight leather pants with matching vest, pants only, or some other appropriate costume/cosplay.

Most, if not all, of the MSWs I spoke with had little public education, and all admitted that they came from rural areas. However, that shortcoming was offset by the confidence of knowing one is handsome, sexy, and stylish. They all saw themselves as successful MSWs who knew how to get the attention of their clients. Very few had facial hair; if they did, it was limited to a well-groomed mustache. No beards were seen. Most (around three-quarters) kept their hair stylishly short, although perhaps a dozen or more grew it out to shoulder-length to look feminine. Only three had their head shaved, and they admitted that it was to please clients by making themselves look more dominating and aggressive.

All 151 MSWs interviewed were interprovincial migrants who came from a handful of provinces (Hunan, Hubei, Jilin, Liaoning, Harbin, Shandong, Inner Mongolia) and moved to Beijing and Tianjin as *dagongzai* (working son 打工仔). Many of these men had either been laid off by employers or had willingly resigned from their previous jobs to enter sex work. A total of eighty-nine interviewees completed primary school, forty-three completed junior high, and nineteen participants said they finished high school. More than ninety of the MSWs resided illegally in urban North China for less than ten years, except for eleven men who had lived in urban North China for more than ten years. Domestic migrants have been branded as "the floating population" (*liudong renkou* 流动人口) in China. The number of single adult male migrants at the bottom of the workforce is estimated to be between 100 and 150 million (National Bureau of Statistics, 2019).

Doctors, NGO Directors, and Living with HIV

Perhaps the most significant result of the interviews with Lennon and the NGO workers was finding the clinical HIV doctors and HIV patients. I was able to interview fifteen HIV clinical doctors, twelve directors of gay NGOs, and twenty-five HIV patients from three HIV-designated hospitals in North China. Among the twenty-five HIV patients who were interviewed, three were very sick when they were contacted and interviewed in March 2017. They each wore a mask, had skin problems, and were frail, thin, and weak. They authorized me to tell their stories if they should die before this book was published and were grateful that I was willing to listen and share their stories. The one request they made to me was to keep their identity hidden. This is part of the pain endured by MSWs in Tianjin. They know that much of their lives cannot be openly shared or even attributed to them because of family and reputation.

When I returned to visit them in the summer of 2019, I was told that all three had already died. There have been advances in highly active antiretroviral therapy (HAART), which has been increasingly used in China for the past twenty years (Cao et al. 2020). These treatments have reduced the mortality of HIV/AIDS patients in China from 22.6 per hundred person-years in 2003 to 3.1 per hundred person-years in 2014. However, the MSWs I met came from rural areas and were not eligible for the more effective treatments available in urban centers. These MSWs either did not receive treatment soon enough or did not have the resources to afford effective medical treatment. In addition, some of them struggled with drug abuse, which led to additional complications that undermined their treatment.

The Wives of Male Sex Workers

The other intriguing interviews in this book are the conversations with *tongqi*, the spouses of MSWs. In rural areas, it remains common for parents to arrange mates for their children to marry. This process is advantageous for a man seeking to remain closeted because it ends awkward questions from parents and relatives about when he will find a wife. Once the marriage is arranged, he can quietly participate and avoid probing questions until after the ceremony, although then there will come inevitable questions about having children. Arranged marriages hold both cultural and pragmatic implications. This conventional practice can promote social unity, fortify familial bonds, and sustain cultural perpetuity. Arranged marriages are perceived as a mechanism to conserve traditions and pay homage to forebears through the inheritance of blood ties. However, this practice also presents obstacles for LGBTQ+ individuals striving to be authentic when expressing their identities. This research went through two iterations in arranging interviews with fifty-nine educated and non-educated *tongqi*. Interviews were initially conducted with 151 MSWs. I also collected data from twelve LGBT NGOs in Northeast China. Two sets of comparable data expanded the range of responses and experiences within the target group. Among the 151 MSWs, 111 MSWs said they were married to a heterosexual woman (*tongqi*), and 29 admitted that they were married to a lesbian (*lala*). The other eleven MSWs were free from parental pressure because their parents had died.

To speak with the *tongqi*, I had to get permission from their closeted husbands first. A total of 95 out of 151 MSWs were asked if follow-up interviews could be arranged with their wives. Around half of them refused because their wives were still unaware of their sexual orientation. Nevertheless, forty-nine granted me permission to contact their wives and request interviews with them. Of the forty-nine *tongqi* who spoke with me, ten were categorized as educated (holding at least an undergraduate degree), and thirty-nine were less educated, with only primary school education. In the second year, I successfully interviewed ten *tongqi*—eight less-educated and two educated—based on referrals from the twelve NGOs. In total, I successfully interviewed fifty-nine *tongqi* (forty-seven low-educated, twelve educated) throughout the forty-eight-month ethnography in North China.

As a qualitative research method, ethnography allowed for a deep understanding of the group's shared culture, conventions, and social dynamics. However, this research necessitated careful ethical considerations. It was imperative to ensure that participants fully comprehended the purpose of the study and their rights, including the right to withdraw at any time without penalty. Given the societal stigma and legal challenges faced by sex workers in China, measures were taken to protect the identities of the participants. For *tongqi*, particular caution was exercised to acknowledge the challenges they face, avoiding any form of victim blaming.

MSWs in China face a lack of legal protections against discrimination based on gender identity or sexual orientation. This absence of legal protection can lead to systemic persecution, particularly as the country increasingly espouses conservative values. MSWs often confront heightened risks, including being arrested and questioned by police. There have been instances where advocates providing support to the LGBTQ+ community have been subjected to police interrogation. *Tongqi* face significant challenges in China due to societal norms and legal biases. As of 2020, it is estimated that there are over twenty-five million *tongqi* in China (Tsang 2021b), many of whom endure physical and mental distress. They often discover their husband's sexual orientation only after marriage and childbirth, fulfilling filial obligations. China's divorce law favors men, so even if the wife applies for divorce, the husband often wins custody of the children. This situation is further complicated by societal stigma and the tendency to blame the victim, which extends even to the woman's own immediate family.

The Clients

The entire sample interviewed for this book included fifty-seven male clients (bisexual/gay men) and twenty-seven female clients (heterosexual, single, married) who bought commercial sex services at Pistachio and other places using smartphones and social media apps like Blued and WeChat. The most common reason for buying sex was pleasure. Female clients interviewed said they had strong sexual appetites and preferred having sex with MSWs. Female clients reported four primary reasons for buying sex from MSWs: sexual fulfillment, which they could not get from their husband; attractiveness of MSWs, who made them feel young again (fantasy); MSWs having the right "tools" (penis); and MSWs' carefulness as lovers; they take directions and may be gentle or aggressive on command. These women were not interested in an anonymous bar-fueled one-night stand. They knew what they wanted, and they bought it.

Transgender Women Sex Workers (TSWs)

Interviews with the TSWs took place separately and independently from Pistachio and also separate from most of the MSWs interviewed in this book. I interviewed twenty-five TSWs from May 2016 to August 2019. Lennon introduced me to several transgender NGOs in Tianjin and asked me to talk to them. All the participants were transgender women who were assigned male at birth. A total of twenty-five respondents, ranging in age from twenty-three to forty-eight, were interviewed about their experience with IPV. Interview participants were selected according to three criteria: self-identification as TSWs, eighteen years old or older, and had experienced at least one form of IPV (sexual assault) from their former or current intimate sex partners and were willing to talk about it. All the participants characterized their intimate relationships as romantic, sexual, and emotional. These relationships lasted from thirty days to four years.

In China, the perception and treatment of transgender and gender-nonconforming individuals are influenced by a complex interplay of cultural, societal, and governmental factors. Transgender and gender-nonconforming individuals often face systemic discrimination. They are at a high risk of adverse mental health outcomes due to minority stress, which is the stress faced by individuals categorized as stigmatized social minority groups. This stress is often exacerbated by issues related to interpersonal relationships and medical transitioning. For instance, the societal pressure to conform to traditional gender roles can lead to the stigmatization and marginalization of individuals who do not fit within these norms. This is particularly evident in the case of rural gay men in China, who often face rejection and criticism, fueling feelings of interpersonal sensitivity and loneliness. The stigma associated with homosexuality prevents the queer movement from achieving significant accomplishments in human rights because of society's disapproval and the constant discrimination these individuals and organizations face. Moreover, the Chinese government's increasing push for conformity and traditional values has further marginalized the queer community. Advocates have been arrested and questioned by police, and LGBTQ+ advocacy groups have faced closure without satisfactory explanation or justification. This systemic failure to protect gender minorities, particularly trans and queer people, is a significant barrier to progress.

Embarking on an Ethnographic Journey

The qualitative interviews with the informants employed open-ended questions that were flexible, interactive, and semi-structured. Most questions sought to capture why or how the individual interpreted relevant events and situations. The rich nature of these responses enabled the thick description of a phenomenon that helps the reader identify the concepts holistically. Therefore, analyzing the data collected from the qualitative interviews used a grounded theory approach (Corbin and Strauss 1990). This approach uses open coding, which involves carefully coding the responses to the interview questions, using constant comparisons to ensure code consistency. Subsequently, axial coding is used when the different codes are classified to identify the themes. Finally, selective coding locates the most meaningful theme as the central concept or story. Conventional grounded theory is expected to be more effective than the more subjective constructivist approach, which is more complex and interpretively demanding (Bryant and Charmaz 2007; Corbin and Strauss 1990). Informal methods of data collection, such as mobile phone apps like QQ/WeChat (微信)/TikTok (斗音), were also used to communicate with the informants. The spectrum of data collection techniques included participant observation, including informal interviews, direct observation, participation in group life, collective discussions, casual talks with the informants during their free time, and analysis of personal documents, online and offline activities, and life histories (Bernard 2011). Interviewees were also approached in their workplace when appropriate and in their free time whenever possible. Furthermore, extensive field notes, research memos, and self-reflection were compiled each night while the memories of the interactions remained fresh and accessible (Steier 1991).

Accessing Fieldwork

Finding appropriate individuals with whom to talk about such sensitive topics as sex work takes time, tremendous effort, and a little bit of luck. Because sex work is illegal, finding willing informants is difficult. Earning trust comes in tiny steps. The gay community has a long, complex history in China, and there are mountains of stigma and discrimination to overcome. They are experienced with lies and betrayals, especially from institutions and authority figures like the government and the police.

To establish rapport with this hard-to-reach population, I needed to do more than just walk into the bar and fire off questions. Once I became a familiar face to the MSWs, it was easier for me to talk and approach the clients in Pistachio for their help. The flexibility of my work shifts provided opportunities to speak with people throughout the day or night. In Pistachio, interviews were held in various spaces: backrooms at bars, nearby social spaces, and cafes.

During my first week at Pistachio, I prepared drinks and casually spoke with the men and their clients. As one might expect, a straight woman tending bar at a gay men's club aroused attention and brought many questions my way. I deflected by saying I was an old friend of Herman's, between jobs, and new in town. By the second week, people stopped asking so many questions, and I could focus on being an ordinary bartender. While many of the staff members accepted me, a straight woman in a gay bar, some remained distant and would not talk to me throughout my time there. Developing a relationship takes time and depends on each individual, the situation, and the context. As I grew more familiar with the bar setting and the men became more familiar with me, we began a series of individual conversations about who they were and how they got there.

On my first full day at Pistachio, two MSWs, Sunny (eighteen) and Rain (twenty), approached me, and we quickly established rapport. We had immediate chemistry, and they reminded me of some former students in Hong Kong. They were often cheerful and outgoing, light-hearted, and quick to laugh. They were indispensable with their help and support, regularly referring interviewees to me.

Sometimes, I would arrange to meet interviewees individually at a nearby café. We could sit and talk easily since we had previously met and established rapport. After working at the club for several days, the regulars felt they knew me or were comfortable enough to talk to me. Those who remained unsure talked to Sunny or Rain, who vouched for me. Everyone knew each other by name. Also, most of the MSWs trusted Herman and Lennon, and the interviewees gave me information about nominal marriage, their relationship with their wives, and HIV issues.

Rain and Sunny constantly updated me about their favorite fashion pursuits, cosmetic products, makeup brands, and traveling. One thing about those two: they knew their makeup. They owned more cosmetic products than I do and were better at creatively applying them. We chatted about various brands and why they used which skin cream and which one left a residue. Some of the MSWs fulfilled stereotypes like flamboyant fashion sense. A pimp named Kei once came into the bar wearing a bright green and yellow jumpsuit accessorized with a red bandana and red pumps, looking ready for the stage. Herman had a close relationship with Kei because they were partners, and Kei paid Herman a monthly commission. Despite the loud music and colorful flashing neon lights, I could still identify him. Only Kei would have had the fashion sense to pull off an outfit like that. He loudly asked everyone for compliments, and of course, the other MSWs either cheered him supportively or made catcalls (你看起来好丑, or with poetic license, "You look like a fat parrot, go home and change!").

As I got to know them, the MSWs grew comfortable talking to me. I did not give advice or render a judgment of right or wrong. Mostly, I let them tell their stories in their own words. I would interject and ask for clarification when I thought it was necessary.

As an incentive, I gave cash coupons/noncash gifts (like treating informants to lunch or dinner) to all the informants who talked to me. Cash coupons valued at 200 yuan (US$30) were used to encourage them to participate in the interviews. Lunch or dinner was provided for those who could stay after the interview. Those who had to leave were given the coupons to use at their convenience. Funding for the cash coupons came from a competitive research grant through my host institution.

Most of the MSWs said that when they offered sex to their clients, they did not have a price in mind. A price for the occasion may be reached by mutual agreement, or the client may offer a more comprehensive package deal. The package is very loose at the beginning. For example, a package could be for the MSW to accompany the client for thirty days in Shanghai, plus some short trips overseas. The client might offer the MSW between 100,000 and 500,000 yuan (US$14,700–US$73,650) per month for companionship. Although not committed to paper, the terms are individually negotiated as a relationship proposal. The client will also verbally express when he can terminate the contract, for example, after ten days, twenty days, or even at the end of an entire year. Expected services are typically expressed as round-the-clock companionship and all that entails, plus activities like traveling, cooking, and cleaning. Besides sex, the MSW may be expected to partake in whatever leisurely recreational pursuits the client wants. This has given us the stereotype of the handsome young man sporting sunglasses and a speedo, parasailing or sitting on a jet ski while his sugar daddy watches from his yacht. This is the dream for many MSWs, and more than a few have experienced it.

Navigating the complex landscape of conducting fieldwork in China, particularly in the context of illegal activities such as commercial sex, requires a delicate balance of safety, ethics, and legality. The researcher must be cognizant of the potential risks involved, including the possibility of legal repercussions for all parties involved. According to the local laws and regulations banning sex work, penalties for violating the law range from a minimum fine of US$5,000 to being sent for reeducation or labor-intensive work (Tsang 2019a). Moreover, the researcher must also consider the ethical implications of their work. This includes ensuring the privacy and safety of their subjects who may be involved in commercial sex work. Online payment methods, as opposed to cash transactions, can provide a layer of anonymity and safety for the subjects. However, this also raises questions about the researcher's complicity in illegal activities. Furthermore, the researcher must also navigate the complex social networks within these establishments. For instance, the owner of an establishment like Pistachio may have extensive connections with law enforcement officers, which can both complicate and facilitate the research process.

Finally, the researcher must be prepared for unexpected situations like police raids. The existence of escape routes, such as basement tunnels, can provide a means of evading such situations. However, the researcher must also consider the ethical implications of using such methods. The researcher must balance the need for comprehensive and accurate data with the need to ensure the safety and privacy of their subjects while also navigating the complex social and legal landscape of their research environment.

Data Analysis

Inspired by Riessman (1933), I analyzed the data in an ongoing, open-ended, and inductive way to ensure global and thematic coherence. The client-worker relationship was explored by analyzing the participants' personal responses (global coherence). Next, prominent themes in these accounts were identified and analyzed (thematic coherence). Inspired by Singer and Ryff (2001), I used bottom-up analysis to explore each individual's personal responses and identify significant commonalities and differences between accounts.

The information collected during photo elicitation and through the community walks helped verify and amplify the data collected in the in-depth interviews. To carry out the photo elicitation, I asked the informants to use their photos, stored on their mobile phones or cameras, to help them describe their self-perceptions, cultural values, and sex worker–client relationships. The information obtained while walking with the informants supplemented and enriched the interview data. This method proved successful because informants often hesitated to answer sensitive questions about intimate relationships with clients, wives, and parents. Photo elicitation helped them to explain their relationship when it was difficult to ask them directly.

After the recorded interviews were transcribed, I translated the transcripts into English and used the NVivo Pro 12.0 software for coding and analysis. I conducted a thematic analysis to identify themes and subthemes by grouping and categorizing the coded responses. Quote excerpts and coding memos were developed according to themes. The dominant themes were MSW, nominal marriage, marriage of convenience, *tongqi*, clinical HIV doctors, HIV patients, TSWs, IPV, marriage fraud, and drugs and police. Transcripts were re-read and validated against themes.

All the interviews were conducted in the mother tongue of the participants—Putonghua—which created a relaxed interview environment and allowed for effective communication. Because I myself am a native Putonghua speaker, there was no language barrier. All the interviews were conducted face-to-face rather than using WeChat or long-distance calls. The Chinese government is notorious for actively monitoring calls and text messages for certain types of content. Face-to-face communication was the best way to protect our privacy and circumvent government snooping or censorship.

Interpreting and Presenting Qualitative Data

Ethnographers often face tricky ethical dilemmas, and my experience was no different. Pseudonyms were carefully used for every interviewee throughout this work, and biographies were slightly modified where needed to prevent revealing identities. The overall work flows better using names rather than markers or numbers. I am fluent in English and a native speaker of Cantonese and Putonghua. However, some verbatim quotes may seem odd because some Chinese expressions do not smoothly translate into English. I have tried to maintain the spirit and intention of what was said wherever I could. The book also adopted a clinical perspective to interview some HIV clinical doctors and patients. HIV is a sensitive topic in China, and many Chinese know very little about clinical research regarding HIV doctors and patients.

Data comprised note-taking and post-event field notes. Before being recorded, all the participants signed consent forms and were given my business card with contact details. They were also reminded that they could freely withdraw without prejudice at any stage in the project. To safeguard the rights of the informants, I verified my identity and university affiliation to assure them that I was affiliated neither with the police nor with the government. The informants were fully assured of confidentiality and anonymity as I used only their current ages and the assigned pseudonyms. I did not ask for personal information such as an official identification number or date of birth. Protecting informants' privacy was of paramount concern due to the sensitive nature of the data. Efforts have been made to maintain the spirit and intention of what was said wherever possible.

Fieldwork Setting: The Pistachio in Tianjin

This study was conducted in Tianjin, Northern China, a coastal metropolis with a total population of 11.6 million in 2016 (National Bureau of Statistics of China 2017). Tianjin is southeast of Beijing, only thirty minutes by high-speed rail. Tianjin is one of China's four independent municipalities, with Beijing, Shanghai, and Chongqing. Tianjin recorded China's highest per-capita GDP in 2017 at 17,126 yuan (National Bureau of Statistics of China 2018). As a beneficiary of economic reform, Tianjin attracts large numbers of male migrants, many of whom come from the three Northeastern provinces of Liaoning, Jilin, and Heilongjiang. These male migrant workers usually work in service industries in Tianjin. A prominent NGO targeting the health-care needs of the gay community is located in Tianjin.

Although Tianjin is not renowned for its public bar culture and nightlife compared to its neighbor Beijing, there is a burgeoning gay community. As mentioned earlier, Pistachio is located in downtown Tianjin, near the area of Italian Style Street (Yishi Fangqingjie 意式风情街). It is based on the former Italian Concession (1901–47) surrounded by the Haihe River. Tianjin's gay bars have gradually developed a unique culture, blending or fusing Eastern and Western aesthetics. These bars have blossomed from semiprivate, homogenous, underground clubs into open, diverse public institutions; like LGBTQ+ issues in Chinese society, gay bars are now much more visible in downtown Tianjin. This not only reflects a stronger sense of self-acceptance among the LGBTQ+ community but also demonstrates a greater degree of tolerance for LGBTQ+ people by Chinese society at large. Tianjin's gay identity bears the imprint of an undercurrent of cultural superiority brought about by the experiences of the city's gay community with colonialism and capitalism when it was occupied by Italy during the Scramble for Concessions from 1895 to 1900.

Images from the High-End Gay Bar in Tianjin

Pistachio is a well-known "gentlemen's club" surrounded by other reputable restaurants and bars that are very popular at night. Still, the open displays of affection between and among MSWs can raise eyebrows. Near the building, there were several same-sex couples holding hands or putting their arms around each other, often with a sexual connotation. On my way to the club, I saw many posters on walls promoting "Tianjin Brokeback Mountain" (*Tianjin Duanbeishan* 天津断背山). The posters strategically covered up older paper images of generic topless or near-naked men. One poster left little to the imagination, advertising "ass fucker specialists" (*caopi zhuanjia* 操屁专家). The MSWs pictured were exceptionally attractive and eye-catching.

At first, I was not used to seeing so much fetish wear, half-naked models in red G-strings or some totally naked. Pistachio has a regular naked dance event at midnight. I thought my presence would be a big surprise for them, and I felt slightly disappointed when no one seemed to notice or even care. The members danced passionately and devoted their bodies to their audiences. Some couples left hand in hand to have sex in the corridor alongside the bar. It was like I was a transparent object to them. A mix of locals, expats, travelers, and women visited Pistachio. It is more of a place to start a night out and is often busiest before 3 a.m.

The entrance to Pistachio is guarded by a large, smiling concierge who will politely ask if you have a membership. Admission to Pistachio is by membership or invitation from either an affiliated sex worker or the bar owner. The first floor can accommodate a few hundred clients and provides a full dining menu and bar. The second floor consists mainly of rooms and facilities for every type of activity. The MSWs and clients can enjoy a massage or privately talk in the sauna. The third floor contained fifty-one private rooms for sex. The rooms are well-furnished and clean. The whole place looks rich and successful and expects its clients to be the same.

I was told that the club had around 150 full-time workers, but during peak times, the building could accommodate large numbers of freelance "guest workers" totaling up to five hundred MSWs working in a week in Pistachio. A spacious antechamber social area with furniture and mirrors preceded the restrooms. In this anteroom, one could find MSWs rehearsing songs, practicing dance moves, gossiping, laughing, watching movies from their smartphones, reading fashion magazines, looking up makeup information, surgery information, or muscle training tips. Some just sat quietly and smoked cigarettes or sipped a drink. Pistachio did not provide anti-raid training sessions, as the police generally did not bother them. Nevertheless, I was told that on a few occasions, Herman sent a message telling everyone to quickly leave using the designated safe passageway to avoid an imminent police visit.

The bar owner generally charges the MSWs 30 percent of their earnings to cover the cost of maintaining the club and its services. The men can keep 70 percent of what they earn from their clients. According to Herman, there are, on average, around 150–200 customers per night, maybe more during weekends or public holidays. The Chinese and non-Chinese clients interact only when they indulge in bragging or showing off their wealth by giving large tips. Any hint of physical abuse or violence is strictly prohibited. The boss will not allow any behavior that might hurt the bar's reputation. Overall, I could sense a competitive atmosphere among the MSWs. Each night, they compete to find and catch the "big-fish" client.

Working Conditions in Pistachio

Most of the MSWs who worked in this bar completed high school and can speak only their native tongue. Most are unable to carry on simple conversations in English. Like female sex workers, many of these young men also come from relatively poor rural areas. They must rely on their salaries to maximize their physical assets through technologies of embodiment. Common cosmetic surgeries for men are nose, chin, ear, hair restoration, and skin refinement. Some MSWs may try to go overseas for transgender surgeries like breast enlargement and implantation. These procedures are relatively expensive and unreliable in China, so they travel to South Korea or Thailand to get the procedures done. For example, a nose job in Beijing may cost 200,000 yuan, but the MSWs said that in South Korea, one could get better quality work for half the cost.

There is an identifiable and well-established network among gay men for medical procedures and surgeries. Based on word of mouth, some

MSWs will go to a specific place in Thailand to undergo transgender surgery. Many of the men interviewed spoke of using the same dermatologist with an office in China. This particular doctor will bring his staff upon invitation by a sponsor (in this case, Herman) and stay at a local five-star hotel for one week. During that time, the doctor and his staff will schedule and complete as many procedures as possible. These include Botox face injections, overall skin care, nose jobs, and other technology embodiment procedures for the MSWs. These men receive the latest skin and plastic surgery information from gay-oriented online apps like Grindr, Blued, Jack, Momo (陌陌), QQ, WeChat, Tan Tan App (探探), and iAround (遇见).

As noted earlier, the ages of the MSWs ranged between eighteen and fifty-nine, with the optimal age skewing young at around twenty before demand for services steadily declines as the worker nears thirty. Around this age, MSWs often consider transitioning to other gainful employment, like working in a sauna or settling into a relationship and exiting the business altogether. Some offered that being a masseuse helped prolong their marketability to age fifty and above.

Most of the MSWs interviewed came from rural China with neither cash nor connections to partake in technologies of embodiment. Many of the men I met had earlier worked in sweatshop factories before engaging in sex work. Scrambling for income, many of these men ended up working at Pistachio. The men begin by showing interest in flirting or fantasy. The Pistachio men are on QQ lists advertising male companionship, allowing local men or drivers from Beijing, Shanghai, or Zhejiang to know how to find them. In Pistachio, the men routinely perform stripteases on stage to drum up business. However, they also work the room by walking around and chatting with clients. Afterward, they privately arrange additional services for interested customers.

Migrant MSWs often feel they cannot escape their fate. They all said that they never wanted to be used by men as sexual playthings. Sex workers need education and help to better understand the protected rights and social benefits afforded to all citizens. They are aware of how powerless they are in Chinese society, and many have no means to further their own self-interests. This is where NGOs, guilds, or even the government can intervene and bring needed change.

In conclusion, research involving MSWs, *tongqi*, medical doctors, HIV patients, and TSWs is crucial to understanding significant social forces operating in China. Interacting with informants, getting familiar with them, and winning their trust takes time. I spent more than four years (mainly in the summer) working and talking with the informants about their lives and their struggles. Rather than asking a series of simple preprogrammed survey questions, the ethnographic approach enabled me to collect answers to questions that were deep and difficult to articulate, responses that emerged in the moment about things most important to my interlocutors.

2

China's Male Commercial Sex Industry

Rural-to-Urban Migration

I met Yang, a thirty-year-old MSW, in July 2015 in Pistachio. He had emigrated from Jilin, Heilongjiang Province, in North China, and had worked in a factory for one year before entering the MSW industry. Yang was tall and muscular, with tan skin and six-pack abs. To me, he looked more like a swimming coach than a pimp. However, his clothes were eye-catching: a pink polo shirt and tight yellow jeans. This would draw attention by Chinese standards because conventional guys dress in muted tones and conservative styles. When he spoke to me, I was struck by the sound of his smooth baritone.

This man who seemed to have it all together was a pimp—or *mamasan* in Chinese—in the lucrative underground world of gay prostitution. Yang worked with another *mamasan* at the club, and they were both always swamped. Yang was the most senior *mamasan*, juggling calls on his three mobile phones simultaneously. Yang estimated that he had managed over a thousand MSWs since 2014. He said that he generally trusted women more than men; he always complimented me on the drinks I served him and interacted with me as one professional to another. Over time, Yang became less formal and treated me more like one of his friends. He had been working in the sex industry since he was nineteen. After eleven years, he was now considered an old bird, well experienced, and a veteran.

There is always a high volume of business at Pistachio. Yang said that in today's China, much of the communication and financial transactions occur via online apps rather than face-to-face, although obviously, the actual activity still occurs in bars or clubs. He said apps are more for safety than anything else because some clients can be unpredictable and unnecessarily violent; the club tries to avoid unpleasant surprises. Yang was at the center of the Tianjin MSW world, connecting hundreds of clients with his deep catalog of "boys" (young men, eighteen–twenty-two or so), which typically numbers above two hundred. He said that he kept his ten best young men as long-term contractors while the others rotated through different pimps in town or between different cities. This practice is called "full-mooning," which means keeping the best MSWs under one's guardianship. Yang estimated that up to 20 percent of the Pistachio MSWs would say they were straight and worked there only because of the money, but that is more a reflection of social attitudes about being gay in China. Yang thought most of those 20 percent were actually bisexual. Yang said that since most of his MSWs came from Northeast China, they stayed in the region once their Dalian rotation was over. They commonly migrated to the provincial capital of Shenyang, then to Beijing, then south to Shanghai, Guangzhou, and down to Hainan. To run this circuit, most of those involved are young adult men eighteen or above. They move silently from one section of the prostitution industry to another and from city to city. Although the burnout rate is high, the ranks are continually replenished by youths from rural areas, China's lowest economic strata.

 Rather than operating under the guise of a sauna, massage parlor, or karaoke bar, Yang ran his business by maintaining ten apartments, which also served as workspaces for the prostitutes next door to Pistachio. Herman, the boss of Pistachio, also provided nearby apartments to other pimps. Since Herman's apartments were typically fully rented, he could quickly uproot the operation as needed. Yang said that he had to move often, even though almost every pimp was protected by paid informants in the police force or judicial system, many of whom were also customers. Yang said it was all about connections (*guanxi*). "My customers are from all walks of life," he reported, "like cadres, police, university professors, university students, and entrepreneurs. Some only hire my boys because they trust me."

 Yang spoke with pride about the trust he had earned. Customers prefer to go directly through pimps like him to avoid trouble or attention, like if they belong to the police, a cadre, or a university and need their identity hidden. Yang said many of his clients feared blackmail by someone they met for sex directly or through phone apps and the internet. Of course, his role did not extend to protecting either party from sexually transmitted diseases. Yang and I often talked at parks and cafés, developing a friendship as I learned how the industry operates. Yang regularly flew to Hong Kong afterward for shopping, and we spoke a few times more. Yang told me that many MSWs like him because they identify with his background as a poorly educated rural Northern Chinese. They all come from multiple-child families, and 95 percent worked at some point in the factories.

During the fieldwork, Yang showed me a poem written by a former factory worker who felt isolated from family and mistreated by female line managers. The work has also been translated into English:

> *Everyone said it is good to go to Tianjin and Beijing*个个都说天津北京好
> *Everyone goes to Tianjin and Beijing*个个都往天津北京跑
>
> *Working like a donkey everyday* 天天加班像头驴
> *Working overtime but without extra compensation* 加班超时无报酬
> *Was scolded by female line managers for no reason*天天挨骂无理由
> *Without love, and cannot see parents*没有爱但想念爹娘
> *Life like a prison, like an iron cage*生活像囚笼像鸟笼
> *Dehumanized and suffered mechanical dismemberment*身体像机器样被肢解
>
> *Empty love* 爱空空情空空
> *Empty pocket*人空空钱空空
> *Empty career* 事空空业空空
> *Cannot come out; it is like a jungle* 不能出柜如被困森林
> *Was laughed at by the female line managers*被女人矮化欺负
> *Labor can be sold*劳力可出卖
> *Dignity cannot be sold*尊严不能卖
>
> *Empty love* 爱空空情空空
> *Empty pocket*人空空钱空空
> *Empty career* 事空空业空空

I met Hongyi (twenty-four) in August 2019. He had been living with his "sugar daddy" for six months, enjoying the bounty of a generous monthly income package. Hongyi said that he loved his job and found value and meaning in it. He indulged in skincare products and regularly worked out in the gym. He went to Thailand for a nose job and Botox injections and said he was considering eyelid and chin surgery. Having a regular sex partner and a "good package" were his main reasons for working in the sex industry, and he pledged he would keep working until no clients wanted him anymore. He regularly wired money to his parents to maintain their villa and invest in their properties. Hongyi said he loved his job, exuding confidence and pride in being so cosmopolitan. He told me he would follow his feelings and was anticipating his next adventure for a "big fish" to support him.

Meanwhile, Dalin (twenty-three) capitalized on embodiment and emotional labor technologies to pursue a cosmopolitan lifestyle and escape rural poverty by de-centering the tropicality associated with his peasant origins. Since he did not hold the urban *hukou*, he could not use city services or benefits without paying the full listed price. Therefore, he had to travel back to his village of origin for affordable medical care or social services.

Tropicality and the Demands of Urban Gay Culture

Tropicality means that urban China treats rural China as a colony, as developed nations imperially treat developing nations. In this sense, the urban rich exploit the rural poor by providing low wages and precarious employment and limiting access to affordable insurance. The pursuit of urban masculinity using cosmetics and cosmetic surgery has become increasingly easy for MSWs. Several informants admitted that from photoshopped pictures in mobile apps to plastic surgery, body re-sculpting machines or nutritional supplements (and even prosthetics) helped them obtain an enhanced, more idealized body in terms of tone, shape, and appearance. For these reasons, MSWs employ aesthetic technologies to remove their rural "otherness" and instead equip themselves with the accoutrements of urban masculinity. However, this strategy raises questions about the geographical imaginations of subaltern peoples as well as their spatialities in the city.

As the global recognition of urban gay consumer cultures moves mainstream, the topic of body image—especially regarding gay men—has elicited discussion by scholars. Shilling (1993) has suggested that debates surrounding men's bodies have emerged in tandem with the recognition of the lucrative consumer culture related to gay men. The consumer culture, termed "pink-pound" or "gay economy," refers to the economic power of the LGBTQ+ community (Jones 2005). Within the subculture of the gay community in Western countries, the muscular and neat physique of Caucasian bodies is identified as ideal (Duncan 2010; Wood 2004). The notion of ideal body image relates to Connell's concepts of hegemonic masculinity or body dissatisfaction as contributing to male perspectives of the ideal portrayed in advertising, mass media, and social media platforms (Connell and Messerschmidt 2005; Lanzieri and Hildebrandt 2011; Wagner 2016; Wood 2004). Hegemonic masculinity fulfills the conventional norms and cultural expectations of society. It implies that power, difference, and desire are mapped out not only in terms of gender but also in terms of other social and cultural identifications, such as ethnicity, sexuality, and class (Butler 2017; Connell 1995; Mac an Ghaill and Haywood 2007). These works explain how the "gay male gaze" (Wood 2004) impacts body image disturbance and psychosocial oppression due to established hierarchies in urban gay communities. In China, urban gays shun characteristics defining one colloquially as a "country bumpkin." The urban gay community maintains the standards for physical appearance, behavior, and speech. Rural gay men are shunned for failing to meet those expectations (Kong 2012b) and stigmatized for their peasant origins and rural queer masculinity.

The literature on migrants has often focused disproportionally on female migrants working in manufacturing and service industries. Studies of male peasant migrants note that they typically move to the city for economic and family reasons but face exploitation because they lack skills and end up in unstable jobs with low pay and little opportunity for advancement. Urban perceptions about peasant male migrants lead to overt discrimination, reinforcing attitudes that the rural environment is intrinsically inferior. Once in the city, the migrants' self-perception regarding their self-esteem and their masculinity suffers as they struggle to succeed in competitive urban China.

This chapter addresses male peasant migrants' efforts to escape from rural poverty. Without the help of traditional institutions such as the government or labor market groups, they instead look to themselves to attain their goals of individualized self, freedom, and autonomy. In China, gay male migrants find themselves subject to this tropical gaze whenever their urban counterparts construct them as coarse, unrefined products in serious need of modernist development. They are motivated by their search for urban acceptance and financial independence to escape the primitivity and poverty associated with tropicality (Duncan 2000; Jazeel 2014; Sidaway et al. 2018). As such, a significant number of gay male migrants may choose sex work to survive because they can employ technologies of embodiment to keep themselves physically desirable, which in turn helps them capitalize on their affective labor.

Hence, the rural queer sex worker is forced to survive in the face of metropolitan China's consumerism by identifying and addressing deficits in his masculinity (Ghazian 2014). The MSWs, with the aid of surgery and other urban solutions, mimic traits fetishized by the urban middle-class gay community. The growth of China's middle class has resulted in rural gay masculinities being subject to the colonialist condescension of urban queers (Tsang 2021a). The gay body is synonymous with tropicality, exercising technology of embodiment and emotional labor in the gay commercial sex industry to access urban social hierarchies.

Migrant rural-to-urban MSWs adopt embodiments of emotional labor to enhance their economic survivability in China's urban gay commercial sex industry. Upon arrival to China's metropolitan areas, migrant MSWs quickly learn that to succeed, they must shed all trappings of their former rural life. They transform themselves physically by undergoing various cosmetic surgeries to conform to the soft-masculine urban standards of maleness deemed most attractive and appealing. Since emotional labor is the commodification of private emotions intended to be sold for profit in a capitalist economy, these men seek to quickly remove negative markers reflecting the rurality of their queer masculinity. Engaging in emotional labor while conforming to urban standards of gay masculinity increases their chances of survival in the urban sex industry. Metropolitan gay communities tend to look down upon their rural counterparts (Tsang 2021a).

A significant number of MSWs in China come from rural areas (Kong 2012b). These migrant men grew up in their family villages, where they kept their sexual orientation closeted. Once they began associating with the gay community in the city, they accepted work as MSWs. The MSWs examined in this work sell their bodies to urban gay men and are no different from migrants in the Global South in search of opportunities in the Global North. The embodiment of metropolitan standards of masculine appearances, social skills, and attractiveness are prerequisites to developing their careers in a competitive queer sex industry.

Commodifying Rural Queer Bodies with Urban Embodiments

One respondent, Minmin (twenty-three), lamented the expectations of China's middle-class gay community regarding physical appearances. The economic climate of post-reform Chinese society left him conflicted and always chasing more income. Whoever has money will receive respect and prestige in society, as well as social status and respectability:

> I am a poor and uneducated peasant man from a country village. I am embarrassed to admit my simple past growing up in poverty. But in today's China, no one in the city knows where you came from. I look more urban and cosmopolitan than most people in Tianjin. I live in an upscale neighborhood, and most of my neighbors are upper-class. Sometimes, it is easy to forget that I am a sex worker.

Yong, a twenty-four-year-old MSW, concurred with Minmin:

> I work hard to look trendy and modern. I go to the gym twice weekly and practice yoga on weekends. I also learned how to dance. I can have more plastic surgery to make myself look younger and stay 'hot.' I buy creams, stylish clothes, and accessories to make me look cosmopolitan. I make enough money to travel to Japan, Korea, or Thailand every month . . . Life is good, right?

The conversations about the MSWs reinforce Bourdieu's (1978) observation that working-class men exercise through the manual labor of their blue-collar jobs, while upper/middle-class people train their bodies during leisure time as an end in itself. For this reason, sophisticated body building represents an upper/middle-class lifestyle where the individual uses discretionary time to keep the body fit and attractive. A muscular, sculpted body in post-reform China represents being upper-class/middle-class. Other than adopting a gentlemen or urban lifestyle temperament, physique, and appearance are common ways for gay migrant men to overcome their peasant origins and gain access to the city's middle-class gay spaces. This trend among MSWs coheres with previous studies linking physical fitness with the cosmopolitan image established in the wider urban gay community. The motivations are understandable as to why sex workers use technologies of embodiment to maximize their body image. It enables them to commodify their rural bodies in the metropolitan gay sex trade. Qianjin (twenty-four) is a six-year veteran of the gay sex industry:

> I have learned how to use makeup and different cosmetic products to please all my client's tastes and preferences. If one client wants me to have tanned skin, I can use makeup to darken my skin. Then, I can role-play if he wants me to say I come from the Bahamas, Indonesia, or Thailand. If another client says he likes fine-textured delicate skin, I will lighten my skin accordingly. Whatever they want, I give it to them.

Siu was a twenty-one-year-old MSW who had worked in the sex industry for more than two years:

> I put together my own wardrobe. I select wigs, dresses, and lingerie to suit the different tastes of my clients . . . . Most of the clothes I buy online, but occasionally, I will go to Hong Kong to hunt for name-brand items. My clients seem to love me best in skinny jeans and bright tops, especially pink, orange, and purple.

Trends in the middle-class queer community shape the spaces of China's urban gay sex industry. Having the proper appearance, being physically fit, and having soft skills like listening and being articulate are especially important for sex workers to survive in the industry. Many rural migrants work hard to overcome their lack of education and being perceived as unsophisticated. All the interviewees agreed that they engaged in some physical training to maintain their looks and meet the demands of the urban gay market for prostitutes. The respondents revealed that body training was the most common way for them to meet the gay community's standard for masculine erotic capital. For example, Ming said he regularly trained in a gym to maintain peak physical fitness and attractiveness. He said it is expected both in the gay community as well as the male sex industry. Qiulin (twenty-five) had been in the industry for six years:

> I do it to succeed in this industry. I think all of us go to the gymnasium regularly to lift weights and work out. . . . I also have had cosmetic surgery to make myself look like a K-Pop star, and I use moisturizing creams daily to keep my skin soft and young-looking. I must do these things to survive.

Jinmin (twenty-three) agreed that being young and muscular is necessary to compete in the industry:

> The industry is very competitive nowadays. The trend among MSWs is "younger is better." . . . Most of the clients like young men. . . . I am only twenty-three years old but already regarded as old. On the street, it is easy to grab someone thin, but it is harder to find someone muscular and young.

In addition to physical fitness, some of the MSWs emphasized the importance of male beauty and a soft facial appearance. Jung (2011, 39) referred to the smoother facial features made popular by Korean pop stars as "pan-East Asian soft masculinity." Jung noted that "this soft masculinity is a hybrid product constructed through the transcultural amalgamation of South Korea's traditional *seonbi* masculinity (which is heavily influenced by Chinese Confucian *wen* masculinity), Japan's *bishonen* (pretty boy) masculinity, and global metrosexual masculinity." According to Louie (2012, 932), a macho-looking body in modern China is by itself inadequate when it is the softer facial look obtained through surgery which signifies competitive economic power; it is a symbol of *wen* masculinity. Among the respondents, Jin (twenty-three) was not muscular, did not use cosmetic products, and did not wear name-brand clothes. Jin said his success was due entirely to his pretty face, as his face is everything for him to stay in the commercial sex industry. Beauty does not mean that the MSWs should be extremely handsome or muscular. Possessing stylish and well-fitting clothing is a minimum expectation in the sex industry. Jin said the other criterion was to avoid being sissy and effeminate because most of the clients did not like this type of MSW.

Keeping Clients Happy: Staying Sweet for the Sugar Daddy

Nineteen out of 151 MSWs said they were in situations living with a sugar daddy (an older, wealthy client). One interviewee said he started such a relationship the day before we spoke, while another had been with the same client for almost an entire year. Sun (nineteen) was an outgoing and pleasant MSW with an ultra-modern fashion sense. He wore earrings, metallic wristbands, chains, rings, a ripped white T-shirt, black skinny jeans, and shiny black Oxford shoes with metallic decorations. Sun wore lots of cologne. He said it was an essential part of his sex appeal, especially when his client whispered in his ear.

Sun bragged to me that his current sugar daddy requested his service for three months. He had to take a high-speed train from Tianjin to Zhejiang. His sugar daddy was a tycoon of a listed company with a wife and two lovely kids. However, he had a horrible relationship with his family, especially with his son. Much younger than Sun, the tycoon's son had not spoken to his father for ten years. The tycoon kept his bisexuality a secret. In front of his family, he appeared straight, highly educated, and successful. Sun described the persona he adopted to please his patron:

> He is a very dominant guy and loves to conquer my body. He has excellent muscle tone, a nice smile, and an upbeat outlook. The most important thing is that in front of him, I must act like his little boy so that he can dominate me. I like it! I pretend I am innocent and naive and give him lots of compliments. I have served many clients and know how to read people's minds.

Fa (twenty-two) was proud of his muscular physique. He had been living with his sugar daddy for six months and enjoyed a lucrative monthly income:

> I use cosmetic surgery to keep him interested so that he will return. I also use skin care products and regular workouts at the gym. A few years ago, I was in Thailand and heard that some of my friends had nose surgery, so I wanted it. I did not have a specific reason; I just wanted a better look. In the past, I used to inject Botox. However, I stopped using it because it was so expensive. It costs a few thousand yuan [US$500] for the injection.

You will look older if you stop injecting it and look weird, especially when you smile.... You look "stiff" like a zombie ... that is why I now use the 'face-slimming needle' [*shoumianzhen* 瘦面针]. I am obsessed with eyelid and chin surgery and want to try more.

Another MSW, Pak (twenty-one), had dark tan skin, which his sugar daddy found sexy and attractive:

If my sugar daddy wants me to have tan and coarse skin, I will sunbathe and make my skin dark, so I look like I am from the Caribbean; however, if he wants me to have delicate textured skin, in that case, I will wear lots of [cosmetic moisturizing] masks, use different makeup techniques to look like I am Japanese or Korean, and make myself look cute, docile, and delicate.

Hexiang (twenty-four) said:

I recently put more money into my physical appearance, such as Botox shots and trips to the gym room. I know that clients want me to take care of my skin ... and try to look tan. Thai and Singaporean clients love tan skin! I just made it through a dark time for me, and now I am ready to overcome it and move on.

Chenliu (twenty-five) agreed that skincare helped bring back clients. He said he came from the countryside and did lots of farming. He reported having had recurring problems with acne, some wrinkles on his forehead, and dark spots on his face. Therefore, the first thing he had to do was thoroughly clean and hydrate his skin. To please his clients, he often used white creams, different cleansers, castor oils, and cleaning oils from Japan to make himself look white and delicate. He wore sunscreen and concealer to cover his black spots when he went out. He regularly used whitening needle injections and wore paper masks with whitening lotion and luxury-brand whitening facial creams to lighten his complexion. Chenliu always wanted to appear as an urban cosmopolite. He despised the way city people looked down on rural villagers as uncouth rubes or country bumpkins. The whitening practice reflects cosmopolitanism and assigns a status to those with lighter skin color, highlighting the divide between urban China and rural China. In Chenliu's case, it was not the intersectionality of race, gender, and hegemonic whiteness that drove his practice but a concern with age and desirability. Desirability is one of the privileges afforded to an urban cosmopolitan.

Staying Young to Keep Clients Interested

The West accepts both "hard and strong" and "soft and weak" gay personas. In the same way, a young man who possesses girlish beauty and exhibits stereotypical feminine traits is acceptable in the Chinese gay community. Louie termed it as the "ideal soft male in China, Japan, and Korea" (Louie 2012), which is less aggressive but gentle and caring (Hu 2018). Generally, softer masculinity is considered *wen-wu* in social, economic, and cultural high-status situations. It could even describe the main characteristic of Chinese masculinity. A body-mind balance is a masculine ideal, but the Chinese "prioritizes the mind more than most Western cultures" (Louie 2014). In other words, the ideal Chinese man is represented as cultivated, refined, and physically robust. With the development of popular culture as both economic and hybridized, Chinese traditional masculinity also diversifies into modern ideal masculinity. Louie introduced the concepts of globetrotting Chinese masculinity, which means wealthy, worldly, and worthy men in the post-Mao modernization era (Louie 2012). Louie also offered Chinese metrosexuality, which elevates the urban man with beauty (*dushili nan* 都市丽男) or flower-like men (*huayang-nanzi* 花样男子) with a modernized and internationalized lifestyle, who are also good looking with either middle- or upper-class income (Louie 2012). The popularity of metrosexual standards of masculine beauty is also due in part to the popularity of Western-based men's magazines among China's middle-class men (Song and Lee 2012).

However, bodily reconstruction is not limited to muscle building and physique. Men increasingly consume grooming and skincare products and undergo cosmetic or aesthetic surgery in Western countries (Gill et al. 2005) to look more masculine. Dong (twenty-four) had worked in the MSW industry for five years:

> I know many clients who do not like sissy effeminate MSWs. . . . My voice was naturally soft and gentle, and some clients told me they did not like it.

So, I went to Thailand for throat surgery to give my voice a more robust, more masculine sound. This surgery is called fat injection thyroplasty, which injects fat into my vocal cords, adding bulk and creating a deeper-sounding voice. Now my voice is stronger. Lately, I have been looking at hair implant surgery to make myself look more masculine.

First impressions are essential for MSWs, and they must successfully hide their peasantries to impress urban middle-class clients. Meanwhile, natural beauty or attractiveness is determined genetically. Technological developments and surgical procedures can enhance physical appearances, and cosmetic products or invasive surgery are ways for sex workers to achieve the most attractive and desirable facial appearance. Some rural MSWs impress their clients by undergoing cosmetic aesthetic surgery. Such surgeries give them added erotic capital regarding their appearance and artificial male beauty, which conforms to the performatives of urban gay bodies in post-reform China. Wen (2013) noted that the culture of emphasizing male beauty impacts the cosmetic surgery industry and youth culture. Present research discovered that cosmetic surgery or micro-surgery is more common in the gay community or gay male sex industry. Cunjian (forty-one) described his experiences with cosmetic surgery:

Age is my enemy now. I will use cosmetic surgery to keep clients interested so that they will return. Like plastic surgery, skin care products, and, of course, regular workouts at the gym. Therefore, I will look more masculine but not sissy. My clients prefer I have tan skin, so I sunbathe and go to the gym daily to keep my looks. . . . I will do whatever the client wants, like I am an obedient little child . . . because my clients like it.

One NGO working to help MSWs implemented a micro-cosmetic surgery program. Surgery for eyelids, Botox injections, and similar procedures were extremely popular among MSWs because they helped them obtain the body capital for enhanced first impressions. Less-muscular participants used more cosmetic or grooming products to maintain their attractive physical appearance. Along with beauty technologies, MSWs often compare the quality of the product with the relative price. Increasingly, smartphone apps are being used by sex workers to advertise themselves and their services on dating sites or gay community websites. Jin (twenty-three) was both a worker and a client in the industry and projected a masculine, metropolitan image:

> I discovered that although beauty is an essential criterion for sex workers to attract their clients, authentic and natural beauty draws a line between real and fake good looks. I discovered that some sex workers might use Photoshop to create a misleading or even phony portfolio in their advertisement to attract clients on websites and apps. I believe MSWs should honestly present their physical attractiveness rather than use deception.

The widespread sense of insecurity reported by the MSWs signals an unease with traditional notions of hypermasculinity, such as those reflected in the rugged, hard-bodied male stereotype considered desirable in both the East and the West. For these reasons, a muscularized body obtained through gym workouts but without cosmetic surgery is inadequate. While the ruggedness of the male body conditioned by rurality in Western countries sets the standards of hegemonic masculinity (Brandth and Haugen 2005), the ruggedness of the peasant male (and queer) body formed by agricultural work is symbolic of tropicality and an absence of urban sophistication. There are thus clear limits to the enhancements that can be made to urbanize the queer rural body.

When I talked to the 101 MSWs, most of them strengthened their emotional outlooks analogous to how plastic surgery, grooming, and working out enhance one's physical appearance. These are all processes that maximize the effectiveness of emotional labor. MSWs universally said they wanted to be more cosmopolitan and enjoy a lifestyle marked by success (for self-esteem) and financial independence. Cosmopolites tend toward travel, leisure activities, and luxuries such as being able to afford to live in a gated community.

Naked Yoga and Capitalizing Emotional Labor

All the MSWs interviewed were pragmatic about the transitory nature of their physical attractiveness, no matter their fitness regimens or surgical enhancements. They had control only over their emotional labor and agreed that that mattered most in determining if a client returned or agreed to maintain a long-term relationship. In the gay commercial sex industry, urban clients prefer MSWs who embody soft masculinity. Thus, for MSWs who cannot fully de-tropicalize their gay bodies, emotional labor is deployed as the best means of staying competitively desirable. One notable tactic used to enhance emotional labor was developing mindfulness through naked yoga sessions.

Studio Session and Mindfulness

The practice of naked yoga has been widespread since ancient times. During the 1960s, it made a resurgence among the hippie counterculture movement in the United States. It has also caught the interest of some sectors of China's gay community as a way to bond and safely work with partners on intimacy issues. Although naked yoga classes can be mixed gender, Brian (twenty-four) invited me to his studio, where he has been teaching all-male naked yoga courses. At his studio in Tianjin, a series of rooms were arranged like classrooms accommodating up to ten adults. The walls were lined with mirrors, and the studio was bathed in soft red lighting and candles. Incense and meditation music completed the experience, all designed to project a sense of peace, comfort, and safety.

As a visitor, I was not allowed inside the classroom, and I had to remain in the outside lobby. However, I saw the ten attendees who arrived that night. They were primarily Chinese MSWs and three visitors from Thailand and Malaysia. They encompassed a range of physical fitness and body types, although most were tall, thin, and physically fit. Brian said he instructs them to undress and lie on yoga mats set a few feet apart. Initially, there is minimal touching. Brian wants everyone first to feel comfortable enough to be in a room, naked, with each other. Because the emphasis is on fitness, body beauty, and sexual health, students are directed to engage in a series of exercises. He teaches his students how to practice naked yoga. Everyone lies on their back, puts their feet in the air, and progresses to "yoga in motion" exercises. At first, time is spent on sharing the rules—no staring at others, flirting, or perving. The focus is on body rhythm and what speaks to the heart. Brian regularly invites clients, sex partners, and short-term partners to his studio. He also set up a WeChat group to recruit new clients and interested parties to the studio.

The studio provides a welcoming, safe, and supportive environment for MSWs to bring their clients. In this relaxed space, they are free from the constraints of clothing in a secular studio. Attendance is by invitation only, and only regular attendees of naked yoga know the address. Naked yoga allows the MSWs to cultivate affective labor as they care for clients in a manner that may be reciprocated. As a form of emotional labor, naked yoga is an activity that allows MSWs to help themselves and develop their self-worth. The goal is to empower MSWs and alleviate feelings associated with the necropolitics of social death. By capitalizing on emotional labor from their occupation, they can exhibit resistance and agency to overcome their circumstances (Hoang 2010; Hochschild 1983; Wolkowitz et al. 2013).

Naked yoga aims to help an individual overcome hang-ups or insecurities about their body. The benefits include lowered stress levels and increased self-confidence. It is an intensive form of self-psychotherapy. It allows the whole body to breathe and to feel the air on every inch of the skin. It enables participants to indulge their physical senses and become more aware of pleasure centers throughout their bodies. According to Brian, many men arrive with body issues, weight problems, and poor self-image. They find that naked yoga helps them realistically assess and accept their body. Naked yoga helps address life stresses while encouraging healthy intimacy. Brian said this activity helps MSWs because it helps them solidify relationships and shift the emphasis from purely transactional sex for money to pleasure for pleasure's sake. Pleasure becomes the focus of the experience rather than the money.

As such, the atmosphere focuses on fun, pleasure, and enjoyment among the participants in the studio. Naked yoga is distinctive as it involves a deeper exploration of breathing and provides a more focused mechanism for quieting the mind, enhancing mindfulness, looking inside, and developing a nonjudgmental temperament. Brian said that as a soul-searching technique, it enhances body muscles and builds confidence and appreciation for others:

> Naked yoga connects me with my body. I no longer feel the need to moan uncontrollably with my clients or try to please them with an act, flirt with them, act like a sissy, or talk in a baby voice. Naked yoga makes me focus on what I want for my pleasure. Sometimes, I have had clients steal my iPhone

and credit card; however, with the practice of naked yoga, I can better appreciate myself and scan unwelcoming clients. Now, I am mentally and emotionally relaxed. I am laid back and follow my feelings to work and live.

Experts assert that naked yoga engages the parasympathetic nervous system, alleviating nervous anxiety and stress. Brian described it as "unadorned fleshiness," which allowed him to indulge in the multifaceted experience of human pleasures. He said that there is an entirely different body awareness without clothes. After the class ended, Brian met me outside, and we went to a café. There, he described how naked yoga helped him be an excellent provider of commercial sexual services:

> I feel like when I am naked, without the constraints of clothes, the focus is much more internal. Naked yoga is the ideal prescription for developing serious self-love for my body. I have to appreciate myself first so I can value my job! I feel like I connect myself with my clients in the studio! If I develop a Buddha belly, I will remind myself to be on a diet and exercise more to make my muscles firm, strong, and masculine.

Chujuan (twenty-one) had practiced naked yoga while living with a client for three years:

> I danced for my sugar daddy through naked yoga. He preferred me to dance like a straight guy instead of a slutty girl, no shaking ass or hips. This is what he hated. Money is not easy to earn, ah? My arms, belly, waist, and legs must be straight and show off my muscles. The naked yoga allowed me to feel, touch, and smell my "honey" [his client] without a barrier. The naked yoga made me believe in the unity of love, emotion, and heart. It allowed me to chase a soulmate rather than provide a service to my clients. In the commercial sex industry, it is hard to find a soulmate or a long-term partner, but naked yoga gives me the chance to dream.

Billy (twenty-three) had been working as an MSW for four years. He used his emotional labor to keep his clients returning:

> My honey needs to talk with someone. Last year, I advised him on how to repair the father-and-son relationship. I suggested he spend more time

with his son, perhaps travel together. He could give him some gifts during his birthday or festivals; he could write him a birthday card and give him something he really liked. Last time, I asked him to buy a Japanese cartoon for his trip to Japan, and he did. At first, his son did not like it, but he could tell that at least his dad tried to show his love. I am sure their relationship will improve in the future. I can disclose my innermost feelings to my daddy, and he can do the same with me, too. However, I am afraid this relationship will not last for long. He may dump me for a GoGo boy [gay sex worker in Thailand].

Powei (twenty-eight) sold his naked-yoga and massage skills, working with heart, emotion, discernment, and care, for which his clients paid him extremely well, up to 1,700,000 yuan (US$250,000) a year. According to him, Tianjin, Beijing, and Shanghai were the best areas to live in because they offered the most opportunities and were full of dynamic, energetic people. He described his job as "passion plus excitement." He used naked yoga to focus, engage in mindfulness, and develop a nonjudgmental temperament. The soul-searching technique worked his muscles and built confidence and appreciation.

When I revisited Powei in January 2020, before the outbreak of COVID-19 in China, he confirmed that his relationship with his client had ended. Powei said he went into seclusion and mourned for an hour, then returned to work. He had come out to his parents the previous summer, and his parents had been supportive. He continued to wire them money every month, although his mother still nagged him to marry and become a father.

Successfully Selling Sex with Emotional Labor

This chapter develops the concept of capital within the context of male masculinities pursued by migrant MSWs. Under the development of beautifying technologies, bodily capital can be a crucial means for MSWs to gain benefits through technologies of embodiment and performing masculinity. While manhood or masculinity is commodified to both clients and sex workers, this research evaluates how masculinities develop through the sex worker's body capital. Moreover, the whole process has the potential to allow MSWs to reclaim their masculinity through cultural capital and technologies of embodiment as well as other capital advances.

I met Zeng (twenty-four) in Pistachio in Tianjin in 2017. His appearance and outlook were effeminate, dramatic, cynical, and witty. He was fortunate to escape from the brutality of China's sex trade at a relatively young age to gain a position that granted him meaningful agency. He was a genuine drama king; he loved playing Chinese opera and Chinese drama. He capitalized on his skills and put on a show using Chinese drama and dance, which kept old clients returning while attracting new ones.

One night, I attended Zeng's Chinese opera performance. We spoke after the performance, and he eagerly invited me to see him perform in drag the following night. When I went to his drag show, I saw a very different look. While it is common for men to dress as women in Chinese opera, they tend to wear conservative gowns and exaggerated features that are not sexual. Zeng in drag was totally different. Although still wearing a Chinese evening gown, his dark makeup and long curly hair richly complemented his overtly sexual dancing on stage. He prowled the stage like a large cat, looking aggressive and seductive. Zeng bragged of his lightning-fast cross-dressing skills, which allowed him to change his clothes and face makeup in seconds:

> For my clients, I can be a cross-dresser, transgender prostitute, or even just a naughty student. I have a game where I dress as a girl and find the client at a bar where we pretend to be strangers, and I let him conquer me. My clients love this game! I can change clothes at the hotel or his place. Some clients demand that I dress like a woman right from the moment they see me. They will not stop for a second if I dress like a man. I go to my client's home with my brows and nails done, ready for a dramatic performance. With my hairnet and manicured nails, all my clients love it!

Zeng said he managed risk in his job. He loved risk-taking and thrill-seeking activities. Once, a client suggested they go to the countryside to play in the jungle. He wore camouflage and carried a pink plastic water gun. However, Zeng sensed that something was wrong on the way there and texted his brother to come immediately and get him. His instinct was validated when the client suddenly pulled the car next to a bank machine and stopped. The client pulled out a long knife and demanded that he give him his ATM card and password. Zeng grabbed his hand, and the two struggled for what seemed like an eternity. By the time his brother arrived with the police, Zeng had been cut on his chest and stomach. The client was arrested and charged, but Zeng was in the hospital for two weeks.

Another time, Zeng met some clients who, after sex, threatened and forced him to carry drugs to a dangerous group of users. His occupation routinely put him at risk physically, legally, and emotionally. One client who fell out of love with him retaliated by sending naked photos of Zeng to his sister, mother, and even the mayor of his rural village. His family was then banned from the ancestral halls because he was considered dirty, sinful, and accursed.

Another MSW, thirty-year-old Chester, was strikingly handsome. Although a bit old, he was tall (six-foot-three) and bragged that he could attract a different client every night for an entire year. He said his greatest strengths were his looks and his confidence. In a quiet moment, however, he said this life was not what he wanted. He shifted his tone and said he performed emotional labor with heart, like taking a shower with his client after sex. Or slowly undressing his client before they begin a night of lovemaking. He noted that he can make gourmet dishes for a candle-lit dinner or a full breakfast the following morning:

> Sometimes, if I like a guy, I will not charge him anything. But for others, especially those who are unattractive or annoying—I may charge them double. If the client is creative in bed, I may also charge less; it all depends on how I feel. I can make those decisions because I am a world-class sexy boy!

Chester did everything to make his clients feel welcome and wanted. He said that he was a mind reader and knew at that moment what a client wanted or needed, whether a glass of water and a massage or a commemorative text message celebrating Christmas or Lunar New Year. Chester said that he could be a warm and considerate guy (*tite zhoudao de nangnan* 体贴周到的暖男), a humorous little flesh meat (*youyou fengqe youmo de xiaoxianrou* 又有风趣幽默的小鲜肉), or a very sexy cat (*shenggan shizu de xiaoyemao* 性感十足的小野猫).

I first met Victor (twenty-two) at one of the NGOs that help MSWs. He worked freelance, meaning he had to find his own clients. He grew up poor on a small farm and still had the tan skin and toned muscles to confirm his upbringing. He did poorly in school, failing several subjects. He was finally expelled after viciously beating up a classmate, who was hospitalized for an entire month. Since he was younger than sixteen at that time, Victor was placed in a custody education center. What should have been two years was instead forty-eight hours after his parents paid a bribe to the police. Victor's parents then had him working full-time in a paddy field growing rice, but he quickly became bored and went to North China to earn more money working in a cement factory. However, he soon quit that job because the sweatshop conditions paid him under 1,000 yuan (US$140) per month, working fourteen-hour shifts seven days per week. Victor was already regularly using gay dating apps to meet men after his shift. Soon he found that he could make quick money offering sex services. Eventually, a friend from his school days told him about a gay nightclub. Since then, he has been an active freelancer, soliciting his own clients:

> I confess I feel bored with just one client, so I am always looking for more variety. Of course, I want a big fish and looking in other ponds is the only way to find them. Men like me love a big dick [*paida* 排大], and I will reward my client with pleasure and thrills! I love my job.

Growing up in North China, he had no experience using cosmetic products; even his mother and sister did not use cosmetics. Victor said he recently needed to lighten his skin quickly for a client:

> I went to a dermatologist for treatment and did what he said. He said that twice a week, I needed to inject whitening needles into my skin. I also had to use chilled tea bags, cucumber, potato slices, and some quality name-brand whitening creams to make my skin white. I also added antioxidants to my diet, like berries, cherries, black plums, kidney beans, and prunes. I had to stop drinking, quit smoking, and stop taking drugs. My whitening tips are applying three–four tiny drops of organic cold-pressed rosehip oil after cleansing my face before bed. I also add a few drops to my SPF 50+ moisturizer in the morning to avoid black spots. The procedure was

much trouble for me, but my skin improved daily. It was encouraging and kept me motivated. I will do whatever my client wants.

While many encounters in China's urban gay bar scene are strictly transactional, genuine relationships are also forged, which help MSWs attain their long-term metropolitan dreams. One particular individual achieved almost mythical status in Tianjin. Zhen, a retired Chinese doctor living in Tianjin, now in his fifties, was regarded as a trailblazer and pioneer of success in the field of male prostitution. He was strong and muscular, and he sported a big handlebar mustache, which was his trademark. Self-confident and easy-going, Zhen was easy to talk to, warm and engaging. Zhen's story resembled that of many rural gay Chinese men. He married a village girl when he was twenty-two to please his parents and fulfill his obligation as a filial son. At the age of twenty-four, his first child was born, and Zhen realized that he disliked having sex with his wife. Despite his aversion to sex with her, he did what was expected of him, and the following year, she gave birth to his second child. At that point, Zhen ceased physical lovemaking with her. At first, his wife was annoyed and irritated with him. They argued and spoke of divorcing, but as with most Chinese couples, they decided instead to quietly tolerate each other. Whenever his wife asked him if he was gay, he stayed silent and refused to answer. When we spoke, he reported that he believed that neither his wife nor his children ever knew of his true sexual orientation. With the children grown, Zhen felt relaxed, with ample money and savings. At the time of our interview, he was devoted to a rich thirty-something client:

> All I can do for my sugar boy is to provide him with my shoulder, be a good listener, and pour him a cup of wine. I am very good at humor, and I will never talk down to him. Whatever he says, I will go along with him. It makes him very happy. I feel I am working for my life instead of a disgusting career. I love my job. I have strong feelings toward my sugar boy. It feels like we are a couple, like husband and wife. He respects me and always looks out for me. He keeps calling me Old Daddy (Laobaobei 老宝贝) or even Wife (Laopo 老婆). It gives me emotional connectedness, even though the money maintains our relationship.

Zhen enjoys his urban dream of material sufficiency and sexual acceptance in the city. His community admires him, which is a rare accomplishment for peasant queer men. There is a felt need to overcome insecurities surrounding the perceived intrinsic inferiority of the rural environment. Just as European colonials considered the tropics their environmental and geographical other (Driver and Yeoh 2000, 1), the fast pace of modernization in China's cities has created a dominant, confident urban middle class. The masculinities created by rural, tropical environments have traditionally been considered inferior by those from more temperate regions (Duncan 2000, 2010).

The Chinese new middle class considers their consumption of plastic surgery, fine dining, and luxury goods as the aspirational ideal that takes its cue from their "temperate" counterparts. To join this community, rural queers need time to transform themselves into urban queers. Most of the interviewed MSWs said they embarked on their migratory journeys to the city with the dream of enjoying the lifestyle of their urban middle-class counterparts. However, they first had to gain acceptance (Kong 2012b) and turned to cosmetic surgeries and alterations to help mask their rural, primitive masculinity.

The transition of MSWs to alternative professions, specifically livestreaming, is a phenomenon that has garnered attention in recent years. This shift has been precipitated by a multitude of factors, including the natural aging process, the ensuing struggle to be physically alluring, and the emotional labor inherent in sex work. A significant trend that has emerged is the migration to livestreaming, a profession that offers enhanced control over one's work environment and potentially less physical and emotional strain. The advent of digital technologies and the proliferation of social media platforms in China have facilitated this transition for MSWs. Many of these individuals possess physical appeal and are well versed in emotional or affective labor, skills that are transferable to the livestreaming industry. The livestreaming landscape in China is challenging and still in its nascent stages. However, it provides an alternative for these individuals to earn a living by capitalizing on the skills initially cultivated in the commercial sex industry. This shift in professional trajectory underscores the adaptability of MSWs and the evolving nature of work in the digital age.

Conclusion

This chapter examined how MSWs' efforts to escape from rural poverty led to the nuances of economic and class location in the urban context of post-reform China. To survive without the support of recognized institutional bodies (formal labor market, government services), they must meet the expectations placed on them through social dictates (individualized self, freedom, and autonomy). To survive in the gay commercial sex industry, MSWs must capitalize on technologies of embodiment and emotional labor skills. There is an ongoing tug-of-war between the values espoused by the traditional and the modern and East versus West. Eating Western-style and surfing the internet are products of modernity that are shaping MSWs' view of themselves and others. The pursuit of fashion and style illustrates how acquiring money through sex work allows them to reconstruct themselves "as a reflexive and inward-directed source of valuation" (Sassatelli 2000, 215–16). The peasant MSWs' intention to treat their technologies of urban embodiment and emotional labor as intermediaries of potential allows them to widen their spheres of choice and underwrite their financial futures. These individuals may not be beholden to the dictates of exploitative contracts, but they are bounded by societal expectations and limited by social and material support. This situation places them within a framework wherein sex work is one of the few platforms enabling them to overcome their socioeconomic environment and attain upward economic mobility (Tsang 2014, 2019, 2021). In this context, engaging in sex work is a rational and acceptable course of action despite the inherent risks of that occupation and the difficulties in leaving that trade.

Technologies of urban embodiment and emotional labor offer rural gay men the opportunity to improve their lives, enabling them to make consumer choices that position themselves as modern. Rather than looking like simple farm boys, these men can present themselves as successful cosmopolites, able to purchase high-end smartphones, designer skincare products, and name-brand fashionable clothing. Sex work allows MSWs to join the dominant urban social milieu in a manner previously unattainable (Tsang 2019a). The commercial sex industry provides them with the financial means to consume luxury accouterments that their oppressors—the new middle class—already enjoy daily (Tsang 2014, 2019).

As this chapter revealed, MSWs experience both positive and negative aspects of affective labor related to their occupation. Many MSWs openly stated that they enjoyed the lifestyle of physical pleasure, the sense of excitement, and the rebellious identity that went with being part of China's gay commercial industry. However, others lamented the ongoing risks of violence, abuse, stalking, and harassment from clients, lovers, police, and even gangsters. They must always think about public health risks with STDs and HIV and keep their occupation secret and hidden from outsiders. Still, most admitted that they had followed their instincts, feelings, and affection to use their affective labor skills. Each MSW knew that he must invest in plastic surgery and deploy beauty and sex appeal behaviors as forms of affective labor in their jobs. Attractive physical appearance is only a starting point in this competitive, transient, high-pressure industry. It is their willingness to take part in the affective labor of beauty as a social process that ensures that value is produced in these gay sexscapes.

The concept of necropolitics shows how the body of the rural queer male prostitute is inevitably subject to being marked for death and marked as inferior. With age comes the loss of looks and sexual appeal, resulting in clients being more able to exercise power to render the MSW disposable. When that happens, the MSW faces social death and can no longer enjoy the privileges afforded to the bodies of middle-class urban queers. This social pecking order renders the people from the countryside, particularly those who are gay, as individuals to be disregarded, erased from political representation, and treated as if dead.

3

"I Don't Want to Hurt an Innocent Country Girl, So I'll Marry a Lesbian"

Male Sex Workers, Parents' Expectations, and Face

Liu was a twenty-four-year-old MSW when I interviewed him in 2017 at a Tianjin café. I could see the stress he carried from his parents' constant pressure to get married. Liu regularly posted advertisements on *Tianya* (天涯), a Chinese website where anyone can post a classified ad or announcement. Liu showed me his latest *Tianya* advertisement, stating he was seeking a *lala* interested in marrying him, a gay man. Liu's advertisement clearly stated that a lesbian partner was needed for a marriage of convenience:

> I was born in 1993. I am 180 cm tall and a sunshine boy. I have a very stable job and finished postsecondary school. I am financially independent. I am looking for a lesbian who has a post-secondary education, has a gentle personality, is feminine, loves talking to the elderly, is willing to give birth, and loves children. Filial to both parents. These are the most important criteria for this marriage. I seek a kind-hearted and sincere person. No need for a beauty queen; I will treat you with honesty and integrity. Even-tempered and have a good heart. Simple and pure. If you act like a princess or a queen, please do not apply for this post. There will be no sex between us, but I would expect us to function like a regular couple. If you want to divorce later, you must wait until my parents pass away. I live in Tianjin and hope you are in the same neighborhood. I only go back to Heilongjiang once per year, generally five to seven days during the Lunar New Year.

Besides advertising across social media to look for wives, Liu and other men also use congregating areas like bars and clubs as surrogate matrimonial agencies. Yang, the *mamasan* in Pistachio—took me to another gay bar, which is used explicitly for MSWs to meet and mingle with lesbians. Unlike typical clubs that cater to the LGBTQ+ community, this bar, plain and without decoration, is itself in a bland and isolated area somewhere in Tianjin. From my vantage point near the entrance, I watched around twenty men and women mingle in a private room off the main bar. They were talking quietly to each other, and despite the smiles, giggles, and occasional loud laughter, a palpable tension underscored the gathering. The men seemed to initiate most of the conversations, awkwardly moving around the room, going from woman to woman. I watched one particularly handsome twenty-something in a bow tie. He was visibly nervous and wiped his face with a tissue after each chat, which lasted only a few minutes. This was no ordinary speed-dating forum. This was a gathering specifically for MSWs to meet lesbians interested in entering marriages of convenience.

Each MSW was seeking the right *lala*, a woman compatible enough to satisfy social and familial expectations of heterosexual marriage. They each tried their best to get to know one another, seeking some connection or compatibility. If they could each find the right man or woman, they could fulfill their filial obligation to their parents, perhaps live with their partner's parents, and most importantly, give birth to a baby. The MSWs typically try to find either a heterosexual woman or a *lala* to mirror the legal and cultural changes happening in China against the backdrop of a nation coming to terms with new moral values. When pursuing a nominal marriage/contract marriage/cooperative marriage (*xinghun* 形婚) or marriage of convenience, these MSWs are negotiating a way for their private sexual identity and public social norms to coexist in post-reform China.

Raoyu was a twenty-nine -year-old MSW I met in one of the NGOs in North China. He came from an impoverished family in Jilin and only finished his primary school education because that was all his family could afford. He worked in a factory, did retail sales, and waited tables, but he hated all of it. He finally found a job working in a sauna and decided to sell sex. He said he sold his virginity for 5,000 yuan (US$769) to a "bald fat man in his fifties." Initially shy and unsure of himself, he now admitted that he liked bondage, S&M, and cross-dressing.

Raoyu came out to his family in the summer of 2018, and the experience still haunted him. He told me how it happened. That day, his parents pushed him as usual, demanding he marry one of the local girls. He became so upset that he was physically sick and doubled over in pain. Still, they kept after him for an answer about when he would marry the girl. Finally, he emphatically announced that he could not marry that girl because he was gay. His parents were aghast. At first, his father was incredulous. As Raoyu related his story to me, his eyes welled up with tears:

> I have a very horrible relationship with my father. It came to a head after I told him I was gay. And then it got worse. The next night, around midnight, he sneaked into my room with a knife hidden in his sleeve. Luckily, my mother followed him and stopped him before he could stab me. I was so scared. My father was hurt in the struggle, and my mother was injured trying to protect me. My parents had to stay in the hospital for a week. A week later, he was hospitalized again because he tried to commit suicide. Once again, my mother intervened and saved him. He still hurt his hands and head. Of course, after this unhappy episode, everyone in my family blamed me and said I was a killer. I don't want to hurt an innocent country girl, so I'll marry a lesbian.

Raoyu said he felt that marrying a lesbian was more honest because they could privately keep their relationships. If he married a country girl, he would have to pretend he was heterosexual and remain closeted. He said that afterward, he began sending occasional updates to his parents, who were considerably cheered after he told them he was finally married. He did not mention that the bride was a lesbian, and they were still negotiating how to produce an heir.

Raoyu's story was neither surprising nor uncommon in post-reform China. Especially in rural China, the consensus among the MSWs who were interviewed was that shame does not come from the workplace, government oppression, or even traditional Confucianist values. The discrimination that hurts most comes from their parents, family members, and peer groups (Chou 2000, 2001). In China, filial piety is paramount in defining a person's morality and quality (*suzhi* 素质). The focus of MSW's suppression and anxiety is not limited to gay, lesbian, bisexual, or transgender issues but broader matters involving family and social relations. Perhaps the most active website connecting gay men and women, Chinagayles.com (Zhongguo Xingshi Hunyin Wang 中国形式婚姻网), reported having over four hundred thousand users and took credit for facilitating more than fifty thousand cooperative marriages over a twelve-year period (*South China Morning Post* 2017).

The marriage of convenience and sexuality in contemporary mainland China has drawn scholars' attention (Choi and Luo 2016; Tsang 2018, 2019, 2021; Zheng et al. 2011). Current research has focused on gender performance in contemporary mainland China regarding immigration, family, labor, commercial trade, and media. More study is needed on the pressure felt by MSWs to enter marriages of convenience and how that affects gender performance in the context of modern China. How parental pressure leads to marriages of convenience reflects performative family roles in post-reform China.

This chapter presents insights gained from twenty-nine MSWs (ten from Pistachio and twenty-nine from NGO referrals) who married *lala* to keep up appearances for their parents. It offers an opportunity to study marriages of convenience between MSWs and lesbians in a neoliberalizing China. Some MSWs marry heterosexual women but encounter enormous difficulties performing procreative sex with them; marrying a *lala* provides a way for MSWs to please their parents through this marriage of convenience. The MSW's comments often focused on practical issues like how marriages of convenience can be used to successfully fulfill internalized heteronormative norms, values, and social expectations in society. It is not only pressure from parents but also the desire to legitimate themselves through the facade of a conventional-looking marriage. This chapter embraces a neoliberal approach to marriages of convenience between MSWs and *lala*.

Neoliberalization of the Marriage of Convenience

Neoliberalism is a political and economic philosophy that underscores the importance of free-market capitalism, deregulation, globalization, and diminished government expenditure. In this context, neoliberalism may also be opening up social norms, profoundly impacting life in the globalizing milieu of today's China. Since the late twentieth century,

China's economic reforms have integrated neoliberal elements, including market liberalization, foreign investment, and privatization. This chapter echoes neoliberalism regarding queer studies for marriages of convenience. Choi and Luo (2016) noted six critical aspects of marriages of convenience regarding social expectations. First, those who have not come out to their parents can avoid participating in family gatherings even though they may live separately from their spouse. Second, they can dissuade their parents from expecting grandchildren, attributing it to medical conditions or other reasons. Third, they can orchestrate appearances and deliberately display their conjugal relationship in front of their in-laws during Spring Festival and other family gatherings. Fourth, they can draft prenuptial agreements covering sexual obligations, having children, sharing properties and possessions or inheritances, dividing financial bills and obligations, and sharing domestic labor chores. Fifth, they can postpone their plan if conflicts cannot be resolved. Lastly, if the two parties cannot agree or reconcile their differences, they can choose to have an out-of-court divorce.

The existing literature about marriages of convenience focuses on Chinese culture (like Confucianism) and the expectations from parents (like filial piety obligations) to contrast the strategies and resistance between gay children and their parents. This literature often ignores the cultural aura of neoliberalism in post-reform China. However, the queers in China differ from queers in Western countries regarding the fight for the legitimacy of being gay or the political correctness of gender nonconformity.

Neoliberal China has experienced massive marketization with unparalleled privatization, capitalism, commercialization, and individualization (Liu and Tan 2020; Tan 2016). Capitalism satiates materialistic and sexual desires previously suppressed during the Maoist era (Liu and Tan 2020). However, economic growth coupled with selective political censorship and surveillance has created an environment now driving everyone—including gays—to more materialistic, practical, and utilitarian goals to fulfill parents' demands and expectations. This trend is especially resonant among middle-class and upper-class gays who must reconcile marriages of convenience in an increasingly commercialized Chinese society. For those MSWs, the derogatory culture of being single and not having a child carries enormous stigma, even regarded by some as sinful. To conform to gender heteronormativity, MSWs must embrace heterosexual masculinity, which demands they get married, become the financial provider, and have children to extend the bloodline (Jin et al. 2015). China is more liberal in economic avenues, but ideologically and politically it still enforces the traits of heterosexual monogamous intimacy that discursively erases alternative sexual subject positions and relationships among both women and men (Huang and Brouwer 2018). Brainer (2017) has asserted that such material matters in the reproduction of gender relations. This chapter argues that marriages of convenience are an intensely commercialized and highly transactional practice for the MSWs and *lala* who marry.

However, an emerging trend in today's China is the changing of sexual norms that promotes the "queer self" through cosmopolitanism (Rofel 2007). Kong (2012, 285) offered that neoliberalism is not a political philosophy or economic ideology but a mode of governance. Jeffreys (2006) noted that China's changing sexual culture has enabled individuals to create a new space for sexual entrepreneurship and consumption. Engebretsen (2014) asserted that contract marriages are a way for lesbians and gay men to resist pressure from family and society. The marriage of convenience is a way to negotiate kinship values and familial ideals by manipulating social norms to their benefit in acquiring social and familial recognition (Engebretsen 2014). Wang (2019) said that a cooperative marriage could offer legal protection for her children. Lo (2020) found that gay marriages often outwardly reflect heteronormative family beliefs and fit well into the grand narrative of individualization. Wei and Cai (2012) described gay couples as an egalitarian partnership, a peer relationship, and enjoying individualization.

This raises the question of whether gays are more individualized and transactional when they engage in a marriage of convenience. However, the aura of neoliberalism in post-reform China emphasizes economic gain, and commercial outlets that make wealthy urban queers embrace modern sexualities are highly classed (Tan 2014). Wealth gives urban queers more choices than their rural counterparts, for example, in dining, travel, clothing, cosmetic surgery, beauty products, fitness, and other areas of consumption (Tan 2016). Neoliberalization takes a distinct shape in China. Since the late 1970s, economic reforms and subsequent neoliberalization have bolstered the country's authoritarian political regime (Tsai 2007) while producing a new "desiring China" where sexual and materialistic needs are re-normalized in a consumption society (Rofel 2007). However, Chinese neoliberalism goes beyond what is happening elsewhere (Kipnis 2007). This neoliberalism encourages Chinese queers to be more individualized, even though they remain ideologically and traditionally conservative to fulfill the expectations of Chinese culture.

Pressure from Parents

I met Dongli, a twenty-five-year-old MSW from North China, to discuss the pressures of marriage on him, an only child. Dongli's contact information came from one of the NGOs in North China, and we met at a local cafe. He told me he had married in 2015. Although it gave him a big headache, he remembered his parents' being overjoyed in helping with his wedding ceremony. His parents were delighted to have a daughter-in-law they liked. His parents saved for three years to build a villa for him as his wedding gift because, in today's China, no respectable girl would marry a guy who did not have a house or property.

To arrange the marriage, his mother went to a public park to talk to other parents seeking matches for their daughters. She passed his photo around, and after many tries, she finally found someone willing to offer their daughter's hand in marriage. Before the wedding, Dongli tried to summon the courage to tell his mother he was gay. However, he could not, especially when he saw how grateful his mother was to prepare for his wedding ceremony. On the day of his marriage, Dongli was very unhappy, but he had to pretend he enjoyed the ceremony. His parents followed tradition and gave him several red envelopes filled with cash and prepared cakes, snacks, and gifts for his friends and relatives as they came to his new villa to share his happiness. Dongli described the ceremony in great detail:

> My parents went to the fortune teller to pick an auspicious date for our wedding. Based upon the date and time when my bride and I were born, December 28, 2015, was selected. The morning of the wedding, the bride takes a bath with pomelo [similar to grapefruit] added to the water to get rid of any dirt or inauspicious [bad-luck] items surrounding her. The

ceremonies are rather lengthy affairs with different stages. In the first part of the wedding ceremony, she wore a traditional red bridal gown for the ceremony. Red symbolizes luck, success, loyalty, Maoism, Chinese, and fertility. For the second stage of the wedding ceremony, she changed into a Western white bridal gown. After the ceremony, she changed into an elegant cocktail dress for the reception. In Chinese weddings, several changes of clothes are expected. My parents did not want me to lose face [*mianzi* 面子, meaning prestige and respect from others] in front of relatives and villages, so they purchased lots of gold [2015 meant year-of-the-pig figurines, rings, bracelets, and necklaces]. My bride had to wear them around her neck and on her arms, hands, and fingers. Firecrackers paved the way for the journey from my bride's house to my house. It was also followed by a traditional lion dance, with a troupe leading the procession, holding a lion's head, and a long-flowing train held by others. More attendants with lanterns followed these. My bride was carried in a curtained sedan chair. The curtains prevent the bride from seeing anything unlucky, such as a widow, a dead animal, or any symbolically evil thing. The parents prepared fifty round tables for our banquet, each seating a dozen well-wishers. The menu features several courses, including shark fin soup, seafood, roast pork, and Peking duck. All these dishes symbolize wealth and give us face in our village.

Afterward, Dongli informed me that his wedding ceremony was wasted because he did not touch his bride that first night. He repeatedly made excuses for several weeks, and things deteriorated between them. Afterward, his parents began to bother Dongli about when he would have a baby. Under this pressure, he finally decided to try and have sex with his wife. Of course, he failed the first time. He had no interest in her and could not get aroused. Despite several more failed attempts, he still kept trying. Finally, however, he gave up and divorced her. He still remembered his mom shouting, "I did not care whether you are gay or not gay, whether you loved her or not. I only care about a grandson. Give me my grandson first; then you can do whatever you want." He decided to marry a *lala* in January 2020, and they tried IVF to please his parents. Finally, he had a son in December 2020. His mother was delighted and forgot his sexual orientation.

Likewise, Ruiyang (twenty-nine) described his marriage experience as much silent suffering as his parents took charge and made all the arrangements. He could not imagine that his parents would invest so much in his wedding. They said he was their only child, so they wanted the wedding ceremony to be as grand as possible. He remembered being told to follow all the traditional Chinese practices associated with the wedding ceremony;

> I tell you, I am not a ceremony person, and I hate following all those rules! When my bride combed her hair, a matchmaker sang loudly during the ceremony.
>
>> First comb to wish you stay married to the end; 一梳梳到发尾
>> Second comb to wish you luck up to your eyebrow; 二梳白发齐眉
>> Third comb to have many kids and grandkids; 三梳儿孙满地
>> Fourth comb to have a long-lasting marriage; 四梳永谐连理
>> Fifth comb to have a harmonious relationship with parents-in-law; 五梳和顺翁娌
>> Sixth comb to have a good fortune; 六梳福临家地
>> Seventh comb to avoid all trouble; 七梳吉逢祸避
>> Eighth comb to earn more money; 八梳一本万利
>> Ninth comb to enjoy good cuisine; 九梳乐膳百味
>> Tenth comb to get whatever you want; 十梳百无禁忌

Other than singing songs, my parents and the matchmakers also picked out red pillows, a blanket, pajamas, slippers, and socks. They all contained dragon (for the groom) and phoenix (for the bride) embroidery patterns. Red is the wedding color, symbolizing double happiness and marriage luck.

Ruiyang told me that he could not remember how the wedding ceremony ended. However, he acted very well and at least gave his parents face in front of his relatives. However, he remembered telling his wife that first night of their marriage that he had a cold and did not want to infect her. Therefore, he slept alone on the floor. Although undoubtedly disappointed, his wife dutifully did not say anything that night. Nevertheless, they divorced less than a year later. Throughout this time, his mother continued to badger him about a baby, and finally, he found a *lala* to marry. They hired a surrogate, and in August 2020, Ruiyang told me that he and his wife had a daughter.

Negotiating Marriage Expectations

For many of the MSWs I spoke with, finding a girlfriend, getting married, and having a child were their parents' top priorities for them. Haoran (twenty-six) was an only child from North China. For his parents, he pretended he was interested in marriage. He said his mom called him daily and dropped many hints about dating a girl soon. She urged him to return to North China, where she helped him find a wife. His mom said, "I have lots of experience and know what to look for; the hips must be large and round. This girl I found for you looks very fertile to me. She definitely will give me a grandson soon." Haoran's mother was a simple person who was easy to satisfy. The only thing for her was to urge Haoran to get married and have a baby. Haoran described how failing to marry and have a child would negatively reflect on the family and add to the perceived failure of one's heteronormative male identity.

Renting a Girlfriend

This pressure reaches its zenith during the Chinese New Year celebrations when these migrants return home and relatives relentlessly pry into their personal lives. Yanjia (twenty-seven) found an effective way to distract his relatives:

> Last year, when I prepared to go home for Chinese New Year, I asked my lesbian friend to pretend to be my girlfriend for 10 days. We bargained, and I agreed to pay her 200 yuan [US$30] daily. She did not want to help, but I pushed her. A man like me who is over twenty-seven but still single is considered a sin. However, when I brought this girl home, my parents were thrilled. I will never forget the ecstatic happiness on their faces. For the first time, I gave them hope of having a daughter-in-law. All my pressure was gone during that holiday. It was better than winning the lottery!

The story of Yanjia is not uncommon. Kam (twenty-four), Keki (twenty-five), and Shutao (thirty-one) had similar experiences. Kam described his experience this way:

> I asked my high school *lala* friend to pretend to be my girlfriend last lunar New Year. My mother perhaps knew I was gay but pretended to know nothing; we never talked about it, and she never asked questions about it, either. My mother has struggled with lung cancer for three years. She urged me to marry my friend and give her a grandson before she passed away. I felt so guilty and ashamed, but I could not do it, of course. She has since died . . . although I still feel sorry . . . now, no one is pressuring me to get married.

Kam was not alone, having to deal with the emotional guilt of disappointing his dead mother. All MSWs must choose between satisfying their parents' desire for a daughter-in-law and children versus being true to their sexual orientation and themselves. I met Keki in one of the NGOs in North China:

> If I could find a wife, my father would have more face in patriarchal rural China. My friends who are younger than me are already married and have kids. My neighbors and relatives talk about me behind my back; they say I must have some problems, which explains why I am still single. That comment makes my father lose face and feel shame.

Shutao also felt pressure from his father:

> During the Lunar New Year, my father assigned me the mission to get married this calendar year . . . . He said he had saved for ten years to prepare for it. He offered the girl a two-story house worth $300,000 yuan [US$44,117] as a bridal gift. My father decided to find me a wife as if it were his own marriage and wedding!

There are several stories of dysfunctional responses from parents. Ruojing (thirty-one), an MSW from Shandong, said his parents used emotional blackmail to shame him into getting married:

My parents were wailing and crying every day. They said they had to sell their house and land because they lost face so severely that it was impossible to remain in the village. They cried, scolded me, and even tried to hang themselves in our home. They starved themselves and stopped eating. In villages, many people like to stab you in the back. They are so conservative and blame anything gay as a sin.

Another MSW from Tianjin, Wenwei (twenty-four), was a crossdresser who provided extreme sex-fetish services (bondage and discipline, dominance and submission, sadomasochism, hereafter BDSM) to customers. I met him at one of the NGOs in North China, and he told me that his strategy was to "hide in plain sight" by telling his family and friends in the village that it was part of his job as an actor. For a while, he thought it had worked, and among family members, only his elder sister knew he was gay. However, even she continued to push him to get married. He felt that his parents figured out he was gay but chose to remain silent about it. The rest of the village was not so kind. Wenwei said that in time, the villagers openly teased him, calling him a zombie, a monster, or a pig. They tried to force him to leave the village.

Cultural Expectations in Rural Areas: The Power of Face

Other than the traditional cultural expectation, the political-social context regarding marriages of convenience is also relevant. Keki (twenty-five) said that marriage was a fulfillment of cultural expectations and a glorious attainment in the eyes of Chinese society. He attributed his intention to get married to China's One Child policy. The One Child policy revealed the political and social bias toward males anchored in traditional Chinese culture. A severe gender imbalance among the population emerged because if a fetus was suspected to be female, it was often aborted (Lin and McGill 2018). In 2013, the ratio was 122 boys for 100 girls, a nationwide deficit of roughly forty million women for eligible marriage-age men (Lin and McGill 2017).

Having a wife and family symbolizes face, status, power, and being a man. Wives and kids are more important than money in patriarchal rural China. Since gays are still not publicly accepted by rural residents, MSWs must hide their sexual orientation from family members and protect themselves from negative comments rippling through the community. Mengzhe (twenty-two) said his parents became a stumbling block for his relationship with his boyfriend:

> I do not want to destroy a woman. My father lived a hard life post-Mao, and the only thing that seems to cheer him up is me giving him a grandson. He threatened that if he could not have a grandson, he would commit suicide. I know he is not kidding, which makes me even more ashamed. You only have one set of parents. When they are so relentless about seeing you marry, what can you do except obey them? I married a country girl, but the marriage lasted only one month before I let the girl go. However, it looks like I must marry a heterosexual woman. I hated to make a woman suffer from physical pain, emotional frustration, and psychological upset. I would choose a *lala* to please my father.

Danian (twenty-six) admitted that he had married a heterosexual woman because of pressure from his parents. He said neighbors and relatives constantly criticized his parents because he was not providing any signs that they might become grandparents. It worried him, and he wanted to come out. However, his family was dedicated to China's "harmonious society." He felt that his gay identity put him at odds with the collective culture's emphasis on marriage, family, and procreation. He often remained silent when he visited his parents for short stays:

> For several years, I wanted to tell them I was gay. However, they interrupted me each time and changed the subject as if they already knew. I guess they did not want to face that cruel reality. My mother picked out my future wife. I met her once and refused to date her because I had no feelings toward her. I thought she was shy, cute, and innocent. I am fine having intimate relations with a heterosexual girl, but I still prefer men. In rural China, if you stay unmarried, people will wonder if you are gay or have some disease. The rumors which quickly spread throughout the village were horrible! To be honest, I do not care about social expectations, but having kids and a so-called normal family can shield my identity. I did not want to hurt a heterosexual girl, and finally, I chose to marry a lesbian.

The Confucian value of filial piety is a norm that Chinese families uphold. Children must please their parents and fulfill particular obligations. Internalized Confucianism forces MSWs to obey their parents despite their financial independence. The emotional factors are more potent than economic factors, which impact the relationship between Chinese children and parents. To protect the family's reputation and produce filial piety, MSWs may opt to accomplish this through marriage, particularly when the woman is a *lala*. Once married, they have—at least superficially—met their filial responsibility in the family. Getting married and sending money are the two prime directives. Many MSWs already feel guilt and pressure because of their occupation, selling their body and sexual services to other men. As an MSW, marriage is the next-best way—maybe the only way—to show filial piety. In rural China, people care what others say about them. Positive or negative comments reflect one's status in the village, and a family's fortunes may rise and fall due to the perceptions and judgments of others.

Having to deal with one's parents' expecting a grandchild is stressful, but the stress is compounded for sons in single-parent families. I met Siwen (twenty-eight) in Pistachio. His father died when he was young, and he was raised entirely by his mother, with whom he remained very close. They were so close, he said, that his mother called him each day to ask when he was getting married. Siwen said that in the village, bloodline succession was more important than wealth. Marriage and childbearing were always the topic of local conversation and gossip. Due to the patriarchal view of patrilineal marriage, the villagers criticized and blamed his mother for his staying single. Siwen admitted that it deeply upset him:

> My neighbors think my mother did something wrong since I do not have kids. They think my mom was a monster who gave birth to me, another monster. My mom even went to matchmaking corners in public parks and amusement centers near our village to find someone for me. She was stressed because I was their only child. I have been everything to her. I have to do something to make her happy.

Patrilineal marriage remains common in rural China. Most of the MSWs' mothers came from other villages in North China, married their fathers, and moved to their villages. The native villagers still treat women who marry into the village as outsiders. Fearing they will profoundly disappoint their parents, MSWs avoid revealing either their sexuality or their occupation. These natural barriers discourage them from marriage, but at some point, their true self will be guessed, if not openly exposed.

Negative Coming-Out Experiences

Of the 151 MSWs interviewed, 144 said that they remained closeted to their parents and family members. Of the seven who said they came out to their parents, three said the reaction was positive, and four said it was negative. The three who reported a positive experience worked at Pistachio and enjoyed significant incomes. It seemed that this aspect gave them leverage and more bargaining power with their parents. The four MSWs who reported negative coming-out experiences reported shaming, conflict, and eviction. Since traditional Chinese moral standards have considered same-sex attraction a form of mental illness, it is not surprising that many MSWs are reluctant to admit their sexuality and occupation to parents and relatives. These are significant barriers to intimacy and even basic transparency. The result was an overall sense of failure, failure to meet family obligations by procreating, and inability to manufacture desire for the person to whom you are married.

Not one of the MSWs considered letting their parents know they offered sex for money, but many discussed the pros and cons of coming out to their parents about being gay. Many said they heard from friends that the most common reaction from parents was the silent treatment. In this case, when the son told his parents he was gay (or bisexual, trans, etc.), the parents would blankly stare and show no reaction. Even when the statement was repeated, they would actively refuse to acknowledge that any such thing was said. Sometimes, the response would be a non sequitur, like asking if he wanted soup or had spoken to his grandmother recently.

Some of the MSWs offered that if there was a reaction not involving anger, sadness, or pain, it typically involved either science, religion, or luck for most of the rural parents. For example, the parents may take their son to a doctor to "fix" him. Alternatively, they may visit a temple and light joss sticks (incense) to invoke divine help. A third way is wishing that by some good fortune, a young lady who shows interest in their son will suddenly appear. Xiaolong (twenty-seven), an MSW from Heilongjiang, described his dilemma:

> I told my parents I work in a hotel as a bellboy. . . . Although my elder sister is a teacher and is more open-minded than other villagers, she cannot accept that I am gay. She thinks I am ill and even took me to the hospital for medical treatment. The doctor prescribed antibiotics and asked me to take more rest.

Huaqi (twenty-seven) reported having a similar experience to Xiaolong's:

> I came out to my parents. At the very beginning, they did not know what I meant. I told them I was gay, and they just stared at me. It was not until I held my boyfriend's hands that finally they understood. My father was so angry that he collapsed right there in the room. Of course, my father also yelled at my boyfriend and asked him to leave and get out of my village immediately. My mom could not stop crying. I left the village that day and went to Tianjin. My mother told me my father had a heart attack and was hospitalized. She begged me once more to get married and have a kid. I did not wish to disappoint my mother, so I did—I married a young girl I met in Tianjin. However, I only went home to visit during the Lunar New Year. I had some difficulty getting my wife pregnant, but eventually, we were lucky, and she gave me a son. I was glad because then I could tell her I was gay. That shocked her, and she left me shortly afterward. My father is still furious at me. Up to now, my parents and family refuse to see me and do not allow me to come home.

Because the divorce laws favor men in China, Ding was awarded custody of his son even though he did not really want to raise him. His parents agreed to raise his son, and Ding said this was probably the best solution for their situation.

Ziqi (twenty-eight) also struggled with his family:

> My parents could not believe the truth and took me to the hospital to have a body checkup. I insisted I did not have to go, but my father yelled at me and

used a knife to force me. My brother, uncles, aunts, cousins, and relatives were crying. The house was full of tears, sadness, and tragedy! My parents, especially my mother, got on one knee and begged in front of the doctors to urge them to save my life. I feel like they are so desperate and ashamed of me. Many villagers pointed their fingers at my mother and said she was an inauspicious person. I am very heartbroken as I respect and love my mom a lot.

Wenyan (twenty-seven), another MSW I met in one of the NGOs in North China, had to deal with a sister who was sure his orientation was just an illness:

The doctor prescribed some hormone medicine and told me I had to do more exercise. If I followed that prescription, my so-called "illness" would be under control. I had to laugh out loud. When my parents hear the word gay, it just pushes them away from me.

The MSWs often described the denial exhibited by their parents, who refused to believe that their sons were gay and would not allow it to be discussed further. Many parents took their sons to see a doctor because, for them, a doctor's diagnosis was the final word. However, after the doctor told them that being gay was inborn and not a disease or abnormality, the parents then blamed themselves for not going to the temple enough to give more joss to the Chinese god. The MSWs said that this strain on the relationship with their parents was the main reason for finding a woman to marry.

Supportive Coming-Out Experiences

Of the 151 interviewed, only three MSWs experienced a positive coming out when their parents gave them tacit support and encouragement. Mianjie (thirty-one), Guoyang (twenty-nine), and Qiuxiu (twenty-nine) had positive, affirming reactions from their parents when they announced their sexual orientation. Their experience is a rare exception in rural China. Mianjie said:

My mother must have asked me to find a girlfriend and get married a thousand times before I finally came out. I was not able to control myself back then. I thought, since she was already over fifty, if I did not tell her the truth now, it would hurt her more later when she was older, both mentally and physically. So, I told her I was gay. She reacted calmly and did not say a word to me. My mother even helps mediate between my father and me. For instance, when my father pushes me to go on blind dates, she will arrange for me to run errands to help me escape those dates.

Guoyang said his mother was understanding and reacted as well as could be expected. He had not told his father yet, as his mother advised him to work up to it:

I told my mother I was gay, and she did not say a word. She remained silent and quietly drank her tea when I told her as if she already knew the fact. She thinks that my father is a very conservative and traditional man who will never tolerate, let alone accept, gay. Therefore, she suggested I wait for a couple of years before revealing my gay identity to my father. Meanwhile, she encourages me to subtly expose my father to gay-related books and TV programs so that he can know more about this issue in the way that I want. She always tells me that as long as I am healthy and happy, then I do not have to care about their opinions so much.

Qiuxiu said his brother knew he was gay. When he admitted it, his brother came to his house and broke several pieces of furniture. In the mayhem, Qiuxiu was slightly injured. He had tried to start talking the previous year with his brother about gay communities. His brother tried to be open about understanding what it meant to be gay without the homophobic stereotyping and did not try to force him to get married or see a doctor. Instead, Qiuxiu's brother worried about his retirement because the wife and children traditionally care for men when they are old.

Matches Made in Heaven: Gay Men and Lesbian Women

The pressure from parents, coupled with the reluctance to marry a heterosexual woman, led several MSWs to find a *lala* to contract a marriage of convenience. Xiaolong (twenty-seven) said he married a lesbian (*lala*) because they could be honest with each other about their sexual orientation. Xialong said he did not have to pretend as he would with a so-called innocent country girl:

> I feel sorry for those farm girls as they should not be just a birth-giving machine. I would not dare to hurt an innocent farm girl. In our village, it is very conservative. A woman who was married and gave birth will have a difficult time finding someone to remarry. It is a tragedy [being gay] already, and I do not want to create another tragedy and stigma in my life.

Twenty-nine MSWs who were interviewed said they had married a *lala* to fulfill their familial obligation. The MSWs who married a *lala* tended to be better off financially, which helped them both agree to enter their marriage of convenience. It has become increasingly common in China to find marriage notices for lesbians seeking gay men and vice-versa. Marrying a lesbian is preferred by many MSWs because, as Bin (thirty), an MSW with classic good looks whom I met at Pistachio, said, they "do not want to hurt the naïve farm girls from their hometown." Lesbians also face family pressure to appear in traditional relationships with men, so marrying a financially well-off MSW is a sensible alternative:

> Lesbians willing to marry a man are hard to find. However, one day, I met a *lala* online; she said she was looking for a big, strong man with a sunny disposition. I am that type of man, so I contacted her. She saw my profile picture on *Blued* [a gay dating website]. I met her in a club, and after talking, she said we could have a nominal marriage but have our own lives and sleep in separate rooms. Like me, she was also pressured by her parents to get married. Therefore, we agreed to marry, live together, and form a family using IVF. She did IVF twice, and finally, we had a baby boy. She cares for him, and I do what I can to be a good father. We go home to see her parents and mine during the Lunar New Year. I cannot describe how ecstatic and happy they are. I did not hurt some unsuspecting farm girl.

Man (twenty-five) also married a *lala* and formed a family:

> I am married to a very rich *lala*. Of course, she did not want to be pregnant, but she wanted to have a baby. She told me her poor physical health

prevented her from giving birth herself. We went to Phnom Penh, Cambodia, and found a surrogate mother. It is very complicated to arrange for a surrogate mother in Cambodia, but she found an agent who was able to recruit the right woman to help. This way is much better than forcing me to marry an innocent heterosexual country girl. I am 100 percent gay and have no interest in women. So, when my friend introduced me to this rich *lala*, it was perfect! Now, we can please my mother. At the same time, I do not have to have sex with a woman. It was difficult to overcome my ego. My so-called wife and I live together in the same house, but we are only like housemates. We have separate rooms and separate lifestyles. The only substantive conversations are about how to raise our kid. I do not know how to raise one, and I do not particularly care. I am delighted to enjoy the freedom and flexibility I get from this marriage.

Tiantian (twenty-six) said he did not want to hurt an unsuspecting country girl:

I think marrying a *lala* was the best way to go. My friend introduced her to me. She made it clear at the beginning that we are not a real couple, only a symbolic couple. She set up lots of rules at home. We went to Thailand for IVF. It took us three tries before she had our baby daughter. She is so happy to be a mother. I am not so happy to become a father, but it makes my parents very happy. We visit my parents twice monthly, and they are very proud of me. It is not easy to live with my wife (*lala*), but for my baby daughter, I can tolerate it to please my parents.

Previously, I had met Tiantian while working at Pistachio. One summer night, we were chatting, and he told me he had found a *lala* from the gay marriage app The Rainbow Families Xinghun Mutual Help Friendship Douban Group (Caihong Jiayuan Xinghun Huzhu Jiaoyou Douban Xiaozu, 彩虹家园新婚互助交友豆瓣小组). He said there were several commercial apps or websites for finding a partner for queers, such as, for example, ChinaGayLes.com (Zhongguo Xingshi Hunyin Wang 中国形式婚姻网). These newer options work in tandem with finding partners through traditional avenues like friends and coworkers.

However, not all gay-lesbian couples work out. Some couples who initially get along well end up in disastrous relationships. Ruiquan said he was too old to get married by Chinese standards. He had been married to a rural heterosexual woman for four years, but he could not bring himself to have sex with her, so they finally divorced. His parents constantly berated him to "hurry up, remarry, and give them a baby." They even threatened to cut ties with him and not allow him to return to his village. Ruiquan did some research and finally attended a marriage of convenience gathering. It looked promising at first:

> I met my *lala* ex-partner there. We thought we connected and liked each other, at least superficially. She wanted to have a kid, and so did I. We even thought we could do it the natural way and have sex together. A gay man and a lesbian! But after she moved in with me, we quickly began to fight. She nagged me for wasting time watching a soccer game and criticized me constantly about my hygiene. She said my smell was disgusting and that I did not wash often enough. I always had to wear cologne, but she was still not satisfied. How could we have a baby? I tried to make it work, but our fighting grew worse. Finally, she went to my family and told them I was gay! Therefore, I demanded that she move immediately out of my house. Luckily, we never married, only lived together. Still, my life has been ruined. My parents are distraught because they know I am gay. They say they need to take medication now. I have to be more careful, cautious, and considerate. I do not want to trigger any more fighting.

Sanyan (twenty-eight) married a *lala*, and they were planning to have a baby using IVF. He said this cooperation could solve many of the problems for both sides. Even if divorce is anticipated, arrangements can be discussed and prearranged. Although his parents wanted to be grandparents, if there were no children, divorce would be straightforward and uncomplicated. He thought that going through marriage and divorce would ease family pressure considerably:

> Girls are human; they are not baby producers. . . . I want to marry a lesbian and cooperate in tackling each other's pressure. My wife is living with her girlfriends, and I am living with my sex partner. We did not live in the same apartment . . . she lives 10 miles from me. . . . I hired a lawyer to draft a prenuptial agreement. The agreement said we would divide everything equally, except we keep what we brought into the relationship.

The main thing is we want a baby. . . . Therefore, I must obtain a genuine marriage certificate. Otherwise, I would take a counterfeit one.

Early one evening, a bisexual client named Yidan approached the bar and sat down to chat. He ordered his favorite drink and shared his story of how he and his lesbian wife became married. Despite his initial reluctance to enter a relationship of convenience, he found that he and Dingyu (twenty-eight) were very compatible. Dingyu was slim, petite, and soft-spoken, with long black hair. Her gentle demeanor and feminine appearance were stereotypical of Chinese women. She came from a well-to-do cadre family, and her parents were anxious for her to marry a successful man and start a family. But Dingyu was undeniably lesbian, having dated only other women. Yidan met Dingyu in a chatroom at a gay bar in Tianjin where gay men and women could meet. After chatting and sharing their stories about family pressures to get married, Yidan said he felt a chemistry between them for a successful marriage of convenience:

When I first met Dingyu, she spoke softly and did not seem to have a strong opinion about anything. I thought she was a perfect match for me. I liked talking to her and found we have the same goal: to form a family, have a baby, and please our parents. We drafted the prenuptial agreement and negotiated our plan for how to please our parents. I live in Beijing, and she lives in Shanghai. My parents live on the outskirts of Beijing, and we agreed to see them twice a year. I also agreed to see her parents twice per year as well, usually during the Lunar New Year and Autumn festival. She worries about whether she can carry a baby. I have to take her to see a Chinese doctor to regulate her body. If not, we plan to have IVF in China or Thailand. We have never slept together, and we only see each other twice per year. We communicate daily online using WeChat and our phones. It seems perfect for us.

The phenomenon of lesbians and gays marrying each other has been documented in the literature (Choi and Luo 2016), but it is not the solution for everyone. Reservations regarding financial status and education level have been expressed among the MSW community. Only three interviewees heard of such a possibility, and only one was open to trying it.

When gay men and lesbians marry each other, the relationship tends to be strictly transactional. They usually enter the marriage of convenience simply to escape the stress from their parents. They rarely bond as a family, even after having a child. Typically, the MSW husbands and their *lala* wives do not live in the same city; some may meet only once before contracting their marriage of convenience.

Many of these couples seemed to manage their relationships and marriages in a pragmatic, utilitarian manner. While officially married in the eyes of the outside world, most live separate lives with their same-sex partners. They only meet up with their spouse during holidays like the Spring Festival and fulfill their filial piety when visiting their parents. Simen (thirty-four) described it like this:

> I met my so-called wife through a dating app for queers. Before we got married, we signed the prenuptial agreement and agreed on how we would cooperate in our marriage. I agreed to pay for the wedding ceremony and pay for IVF to have a child. I think that if we have conflicts over things like buying an apartment, or we cannot solve problems together, we may decide on an out-of-court divorce. . . . I know, I act every day. . . . I am a drama king.

Zhaolin (thirty-one) married a lesbian he had known since they were children:

> I live with my boyfriend, and my wife lives with her girlfriend. Most of the time, my wife and I are apart except on occasions like my parents' birthday or spring festival. One day, my parents called my wife and asked me where I was. My wife answered that I was out of town in Beijing. Then, my mom called me immediately, and I said I was in Tianjin. She was obviously suspicious of us. Therefore, my wife and I agreed to coordinate and communicate better. Otherwise, my mom will know the truth. I got a false marriage certificate from Taobao [淘宝] and showed it to my parents to entertain them. We do not want to have a child. A genuine marriage certificate sounds very troublesome, but we decided to get a real one in case we decide to have a kid later. I can always find an agency to have a baby using IVF.

Simen's and Zhaolin's stories are typical of mixed gay couples. Many of the MSWs interviewed are financially independent and often willing to fulfill their role of supporting the household. Likewise, many of the *lala* take on the role of normative homemakers (Yang 2010). They act every day and try to perform their scripts well.

Conclusion

Since 1949, there have been seven decades of state engineering, globalization, and economic reforms that have dramatically changed the institution of marriage and sexual values in China. Consequently, people's expectations and practices regarding gender and sexuality have changed (Davis and Friedman 2014; Yan 2003). Under the influence of Confucianism, marriage and having children are still of utmost importance in Chinese culture as a means of verifying male masculinity. This is particularly true in rural China, where decades of economic reforms have not changed people's traditional values. China still experiences tensions between touting the highly individualized self and the continuing importance of marriage and having a family. Traditional Chinese cultural values highlight the importance of romantic coupledom and family status, making extravagant wedding celebrations imperative. This pressure to please their parents is compounded by the expectation that the sole gateway to childbearing is through marriage.

The notion of a loveless and primarily pragmatic marriage is not viewed as problematic within a Chinese context; intergenerational harmony, rather than conjugal love, is deemed essential for the family. Wealthy MSWs and *lala* have more freedom and choice. However, MSWs still struggle with the Chinese cultural characteristics of being people-oriented, patriarchal, rule-abiding, morality-valued, and Confucianism-centered (Yan 2003). Enlightened by these traditional Chinese values, filial piety through marriage is vital to both gay men and gay women within the context of Confucianism and Chinese culture. They still blend East and West and cannot wholly embrace Western modernity nor reject Chinese Confucianism and ideologies. These ideologies, like filial piety and collectivization, are especially evident in appearances at family gatherings, pleasing parents by getting married, and having children. Queers of both sexes desire to conform to the expectations of their family and the outside world. Many of the men interviewed saw the benefits of living the so-called normal life consisting of a successful career, a family, a wife, and children. The conventional literature about Chinese marriages is practicing compulsory heterosexuality: they married mainly to satisfy the Confucian imperative to procreate, extend the patriline, and socially legitimatize their offspring (Rich 1980). The ultimate goal is the production of extending bloodlines or (male) offspring to fulfill the demands of filial piety (Liu and Tan 2020).

4

A Phoenix Rising from the Ashes

China's Tongqi, *Marriage Fraud, and Resistance*

Male sex workers must deal with family pressure to marry and have children. In rural areas, it has been common to arrange marriages between adult male sons and local women. This structure enables gay sex workers to hide their orientation and occupation in often loveless marriages. Even if a wife discovers her husband's true occupation, divorce is often not an option. This chapter discusses the situation of the wives of MSWs, *tongqi*. Around 80 percent of divorces in China are typically settled out-of-court without lawyers for divorce litigation and settlements (Li 2015). Even though the divorce law was amended in 2001, subsequent Supreme People's Court interpretations still favored men and their parents in both out-of-court and in-court divorces (Li 2015). For out-of-court divorces, women have been at a disadvantage in several ways. Since women are likelier to stay home, they have weaker social bonds, lower social status, and less financial resources or power. They are often unfamiliar and thus ineffective in engaging with the legal system. Females, especially those from patrilineal rural areas, are particularly disadvantaged. For example, the persistence of the patrilineal and patrilocal tradition in rural communities leaves a distinctive mark on the legal profession's attitudes and conduct toward women disputants (Li 2015; Li and Friedman 2015; Ren et al. 2019). Lineage also constitutes a core attribute of the traditional Chinese family system, where men have dominated manual farming labor and have thus retained exclusive inheritance rights to ancestral properties. Since women have been excluded from these rights, significant gender inequality has been maintained (Cheng 2016).

For in-court divorce, neither the Marriage Law nor related judicial interpretations provide clear guidelines for assessing evidence related to child custody, marital property, and domestic violence. The Chinese courts have awarded custody based on the father's financial ability rather than the mother's emotional attachment or bond. However, it is unlikely that a woman would initiate an affair when she is pregnant. Adding insult to injury, the children may become *tuoyouping* (拖油瓶), a derogative term for those who follow divorced mothers into remarriages.

The courts also tend to favor situations where the *tongqi* give up their property claims rather than seek a more equitable distribution. The courts frequently award the men family and property control, and the *tongqi* often end up with no housing, no property, and little or no financial compensation (Li and Friedman 2016).

Regarding domestic violence, China's divorce law has also skewed toward men. As noted earlier, Chinese law does not recognize adultery as occurring between two men (Li 2015). Vague wording must be made more precise to evaluate domestic violence cases fairly. For example, current law has not acknowledged the existence of marital rape, much less defined when it has taken place.

Three strategies used to oppress women are diversion, normalization, and legitimization. Diversion occurs when the court shifts the topics when gathering evidence in divorce settlements. Normalization occurs when the husband's physical violence is framed as "arguing" or "couples fighting," which is implied to be expected. Legitimization justifies a behavior by altering the context (Li 2015). For example, violently forcing the wife to have sex may be excused if the motivation was for the couple to fulfill their obligation to produce an heir.

Low-Educated and High-Educated *Tongqi*

I met Xiaojun, a petite Chinese woman of twenty-eight, inside her modest apartment in her village in North China. It had been only six months since she was infected with HIV from her husband. Upon arrival, I saw that wedding photos still adorning the living room. As we spoke, she wistfully looked at the large wedding portrait typical in Chinese homes. Just looking at the wedding photo still made her voice crack. More than once, she lamented that even though she was the one wearing a white veil that day, the picture showed that she was not half of a happy couple. The photo portrait shows Xiaojun and her husband smiling happily, flanked by the maid of honor and best man. She remembered that they accepted the blessings from their relatives and villagers and recalled sitting in her red Chinese wedding gown in the sedan chair. The firecrackers paved the way for the journey from her house to her husband's house in the countryside in North China. It was followed by the dancing lion and attendants who hung lanterns to follow the procession. Tears welled up as she reminisced about her wedding ceremony from eight years ago, and her face turned ashen and grew dark when she said that this past year had been a sexless, loveless marriage because she discovered her husband was having a torrid love affair with the best man:

> I do not remember how long he did not touch me . . . but his parents kept pushing him to have a second baby for us. We had sex occasionally. When my husband came home for the Chinese Lunar New Year, I found some pills in the bathroom. I looked up the label on *Baidu* [百度, a Chinese search engine like Google] and discovered they were drugs for HIV treatment! I could not breathe. My husband has AIDS? I was worried I was infected, too. Therefore, I went to the hospital to have a blood test. It turned out positive. I wanted to step off a high building and commit suicide.

Many of the people I spoke with mistakenly used the terms HIV and AIDs interchangeably. Human immunodeficiency virus (HIV) is an infection that, if untreated, can worsen into acquired immunodeficiency syndrome (AIDS). For example, before I went to meet Xiaojun, I knew she had contracted HIV from her husband, a former MSW who had to quit his job after he tested positive. He permitted me to contact her, and she admitted that she was taking medication and treatment. Xiaojun said her life now was like stagnant water:

> My face was pale when I knew my husband was gay. I was completely shocked, angry, and desperate. Why did he choose me but not the other women? Why did he destroy my life? I could have had a normal marriage if I did not marry him. I am only a farm girl, and my philosophy about life is straightforward. I just wanted to find a regular guy to marry and have a kid. I never imagined I would have AIDS. I did not even know what AIDS was! However, I have my son to take care of. I have no right to commit suicide.

Another interviewee who was infected with HIV was Zhuoyin, age thirty-one. She had married her husband in 2009 and had two girls; when we spoke, one was seven and the other five years old. She discovered she had HIV in the winter of 2017. She took medication and visited doctors regularly. Her in-laws knew that her husband was an MSW and also had HIV:

> I have no right even to die! The villagers and my neighbors already gossiped about my AIDS and husband. The villagers even wanted me to leave the village. I had nightmares every evening. I wanted to commit suicide, but I did not want to leave my two daughters and parents. I could not sleep and suffered from severe depression. I am just a countryside woman. I am very fragile, vulnerable, and unstable. I do not have a weapon, no gun, and no money. I only have a dream to take me to a simple but happy life. Why does my husband have AIDS and still want to kill me?

Xiaojun and Zhuoyin were two HIV patients infected by their gay husbands. Siyuan (twenty-three), another *tongqi* I interviewed, was the most educated among the fifteen interviewees, having finished high school. I met her in one of the cities of North China at a café near downtown. She did not look like a simple country girl. She wore a striped yellow-and-white short-sleeve blouse and matching skirt with oxford shoes. She was bright and cheerful when she spoke and, coupled with her youthful appearance, did not appear like some of the older, more depressed *tongqi* I had met previously.

Siyuan said that she was married in 2016 when she was only twenty-one. After marriage, she suspected that her husband was gay and did some searching. She opened accounts in Tianyan (天涯), Douban (豆瓣), and Zhihu (知乎) (Chinese apps for people seeking partners and related questions about relationships). These are search engines to know people's sexual orientation and sexual problems. She finally found her husband's photos on Tianyan. She put up a generic male photo as her profile picture, and sure enough, her husband made contact and kept flirting with her. She felt betrayed and saw that she was being used. She called her husband the next day on WeChat and showed him their conversation. He was shocked and admitted everything, even that he was not actually employed as an office manager but turned tricks as a "money boy" in Tianjin. He said he did not want her to disclose his secret:

> Initially, I did not know what money boy meant when he told me. However, he kept explaining things to me, and now I know. I feel like he is so dirty, and he destroyed my life. Right now, it makes perfect sense why he never showed interest in me and would not touch me. He has no interest in any women, not just me. It explains why he could not get aroused with me. Even when I wore sexy panties and lingerie, with lots of perfume and roses, in our bedroom, I could smell him drinking *maotai* [茅台 80–100 proof Chinese rice liquor]. Finally, everything made sense. I was so stupid. He is gay! A male sex worker! He sleeps with men! Oh my god! This is too complicated. I think I had the right to know the truth before marrying him. It is too unbelievable, and I have been treated like garbage!

After reading up on this phenomenon using Chinese search engines like Baidu (八度), Weibo (微博), and WeChat (微信), Siyuan estimated that there were millions like her. She was right. There are an estimated 13.6 million *tongqi* in China (Tang et al. 2019), and the legal and social predicaments of *tongqi* demand critical public policy and scholarly attention. While the estimated number of *tongqi* remains a fraction—around 3.5 percent—of the four hundred million married women in China, they represent a greatly distressed group who suffer both physically and mentally (Wang et al. 2020). *Tongqi* report higher rates of IPV and associated behaviors, including attempted suicide, chronic depression, coerced anal sex, exposure to sexually transmitted diseases (Cheng 2016; Wang 2017; Wang et al. 2020; Zhang et al. 2014, 2015), and being more susceptible to be infected with HIV (Wang et al., 2020).

The culture is at cross purposes with itself as individuals wrestle with holding to traditional gender roles. The rapid rise in women's education has created an environment of low marriage rates among older, highly educated women (Qian and Qian 2014). The term used to describe single women over the age of twenty-seven is "leftover ladies" (Wang et al. 2020; Zhu 2018). These older women are ripe for falling into a marriage of convenience because of the persistent pressure to marry and produce a child. During the years China enforced its One Child policy, those with rural hukous were exempt from this constraint, primarily enforced in urban areas. China's *hukou* household registration system assigns each individual a permanent identification number comparable to a birth certificate and social security number in the United States or a permanent identification card in England. Before 2016, the policy was widely enforced more in urban than rural areas. In rural areas, the most significant influence for procreation still emanates from family and even neighbors in the towns, villages, and farms, more so than the One Child policy. Parents continue to urge their adult children to marry and secure bloodlines (Cheng 2016).

Most *tongqi* come from rural backgrounds with little education or financial resources. When they discover that their marriage is a sham, they have few options to resolve their situation. Besides the legal hurdles, the stigma of being a *tongqi* will remain. In terms of queer necropolitics, the precarity of their husband's lives has been transferred onto them. While gay husbands can secretly indulge themselves while hiding their sexual orientation in their fake marriages, the wives are left to fend for themselves in a loveless marriage from which they cannot escape. Besides depression and loss of self-esteem, they must endure the stigma of a failed marriage from their family and friends in their home villages.

Necropolitics and *Tongqi*

This chapter extends necropolitics to the social death situations of educated and low-educated *Tongqi* and reveals how they resist and overcome their circumstances. *Tongqi* are the victims of human rights violations involving their marriage, but they are not simply waiting for death. In many rural villages, divorce creates the perception that *tongqi* are damaged or spoiled goods. Even worse, if rumors emerge that the woman is a possible HIV carrier, neighbors, friends, and even family may say she is undeserving of a second chance for love. The predicament of *tongqi* and the reproductive imperative reflects the gender inequality that persists in China. The reproductive policies and societal expectations disproportionately affect women, particularly in terms of their sexual and reproductive rights. The challenges faced by *tongqi* and the societal pressure to reproduce are manifestations of gender inequality in China. This inequality is perpetuated by societal norms, expectations, and even legal structures. Heterosexuality and extending the family bloodline are deeply rooted in the culture, and the nuclear family remains the cornerstone of collectivist China. Gay men still rarely come out to their parents but engage in marriages of convenience to fulfill their parents' wishes for grandchildren. As such, *tongqi* are, in a sense, defrauded in marriage because the gay husband merely enters into the relationship to deflect social and family obligation pressures.

The social death perspective can include social aspects that recognize *tongqi* as victims and include the ways they may exhibit resistance and agency. To date, there is limited literature studying *tongqi*. *Tongqi* and their closeted gay husbands are often omitted from sociological research, but there are profound public health implications. In extreme cases, *tongqi* have committed suicide after discovering they had contracted HIV from their gay husbands. Still, despite the challenges of social stigma and HIV risk, *tongqi* are often resolute in finding ways to resist, cope, survive, and eventually overcome their situation to achieve a new "normal" life. The *tongqi* are not merely passive victims of unfair social and cultural policies in China. Their efforts to escape the slow violence" of queer necropolitics in China represent a brave reclamation of their identity. *Tongqi* should not be deprived of fundamental human rights because they entered into a marriage without knowing their husband's sexual orientation. At issue is how *tongqi* exemplify what necropolitics refers to as "kept alive but in a state of injury" (Mbembe 2003, 21). How this wounding fits with the characterization of necropolitics in China is underdeveloped in East Asian studies of culture, sexuality, and migration.

By framing *tongqi* as heterosexuals queered by necropolitics, this chapter can contribute significantly to the services and support provided by NGOs, state actors, and other social service providers. The findings offer strategies to support *tongqi* and protect their mental and physical health. Our understanding of *tongqi* and their gay husbands may be extended in three ways: *tongqi* divorcing and refusing to be socially dead; *tongqi* living with HIV but seeking treatment and medication (addressing physical death); and *tongqi* finding means of support by seeking help from NGOs and the Internet.

Repercussions of Discovery for *Tongqi*

Previous studies about *tongqi* describe their situation as bleak or even desperate. For example, Bie and Tang (2016) have found that when gay men come out to their wives, it is to force two things to happen. Since divorce carries such stigma, that becomes akin to a nuclear option where both parties would lose. Thus, coming out is a gay husband's strategy to force the *tongqi* to turn a blind eye to his gay relationships while also placing the burden on her to maintain the appearance of a heterosexual family marriage. Choi and Luo (2016, 276) and Lo (2020) found that gay husbands with lesbian wives implicitly and explicitly collaborate with their parents to create the facade of a heterosexual family. Liu (2013) noted the increasingly common practice of gay men and women agreeing to a marriage of convenience to meet their parents' expectations of social conformity. Huang and Brouwer (2018) have suggested that nominal marriages of convenience reproduce heterosexuality in socioeconomic and material terms without romantic heterosexual love. Zheng (2015) reported that most "red collar" (government employees) and "gold collar" (wealthy) men marry women who appear sophisticated and educated. The experiences of these women are very different from those of their rural, low-educated counterparts.

After Discovery: *Tongqi* Who Divorce

In-Court Divorce

Of the twelve *tongqi* with education whom I interviewed, nine filed both in-court and out-of-court divorces, while three opted to stay in their marriage. Those who chose to stay married said it was solely because they did not want to lose custody of their children. Of those who filed for divorce, six chose out-of-court divorce proceedings, and three chose in-court divorce proceedings. The three in-court divorce cases were filed by Shanshan (thirty-four), Siyuan (twenty-seven), and Xie (twenty-seven). Shanshan filed in-court divorce in summer 2018:

> I must have accountability; it is my right to know this before we married. I need respect. Therefore, we were divorced last summer. My ex-husband did not confess he is gay and refused to equalize his properties to me . . . and we both wanted the kids . . . therefore, we could not settle it from negotiation. We must go to in-court divorce.

Shanshan said that it was worth it to pursue happiness with courage. Culturally, a married couple is expected to provide an heir for the family.

When Shanshan was first married, her husband dutifully had sex with her until she became pregnant. She remembered that his reaction to the news was more relief than joy. Then their lovemaking abruptly stopped. As the baby's delivery date came closer, they argued and fought until he demanded a divorce.

For a woman who unknowingly marries a gay man, a divorce can be difficult to obtain because according to Chinese law, infidelity cannot occur between two people of the same sex. Still, Shanshan filed for divorce, and the court rejected her claim that her husband was guilty of infidelity, declaring him innocent because he was not sleeping with another woman. Therefore, the court awarded primary custody of her nine-month-old daughter to her ex-husband and ruled that the daughter could stay with her mother four days per month. There is no typical or standard divorce agreement in the context of Chinese marital dissolution. The terms are often contingent on the negotiations between the couple involved. This variability is exemplified in the case of Shanshan and her husband, whose divorce terms were the product of specific negotiations. This case underscores the importance of considering individual circumstances and agreements when examining divorce practices in China. Financially, Shanshan lost as well. Although her husband agreed to pay alimony of 700 yuan (US$114) per month, Shanshan said that accounted for less than 20 percent of her monthly expenses. She said she had to agree to the terms because her husband's family threatened that if she did not, they would restrict contact with her daughter further:

> There is no such thing as a man having an affair with a man! He has never admitted he is gay. If a man and a woman get a room [in the hotel], we can say it is an extramarital affair, but if it is two men, I can say nothing. China's marriage law discusses cohabitation with another person, resulting in divorce and compensation to the other party. However, judicially, according to my knowledge, "another person" is always interpreted as "the opposite sex."

Siyuan echoed Shansha:

> The lawyers in court even denied me to share my husband's properties, denied his adultery, denied his violence, and I lost custody of my two

sons. Only men are still considered legitimate heirs of ancestral properties and are still the primary labor force in rural China. The court still favors men in divorce cases. What can I say? I am very frustrated.

When we spoke in downtown Shenyang, Xie discussed how she had filed for an in-court divorce with her husband but admitted that she was unprepared for what followed:

> My husband hired a lawyer to prepare the divorce document. He colluded with gangsters to attack me and beat me up. I was in a hospital for three months. However, his efforts were futile, and I was not scared. Still, he was clever and transferred all his assets to his parents beforehand. I was not able to get anything. Since then, I have worked as a clerk. I still suffer psychologically. I have insomnia and depression. Nevertheless, at least I felt some release and have become more relaxed.

Xie lost custody of her five-year-old son and could see him only once a month. Life was getting back to normal, albeit painful and lonely. She had trust issues and admitted that she was not ready for another relationship. She said nightmares, depression, and thoughts of suicide still haunted her. Still, she felt that divorcing her husband was the right thing to do as the marriage law in China has not been updated since the 1980s. Xie told me that after she divorced, her family criticized her because she not only was denied alimony, but even worse, she lost custody of her son. The law in China states that only a woman can be a mistress; Xie could not sue her ex-husband for adultery because his "mistress" was a man! Although it has consumed all her savings to pay attorney's fees, the uphill battle for her dignity and justice was the right thing for her to do, and she had no regrets.

Out-of-Court Divorce

Divorce for women, especially for mothers, has far more severe consequences than for men. Old traditions and values persist, as do old stereotypes. Huahua (thirty-one) was an educated woman who took two years to end her marriage through out-of-court divorce. Her story was similar to the other nine educated *tongqi* who filed for out-of-court divorce. Her divorce continued to wreak havoc on her life:

> I made the mistake of being involved in a failed marriage. However, I have a right to cut my loss! My ex-husband and his parents collaborated to bully me, and I was not allowed to see my daughter. I do not have money to hire a lawyer! Although my closeted husband destroyed my life, I did not destroy myself. I have to repack, rethink, and move on.... I remained his wife, so if I fell in love with another man, I could not get married. However, it has been worth it, as at least I have my freedom.

The nine educated *tongqi* who filed for out-of-court divorce suffered tremendous physical and psychological impacts upon themselves. However, only by filing for out-of-court divorce could they find dignity and self-respect.

After Discovery: *Tongqi* Who Remain Married

Xiaojun and Zhuoyin, both of whom were infected with HIV from their husbands, opted to maintain the status quo rather than divorce. For these two *tongqi*, hopes of a sexual relationship were dashed by their husband's dishonesty. Subsequently, the stigma of having been duped into marriage by a gay prostitute left them unable to speak to friends about the matter.

The other *tongqi* did not contract HIV from their gay husbands, but they still suffered from depression. When Qiaoxian (twenty-five) was first married, she felt that her husband cared for her, but the lack of sex was disappointing. Her feelings changed drastically in a single night:

> We were married for more than one year, but still, he would not touch me. One night, I told him I would probably not come home because I had to care for my sick sister in our village. He seemed very pleased, even excited, when I told him about this. However, my sister seemed much better that night, so I returned home sooner than planned. I entered our home and found it was quiet. When I came to our bedroom, I could hear him talking to someone on his cell phone. My husband was having an intimate conversation and saying how much he would charge for specific

sexual things! I could hear him say things like darling, sweetie, sweetheart, and I love you. I was so shocked. He never used words like that with me and did not even refer to me as his wife! I just walked in and pretended I heard nothing. He quickly hung up and told me it was a call from an old friend. The critical moment was when I caught him in a QQ chat room. I entered the chat under the guise of a man. As we talked in the chat, he began flirting with me. I played along and then he became explicit. Afterward, I confronted him, and he admitted he was gay. I am lucky; he could have infected me with HIV or syphilis. He told me making love to a woman repulsed him psychologically, and he could not get an erection. . . . I witnessed that sometimes, he had to take two Viagra pills [Waige 伟哥] to stay erect and consummate the act with me.

Meiqi (twenty-four) finished only grade three in rural China. When we spoke, she said that she had been married for six years. She insisted that her husband not only did nothing on their wedding night but also continued to avoid all sexual activity into the third year of their marriage. At first, she regularly complained, but he always had an excuse. After a few months, he would not even respond to her. By the third year of the marriage, his parents were pushing incessantly for him to give them a grandchild. However, still he would not initiate sex and was reluctant even to touch her. During that third year, they finally began to have sex. He would begin with a glass of wine in the kitchen and tell her to wait in the bedroom with the lights off. After a few minutes, he would enter the bedroom but always finish very quickly, then go immediately to sleep. He said he had a medical condition, and this was the best he could do. Still, it worked, and in the fourth year of our marriage, she gave birth to her son. However, throughout the marriage, she felt strange that they rarely kissed, touched, cuddled, or flirted. After she gave birth to her son, all physical contact stopped. Two years later, he admitted he was gay.

Meiqi openly identified herself as a *tongqi*. Reflecting on her marital life, she estimated that approximately a decade of her life had been spent in a relationship that lacked the typical intimacy between heterosexual couples. This period of her life, she believes, was lost due to her husband's sexual orientation. The couple ceased to have sexual relations following the birth of their child. She described herself as feeling hopeless and desperate.

Only three of the less-educated women in the sample divorced their husbands. They divorced because they wanted dignity, respect, and to be able to repack themselves to have a new life after cutting their losses from their failed marriage. Miumiu (thirty-four) was an educated *tongqi*:

> I need to live in dignity! Why would I want his money if a man did not love me? Of course, my husband gave me nothing, no alimony, and I lost custody of my daughter! I do not care. Once I could see my daughter twice per month, I was satisfied. I do not have an education, but I have my hands. Every woman is a hero! I will not be starving. I can become a cleaning lady or return to my hometown and be a farmer.

The other forty-four low-educated *tongqi* opted to remain married because the stigma of divorce was still a problem in rural China. The social pressure to avoid divorce and the shame associated with it are powerful motivators. Caught between two bad options, they feel unlucky and ill-fated. Ping (twenty-five) finished grade four education:

> I did not have a job, and I never finished primary school. It will be difficult for me to find a job and leave my village. . . . Still, my husband has been good to my family. He gave my parents around 300,000 yuan [US$50,000] to help them with their financial difficulties last year.

For twenty-three-year-old Yinxin, a rural girl with a primary school education, the transformative effect was, in essence, the death of having the autonomy to lead a simple and uncomplicated diurnal existence in the village; Yinxin said she would not be so stupid as to divorce him because then she would get nothing. She said maintaining the status quo would mean that she could at least live with her son and daughter. If she divorced her husband, she would never get custody of her kids. She asked me whether she could have received counseling from some service organization. She was very stressed and did not know what to do.

Tongqi: Resistance and a New Life

When I interviewed the *tongqi* in 2018, the ages of the educated and less-educated *tongqi* ranged from twenty-three to thirty-four years.

Each of the fifty-nine informants had at least one child, and three reported having two children. All the interviewed educated and low-educated *tongqi* and their husbands came from rural areas. There were two low-educated *tongqi* who admitted that they had been infected with HIV. Nine out of twelve educated *tongqi* were separated from their husbands. Three out of forty-seven low-educated *tongqi* initiated out-of-court divorce proceedings, and forty-four low-educated *tongqi* chose to remain married but sought emotional counseling or support either online or from NGOs.

Interviews with the fifty-nine *tongqi* confirmed that many were not just waiting for death. These *tongqi* rose from the ashes to start a new life by taking action in at least three ways. One way was to file for divorce, thereby regaining their self-respect. Changing their social and legal status helped them become emotionally stronger and stop being socially dead. For those infected with HIV, a second way was to get medical treatment and stay physically healthy. With physical health, they could raise their children and chart a new life course if they wished. A third way was to seek help and support from NGOs and online groups to share their stories with those having similar experiences.

Divorcing and Refusing to Be Socially Dead

The nine educated *tongqi* divorced their husbands because they had jobs or knew they could find jobs afterward. Education and marketable skills made it more likely that a *tongqi* would end her dysfunctional marriage. These women have the means to hire divorce lawyers, find or hold stable jobs, and become financially independent. The three low-educated *tongqi* filed out-of-court divorces with their husbands. They were motivated by their need—their demand—for dignity and justice. This motivation helped them take control of their lives. Many of the low-educated *tongqi* admitted that they remained in their marriages because of concerns about child custody (Wang et al. 2020) and being financially dependent upon their husbands (Wei and Cai 2019; Zhu 2018). This constraint was especially relevant for older *tongqi*. Regardless of education, all twelve educated and low-educated *tongqi* who divorced noted their disadvantaged status in the legal system.

Living with AIDS: Getting Treatment and Medication

Two low-educated *tongqi* admitted that their husbands had infected them with HIV. The incidence of HIV in China has increased dramatically, growing almost twenty fold between 2004 and 2017, from 0.23 to 4.2 per hundred thousand people (Li 2015; Wang et al. 2020). *Tongqi* are a particularly high-risk group because their husbands are a bridge to exposure and infection (Zheng 2015). All the *tongqi* I spoke with complained that Chinese marriage law essentially presented them as subjects of scrutiny and disgust, as potential vectors of HIV, or as those who would ruin the fabric of collectivist Chinese culture. Educated *tongqi* may refuse to subsist in loveless marriages and be able to find social acceptance from their family members. In the following narratives, the low-educated *tongqi* find themselves legally disadvantaged yet determined to overcome the hurdles by refusing to succumb to the slow living-death worlds. Zhuoyin (thirty-one), said:

> My mother understood and encouraged me to divorce my husband. She took me to the hospital and encouraged me to fight my AIDS infection. Without her understanding, I would not have survived.

Xiaojun (twenty-eight) echoed Zhouyin:

> At first, my brother abandoned me and did not want to help me look for different NGOs. However, after I was rescued from my attempted suicide, he finally understood my feelings. Then he used his social and professional network to find a good doctor for me to get counseling.

The two low-educated *tongqi* infected with HIV were not simply waiting for death, despite feeling hopeless and desperate. They actively consulted with doctors and sought professional advice and treatment for their HIV. Their parents and family members forgave them and became the primary source of strength for them to overcome the hurdles and darkness of dealing with HIV and starting a new chapter of their lives.

All the *tongqi* interviewed tried to find space to survive and find their own political, social, and civil life. They could survive, even thrive, within these necropolitical lives with the help and interventions of NGOs and social workers.

Efforts to Change with NGO Support

It has been estimated that over 20 percent of the 13.6 million *tongqi* are emotionally strong enough to maintain the facade of heterosexual marriage (Li 2015; Song 2016). These women are willing to keep their husbands' sexual orientation a secret so they can stay together and raise their children. However, most educated *tongqi* choose to leave, refusing to accept being the unwitting party in queer kinship. To them, the dishonesty justified the search for a new future. Meifang (thirty-four) said:

> I am not waiting to die, nor will I try to commit suicide, although it was a very tough and complicated procedure to divorce my husband. I lost custody of my two sons, but at least I have my dignity. I use my phone and social media to share my experience through different NGOs. I hope I can get more help from NGOs for my job hunting.

In 2017, the educated *tongqi* Siyuan attended the National People's Congress (NPC) to lobby for legalizing gay marriage. According to Siyuan, only thirty delegates out of around three thousand supported her, which was insufficient for a formal debate. Since then, she tried several times to bring the matter to an advisory body of the NPC. When she first began, delegates bluntly told her that gay marriage was wrong. One officer said that the time was wrong and other problems were more urgent. Siyuan and others were pessimistic yet determined because these marriages of convenience remained widely accepted among gay communities as they reinforced heteronormative traditions. *Tongqi* will need to find a way to galvanize the public and the government to action, perhaps by attaching their circumstances to public health.

Xiaojun was one of the tongqi who contracted HIV:

> I have contracted AIDS, and my husband betrayed me. My life is a mess. I almost committed suicide. However, I will never think I have to wait for death and kill myself. It is what it is. I must cope with it and move on.

Zhuoyin echoed Xiaojun:

> I know full well the shame of having a failed marriage in my hometown. The situation for us *tongqi* is improving as we have more online support, and I know I am not alone. . . . My failed marriage does not mean I have a failed life, even though I now have AIDS. Therefore, I remain silent and stay married; I do not want a divorce. As long as he provides monthly support for me and our kids, I am OK with how things are.

In sum, most of the low-educated *tongqi* felt that they did not have the means to leave their sham marriages. These women faced extraordinary emotional and physical challenges because they had limited resources, assets, or marketable skills. To incrementally gain financial independence, their options were often limited to sweatshop factories, entry-level retail sales, or the illicit sex trade. Shi (2019) and Gao (2017) reported that rural-to-urban migrant workers in China suffer from severe social insecurity in the absence of *hukou* in the cities to which they move. Under the *hukou* system (Kong 2012b), they are not entitled to medical benefits or insurance. This has led some low-educated *tongqi* to approach NGOs, such as the China Wives of Gay Men Mutual Aid Studio (Tongqi huyuan gongzuoshi, 同妻互援工作室), Xiao Delan (Little Teresa, 小德兰), the Sister-Brother Voluntary Group (jiemei xiongdi zhiyuanzhe yizhan, 姐妹兄弟志愿者驿站), and the Tongqi Group (tongqiqun, 同妻群) for professional and legal advice. Others have joined QQ forums, Weibo, and WeChat groups, demonstrating their resistance and agency despite their difficult situations.

Conclusion

There are significant cultural differences between today's China and developed Western nations, and closeted queer men who marry women are just some of the myriad skeletons in China's closet. The relationship between *tongqi* and their closeted gay husbands in North China has been a significant issue needing the attention of scholars researching sociology and sexuality. Research based upon Mbembe's characterization of necropolitics helps us understand *tongqi* as subjects "kept alive but in a state of injury" (Mbembe 2003, 21). This condition describes social death, not physical death. The literature on gay men marrying *tongqi* in China often ignores how these women are subjected to necropolitical conditions once the truth about their marriage is revealed. Robbed of their expectations of a traditional marriage relationship, these women become victims of necropolitics, living a social, if not physical, death (McKinnon 2016; Puar 2005). For instance, these women often face a multitude of adverse consequences. They may lose custodial rights to their children, contract sexually transmitted infections, and experience stigmatization. Additionally, they may suffer a decline in social status, transition into the role of a divorcee, and lose the support of their family. These outcomes highlight the complex and multifaceted challenges these women encounter. They must deal with significant stigma and loss. They lost their marriage, their husband, custody of their children, perhaps their health due to an STI, and even the respect of their family and friends who blame them for initiating the divorce without knowing the actual reason why (Rofel 2007).

The literature has framed the life of *tongqi* in China as bleak. For example, *tongqi* have been portrayed as physically at risk for HIV infection, psychologically depressed, socially stigmatized by family and friends, professionally unskilled, and financially dependent; no wonder they have been dismissed as those waiting for death (Bie and Tang 2016; Huang, 2015). Nevertheless, despite these massive disadvantages, many *tongqi* have resisted and eventually overcame their situation. The data presented here confirm that *tongqi* survived and found fulfillment, joy, and success. The findings fill a research void by revealing how these women have overcome their predicament. The necropolitics of social death provides some hints as to how conditions designed for death can ironically become life-giving. This conceptualization allows researchers to examine how some women resist overwhelming adverse circumstances, overcome them, and make changes resulting in a positive new life.

This chapter addressed the social forces leading to dysfunctional marriages of convenience between gay men and heterosexual women. Gay men should not be driven to marry to escape the pressure and obligations demanded by their families and the village. Likewise, these women have a fundamental human right not to be defrauded in their marriage. The heretofore bleak life of *tongqi* that stems from China's social and cultural policies on heterosexuality reflects a deep-rooted enmity toward gay men that requires further investigation. The literature indicates that Chinese cultural factors reinforce the stigma associated with being gay, encouraging men to hide their sexual orientation by marrying women. However, the way straight *tongqi* have been saddled with some of the same stigma assigned to those in the gay community demands urgent attention to advance theories beyond the straight/queer binary.

In the dominant Chinese culture, the authority and the general population treat *tongqi* as members of queer communities even though all the *tongqi* represented in this book despised this label and asserted that they should not be treated as such. One of the objectives of this book is to explain why *tongqi* are treated as members of queer communities by mainstream Chinese society. For example, *tongqi* suffered both enacted stigma and felt stigma (chapter 6), leading to feelings of shame and victimhood. They often asked rhetorically why they were selected to be *tongqi* while other women were not. Family pressure to marry increases as they approach the age of twenty-seven. Once a woman is twenty-seven years old and unmarried, she acquires the label of leftover lady. In this context, these rural women are typically eager to marry and do not carefully observe whether their fiancés are gay. The one-sided emphasis on the hardships faced by *tongqi* highlights the intransigence of social and cultural policies that treat gay communities as a threat to Chinese values. These sham marriages have been a loophole that must be closed; they have been an easy escape that ultimately does more harm than good. The issue can be more honestly addressed once gay men are discouraged from marrying heterosexual women to extend the bloodline. The stigmatization and alienation of gay communities in China must evolve toward the understanding that all citizens have the collective and mutually engaging goal of eradicating prejudice. By focusing on remedies rather than blame, possible solutions may come from policy changes, cultural changes, and counseling strategies.

This chapter provides insights into NGOs, state actors, and other social service providers that help *tongqi*. Protecting the physical and mental health of *tongqi* can reduce the need for taxpayer-funded resources to combat HIV transmission. This chapter addresses how to simultaneously reduce the social stigma associated with being gay while addressing the filial obligation for men to give their parents a grandchild. Although

China's marriage law was revised in 2001 and tried to address adultery, divorce, child custody, property arrangements, women's interests and rights, and domestic violence, it failed to address mismatched sexual orientation within the cultural context or how this might impact divorce. It is time for policymakers to evaluate marriage and divorce laws to meet the needs of China's 13.6 million *tongqi*. These findings provide direction for the government to help *tongqi* cope with divorce, look for jobs, and find hope in their lives.

5

"Buying Sex Makes Me Sky-High"

Relationship between Male Sex Workers and Male/Female Clients

It was a warm, rainy day in Tianjin. Gaoling (fifty-five) was a frequent client and always visited Pistachio to find his favorite MSW. Born in China but living in Australia since he was two years old, he was a bisexual man who had been married to his heterosexual wife for more than ten years. He ran a trading company in Beijing. Gaoling said that he dated men and women as a teenager. He particularly enjoyed sex in outdoor places like public restrooms or the beach and regularly engaged in casual sex with other young men in places like the sauna or yoga rooms. However, now he was older and no longer at his physical peak. To fulfill his physical desires, he bought commercial sex at Pistachio:

> I tried to be a good husband and father of two sons for over ten years. My two kids are currently studying high school, and I feel I have to do something for myself. I have my sexual needs. When I was younger, I married my wife as a cover for my lifestyle. This is important in conservative China. I like sex with men, young men, especially bondage; I also like having sex with transgender people. . . . I used to love quick sex with a hot guy. It was so easy when I was young. However, I am over 50 now and not in shape. I cannot just go to the beach or public toilet and flirt with young guys.

Gaoling's situation reflected his inner struggle. Part of him needed to fit in and be seen as a typical heterosexual family man by those around him. He had taken great pains to please his parents. He married a woman, and they gave birth to two sons. Having fulfilled that obligation, Gaoling now regularly took private trips to surreptitiously get away and feed his true self, nurturing himself as a client at Pistachio.

Besides the parade of men like Gaoling at Pistachio, I also saw a surprising number of female clients. Although the numbers were small, some women regularly bought sex from MSWs. After talking to several of them, I discovered that their reasons were logical and understandable. One night in April 2017, my friend Yang (thirty) and I chatted with some MSWs and listened to their stories. Male and female clients came to Pistachio to find MSWs. Most of the male clients were both gay and bisexual men. Most of the women were well-to-do middle-aged executives. Women buying commercial sex was admittedly uncommon in Pistachio, and these clients were greeted with great fanfare and attention. Yang told me that these women were married but unhappy in their marriages. They told me about their experiences with their tycoon husbands routinely inflicting emotional abuse and neglect. Sometimes, there is physical abuse and violence. When they first come to *Pistachio*, many of these women feel depressed, psychologically and emotionally empty, and hungry for love and affection. One of the women interviewed had become a regular patron and was particularly outspoken. She demanded Yang to "recommend your best men. They must be young and strong, hot, and sexually creative. We want to enjoy ourselves through the night." Such candor reflected their pragmatism and no-nonsense approach to buying sexual services.

Given the nature of their occupation, MSWs often have trust issues due to poor relations with parents and family. All 151 MSWs interviewed generally agreed that the straight life was performed publicly to avoid being shunned or disowned by their family. Their true selves had to be kept a secret. They also agreed that their relationships with clients should be just as superficial and transactional. This raises several core questions about the nature of male-to-male relationships and the dynamic interplay between MSWs and their clients. The motivation for being an MSW is primarily financial, and client gender may be more important for some and less for others. The bottom line is that MSWs provide services for the sexual pleasure of any client. There is ordinarily little or no effort to have authentic intimacy or emotional connections. But naturally, neither the worker nor the client knows when a connection might occur, sparking a potential long-term romance or relationship.

This chapter presents stories and experiences of fifty-seven male and twenty-seven female clients buying commercial sex from Pistachio and other places. As noted earlier, sex work is illegal, as is the purchasing of sex. However, first and foremost, the clubs protect the clients and have procedures to get them out quickly and away from the police. Police are typically not interested in clients because the richer the client, the more likely it is that a higher-up gets involved and the case is dismissed. Understandably, cops on the street know that it is usually a waste of their time to arrest clients and can even get them in trouble if they are not careful.

Still, the purchase of commercial sex in China's gay sexscapes needs to be researched because the male and female clients' voices and their narratives are under-represented in the literature about MSWs. MSWs and client relationships, especially regarding money or bounded authenticity, are, at best, understudied. Sexual encounters with clients are typically cast as simple pecuniary transactions: payment for pleasure, excitement, and sexual thrill. It rarely, if ever, involves trust and fidelity. Just as male clients typically take charge and dominate MSWs, so also female clients will dictate the time, place, and manner of sexual services they will receive. Female clients can request cuddling and soft, gentle pampering or demand an evening where they can be aggressive and dominant.

Studies on the Purchase of Sex

Some have framed MSWs and client relationships as transient and lacking long-term commitment (Tsang 2019a). In the existing literature on clients, most literature disproportionally focuses on female sex workers and their male clients (Farley et al. 2017; Joseph and Black 2012; Monto and Hoteling 2001; Monto and Milrod 2014). Other scholars argue that female sex workers and their clients tend toward a more "bounded authenticity" with rational bounding to each other, contract-based fulfilments of needs, and sexual liberalism (Bernstein 2007; Brents 2016; Joseph and Black 2012; Milrod and Weitzer 2012; Peng 2007; Pettinger 2013); selling sex for sexual gratification, companionship and emotional support (Tsang 2019a); buying sex for pleasure (Sanders 2008); and buying sex for edgework (Kong 2015).

There has been growing interest in studying MSWs and male clients (Mai 2017; Minichiello and Scott 2014; Minichiello et al. 2013; Niccolai et al. 2013; Okanlawon et al. 2013; Smith and Grov 2011; Vanwesenbeeck 2013). Buying sex provides consumers with experiences of power and control in terms of gender, race, class, and nationality (Kempadoo 2001; Sanders 2008). These experiences of fantasy and domination have cultivated an entire clandestine industry built around sex tourism, where people (mostly men) from one country go to another country to exploit Indigenous young women or men who are not able to assert their own identities and positionalities (Johnson 2007; Kempadoo 2001).

As such, the literature portrays the MSWs and their clients' relationship as simulations of intimacy and companionship without commitment (Mai 2017; Rivers-Moore 2012). Some American male sex tourists try to justify their behavior by blaming feminism, which they say has made American women unattractive and unappealing (Rivers-Moore 2012, 2016). These sex tourists argue that feminism has robbed them of their masculinity (Kempadoo 2001). MSWs typically describe female clients as aggressive pursuers (Berg et al. 2019). In commercial sexscapes, men are typically limited to traditional gender roles (Kempadoo 2001). Women clients also engage in sex tourism, as documented both in Taylor (2001) and Kingston, Hammond, and Redman (2020). Taylor (2001) offered an in-depth analysis of North American and Northern European women who buy sex services from young men in the Caribbean for what the women describe as "romance holidays." The women who bought sex services were reluctant to label what they engaged in as prostitution. Their ideas about the young men they bought were also deeply rooted in racist ideas about Black men and sexuality. Most of these studies focus on sex tourism websites and their advertising strategies, examining websites generated via Internet search engines at a specific time (Gezinski 2016). More information is needed about MSWs and their clients, both male and female.

Sex Workers Tactics for Long-Term Sexual Services

Rain (twenty) said he used his youthful good looks to entice clients to offer him long-term packages of up to several months. Rain boasted about his collection of cosmetic products and provided an unsolicited rundown of his cosmetic surgeries. He ticked them off using his fingers: invasive rhinoplasty, eyelid surgery, liposuction, hair implants,

Botox injections, and collagen injections. Finally, he provided his list of supplements to stay lean and muscled. Rain said these were investments in himself to stay competitive and marketable as an MSW. Although expensive, he felt good about himself and his occupation. At the end of our last conversation, he finished with a rhetorical flourish: "You think it is easy to stay so desirable? You must invest in yourself and work hard to stay in demand! Although the time is short, I enjoy every moment in this playground."

Rain said that in the beginning, his sugar daddy seemed captivated by him, perhaps because of his smile, youth, tan skin, muscles, and sweet and sunny personality. Rain said he went sunbathing daily and did what he could to please his sugar daddy, attending to his needs and obeying all his wishes. In return, his sugar daddy bought him everything he asked for. He promised to buy Rain an apartment in downtown Shanghai and set him up to run his own business sometime on his twentieth birthday.

Days later, while on a solo trip to Thailand, it all suddenly changed. Rain had been on a Bangkok shopping spree that day, picking up designer brand items like Hermes, Cartier, Chanel, Gucci, and Prada. He remembered that the bill was over a quarter million yuan (US$38,461). He returned to the hotel in the afternoon and was relaxing when the credit card company suddenly called him to say the payment was denied, and he had to return all the items immediately. Rain was stunned. He then tried calling his sugar daddy back in China, but his mobile phone service was also cut off. He realized at that moment that it was over. Everything he bought had to be returned, and he had to pay all the trip expenses, including the hotel room, meals, transportation, and more. When he returned to his Tianjin apartment, he found it almost empty; all the gifts had been removed. His sugar daddy had vanished without a simple goodbye. He never thought their relationship would end in such a way. Looking back, Rain was philosophical,

> I was not sad. Money comes, and money goes [*caisan renanle* 财散人安乐]! I learned a great lesson. Everyone is a hypocrite. It is all theater. We act, we lie, our clients lie, and we should all go to hell. Anyway, I washed my hands and came back to the club. I will not be so naïve and innocent anymore.

When Rain returned from Thailand, he was deeply in debt and resumed his old position at Pistachio. He also worked the streets and parks to pay his bills so he could hustle extra money. Soon, Rain met his second sugar daddy, a thirty-year-old university professor. Rain said this client was also married with a young daughter, and the wife did not know that her husband was bisexual but preferred men. Rain said the man was intelligent and enjoyable but conflicted about his wife. He told Rain that he had stopped sleeping with her after she gave birth. With Rain, the professor was sexually aggressive and dominating. In return, he quickly set Rain up in a Beijing apartment with a monthly allowance of 10,000 yuan (US$1,612). While not a great package, Rain was desperately in debt and grateful. During that first week, he saw the professor twice, and then, like before, suddenly, it was over. After one short week, Rain's second sugar daddy had found someone else.

Rain's third sugar daddy was a professional and worked in a bank. He was tall, handsome, gentle, and, of course, rich. While he loved chasing different MSWs, he said he wanted to rescue Rain from being beaten up by so many others. He told Rain to move in with him so he could take care of him:

> We lived together for a week, and then he asked me to leave his house. He already felt bored with me in bed. He wrote me a cheque for 200,000 yuan (US$29,411) to pay for my seven days with him. I was hurt, but when I saw the cheque, I shrugged my shoulders and thought, "That's life." I am ready to find some other clients. Although I am a little bit older, I am already planning my next adventure.

I met Rain's ex-sugar daddy, Kiu, a forty-nine-year-old Chinese man from Zhejiang. Kiu went to Pistachio because Rain asked him to as a favor for me. We met in August 2018:

> You asked me if I fell in love with Rain, but it was just curiosity. I love my family, and my wife treats me as if I were 100 percent her man. I do not want to come out to my wife. Does it make sense? In this modern age, if you want to find a partner, find one. However, do not throw your life away. Money boys are just for sex.

Kiu's account reflects a common refrain about marriage. Large parts of Chinese society remain very conservative and probably would not accept a listed company director as being gay. For someone in business or government, the fear of being outed is enough to keep one in hiding. For MSWs like Rain, that only leaves living in the moment and enjoying the sexual thrill. Both Rain and Kiu seemed to agree that there is no such thing as love between a client and an MSW.

Master Zhen and His Sugar Boy

A counterpoint to the transactional cash-for-sex approach is used by the MSW who was highlighted earlier in this book. Zhen, the fifty-something retired doctor with his distinct handlebar mustache has remained popular in Tianjin because he knows how to connect and create a relationship experience.

To recap, when Zhen was young he fulfilled his filial obligation, marrying a village girl and having sex to produce children. As he realized he did not care to have sex with his wife, he instead found he had strong urges to have sex with men. After the birth of his second child, he began visiting gay clubs and stopped all lovemaking with his wife. At that time, Zhen was earning a modest income working at a hospital specializing in plastic surgery, massage therapy, and general wellness. Over time he also started earning money for providing sexual services. In 2019, after his children became adults, he closed his clinic and transitioned to full-time sex work. He kept his secret from his wife and children.

Zhen uses his age, wisdom from experience, and his massage skills to fulfill the needs of those clients who seek him out. He has been able to enjoy steady and recurring visits from clients and admitted he tries to be open for a deeper and more serious relationship.

When he started at Pistachio, Herman hired Zhen because of his mature outlook, age, and Thai masseuse skills. Zhen was considered too old to be a sex worker, but he capitalized on his knowledge of consumer psychology. Customers were always looking for fresh new blood in Pistachio, even though it was packaged in an older body. To Herman's surprise, Zhen quickly became the top-earning sex worker there, if not in all of Tianjin. It was not long before Zhen became somewhat of a legend.

> I only want passion and excitement. Sex work is like getting high and riding a rollercoaster. I do not want any attachments when I am with a client. . . . What I sell is my massage skills, my heart, and my sincere care. That is what keeps my clients returning. . . . Beauty, muscle, and caring make me a success at Pistachio.

Zhen said that he was not overly attentive to his physical appearance. What he sold to his clients was his affective labor and massage skills. Each month, his income ranged between 20,000 and 40,000 yuan (US$3,076–US$6,153), with an average monthly salary of 30,000 yuan (US$4,615). At Pistachio, he was provided a room and meals, and his salary was almost three times higher than at the hospital.

> That I could become a top MSW in a club like Pistachio at age fifty is indeed a miracle. I am happy with my work and would never go back to my old hospital job or return to my dead-end marriage. The club is always exciting. My children are adults and they have their jobs. I remember the first time I had three clients at the same time. They loved my massage and our lovemaking. I do not think I am old. I am still very hungry for sex.

One night in the summer of 2016, I met Zhen in the nearby public park and talked with him as we returned to Pistachio. He was upbeat and talkative about his profession. That day, he was sporting a tight tank top that accentuated his well-defined musculature. His physique drew the attention of people around us. He looked much younger than his age. He looked glamorous, charming, and wise. He was optimistic about the demand for his services at the club.

> I am happy to help my clients get rid of their fatigue. They love my massages. . . . I feel like I am rejuvenated; I have a new life. At this stage in my life, I enjoy both passion and pleasure. I feel my body dancing, laughing, and enjoying every moment in Pistachio! I love what I am doing and will continue to follow my feelings.

Zhen said he had even found himself a "sugar boy," a wealthy businessman twenty years younger than he. Zhen said his "boy" had a frayed relationship with his cadre father and that his younger partner needed someone stable to listen to and maintain the home:

> He loves what I do for him, like cooking, laundry, massaging, talking, listening to how his father treats him, and how he feels so stressed about being gay in today's China. His father has lots of mistresses, and he grew up in a complicated family environment. His mother was one of his father's early mistresses. I listen to what he tells me and do not judge him. Of course, afterward, I make sure we have our passionate moment every night. He wants me to be exclusively his, but he will not intervene with my job. He says I complete him and give him what he looks for in a daddy.

Zhen provided round-the-clock cooking, cleaning, laundry, and sex services. He connected with his younger partner by developing intimacy through emotional labor. Zhen lavished attention on his client in every way, from regular body massages to singing romantic songs. In return, Sugar Boy took care of his living expenses, entertainment fees, and other amenities. Some months, Zhen received a large cash stipend that allowed him to buy property, travel, or invest in setting up his own massage business.

Zhen was pragmatic about his services. He combined thrilling sexual activities with a range of interpersonal services requiring unique skills. Personal relationships were essential to the negotiation process between him and his clients. His skill at negotiating client relationships gave him the confidence and freedom to feel he was contributing to society. However, Zhen remained cognizant that his sugar-boy relationship was fragile, and he tried to be ready for the day it would inevitably end:

> I am afraid he will leave me for a younger man one day. However, whenever I tried to break up with him, he threatened to commit suicide. One day, he proudly showed me he had put a heart-shaped tattoo on his chest for me. I was touched, but I still had to be pragmatic. You never know what the future holds. My instincts told me that one day, this love would end.

The desire to have a relationship marked by everlasting passion is a fantasy that is both improbable and impractical. I asked Zhen to introduce me to his sugar boy, and two days later, he surprised me. "This is my sugar boy," Zhen said when he introduced Yifei (thirty-one). "Handsome and young. Beauty and brain? Huh?" Yifei chatted about my role at Pistachio:

> It is not easy to fall in love with one man. I do not know how long my love for Zhen will last. I only know that, at this moment, we connect. That is important. I confess my love to him may be intensely physical but short-lived and ephemeral. . . . I think it is related to my own family. My father had lots of mistresses, and he acted like he suspected I was not his son. So maybe I am looking for a father-like man to be my sex partner. He cooks and cleans, and we have fun together. This is what matters. I even have a heart tattoo on my chest for him.

When I returned to Tianjin in July 2019, I found that Zhen and Yifei had already split. Zhen had fallen into the typical cycle of disposability exercised by his sugar boy as the pleasure and excitement faded. He had predicted this from the beginning, stating, "There is no lasting love in these commercial sexscapes." Zhen secluded himself, mourned for a week, then returned to Pistachio.

The last time I spoke to Zhen was January 2020. He was living with a wealthy client in Tianjin. I asked him if he thought he was now too old to be a sex worker:

> I get all manner of pleasure, thrill, and excitement from my job. I have nothing to be ashamed of; I am definitely not a "dirty boy." I work from my heart for my clients. At my age, I follow my feelings, do my job, catch my dream, and find my life. I know that clients come and clients go.

Zhen and his client are typical examples of sex worker and client relationships in Pistachio. He does what he can but does not expect a lasting relationship. Zhen may continue to be a legend among MSWs in Tianjin. Although he does not have a handsome face, his massage and plastic surgery skills made him an icon in Pistachio. It is unusual for a fifty-year-old man to be in such demand as a sex worker. Zhen has been a trailblazer and a beacon of hope to the younger men who think they may wish to keep working in the industry for years to come. Zhen's life was all about learning to delay client disposability as far as possible and to be resilient in "bouncing back" by looking for a new relationship that will unfortunately end in the same vicious cycle.

The Male Sex Worker's Golden Rule

In August 2016, I met Guo (twenty) during my night shift in Pistachio while he was working. Everyone has their favorite drink, and as a bartender, I found that light drinkers often ordered a beer. The MSWs who were working were limited to one free drink with a 20 percent discount for anything afterward. The clients typically wanted to order something expensive like brandy, champagne, or *maotai* (茅台). They also competed with each other in drinking contests. Some light drinkers would order one glass of champagne. Coffee, tea, and energy drinks were provided throughout the night.

When Guo sat down for his free drink, I asked questions about client relationships. He wore his usual outfit: a red crop top to show off his abs and tight denim shorts highlighting his clean-shaven legs. His face was adorned with makeup to accentuate his youth. I asked him if he ever fell in love with his clients. He made a face and pursed his lips. Guo said he used to dream of meeting the perfect rich guy and that they would live a wild and fantastic life together. Then he smirked and said that dream died long ago. The times he tried, each time it ended in pain.

A year later, I was making drinks for clients when Guo suddenly came up to me in a panic. He said his current sugar daddy, a businessman from North China, suddenly vanished and changed the lock at the apartment where they had been staying. Guo could not even get inside to retrieve his clothes and other personal belongings. I told Guo to stay calm. I knew he could find a room at the club, and I offered to go with him in the morning to find the landlord.

During our journey the following day, Guo told me his story. He had broken the golden rule among sex workers never to have genuine feelings about clients. This holds for men and women, despite the occasional success story (Tsang 2017, 2019) or Hollywood movie script. Guo said the common saying among clients is that they seek a "fresh flesh man" (*xiaoxianrou* 小鲜肉), which means young, cute, cheerful, and having a good figure. To stay emotionally uninvolved, Guo said he prefered to change sex partners frequently. "I try to show my client a good time," he said. "It is just for one night. A bird in the hand is better than a bird overhead. But when the dream is over, I have to wake up." He said it was too difficult to sustain an intimate relationship with clients in the gay community. Even though some clients wanted to have a relationship with him, he had to be on guard and stay rational. The goal is to negotiate a long-term package deal for services that do not include emotional intimacy, only physical intimacy. To get emotionally involved with someone, MSWs find boyfriends on other gay dating apps or meet them through friends and social gatherings.

Clients in Pistachio

I met some clients in Pistachio and through referrals from the NGOs. Most of the clients said buying sex at the club was safer for them than anonymous club hookups, which could end in violence, disease, or, worst of all, blackmail. Many clients at Pistachio were married with children and held high-profile positions. Since being gay is still widely taboo in many sectors of Chinese society, being serviced by an MSW at a club like Pistachio is discrete and private.

A client named Xiyang (forty-nine) visited Pistachio during Christmas in 2017. An entrepreneur running his business in Tianjin and Beijing, he had a traditional wife with two children and hid his sexual orientation from the world. He said it was not practical or feasible for him to seek a stable gay relationship. He said it was impossible in China to sustain anything other than his traditional family back home. In terms of desires, Xiyang said he kept his wild side hidden from his wife:

> I like my boys to dance more conservatively, as if they are straight. I find that more arousing than him shaking his ass like some slut. I like outfits that show off their figure, especially their muscles. I do not like sissy types. I like guys who are tanned and fit from working out at the gym.

Another client I met in one of the NGOs was a Caucasian American named Mathew (fifty-one), who had run a trading company in China since 2012. Mathew often visited the club to enjoy the services there. "I enjoy those boys," he told me, "and I am never disappointed. I want pleasure without baggage, and I get it. I do not have to be on my guard or worry about anything."

Some clients' approaches to sex fell along a continuum between domination and being physically aggressive versus a more relaxed, fantasy-oriented approach conducive to emotional connectivity. These drives reflect similar client motivations in the heterosexual commercial sex industry (Tsang 2017, 2018, 2019). The physical mechanics of sexual stimulation and pleasure drive the gay male sexual experience. The sheer physicality of sexual activity can be marked by domination and aggression. For gay men, sexual encounters have increasingly become mediated by mobile applications like Blued. One client, Zhangyan (thirty-nine), a government officer, said he regularly buys commercial sex through his phone using apps. He tried to be discrete so his wife would not know:

> I have a wife and two children at home. It is so painful to pretend I am not gay, and I have to act like those other husbands in the general population. I love sex with men, but I cannot tell my family or coworkers. Since I have to hide, I buy commercial sex to forget my pain. I know I will never find a long-term sex partner in a gay bar. I am simply pursuing sexual thrills and excitement. Having sex this way is like fast food. I place my order and eat until I am full. Each new boy is like trying a new dish.

Animus (forty-nine) was an English teacher from Ireland. He said that for a long time, he went to the club to find love. However, as a self-described incurable romantic, he had problems controlling the encounters. In those days, he would arrange elaborate private dinner dates at his home with fine wine, scented candles, and decadent desserts. Afterward, there was slow dancing, caressing, and sexual flirting. He said that this erotic environment enhanced his arousal and sense of sexuality. Having sex with a young MSW in this environment was a way for him to perform masculinity vis-à-vis the dynamics of sexual exchange. Unfortunately, it never worked out to his satisfaction. The MSW would either refuse to kiss him or briefly half-heartedly kiss before moving straight to sex, then ask to go back to the club. Animus said that eventually, he gave up trying to be intimate and resigned himself to buy sex to satisfy his physical needs.

Animus described how repeated rejection left him jaded and cynical about romance. Money cannot buy intimacy, and definitely not from MSWs. When he buys commercial sex now, he is cruel, sexually aggressive, and dominant. He bragged about his sexual ability and drive, that he could play with five or six MSWs per night. Perhaps he was merely a braggart and his claims reflected his frustration. He said he was always the dominant one, passionate and sexual. He said he preferred "Oriental men," defined as an MSW with a flat face, a flat nose, small eyes, and dark skin. Animus said that men who were short and thin made him feel strong:

> I used to fantasize that those boys would fall for me and I could have a life with them into my retirement. Now I am older and wiser. There is nothing there. I cannot communicate with these Chinese boys except by eye contact and physical touch.

MSWs, like their female counterparts, said that they charged foreign clients higher rates for sexual services than locals, ostensibly because of being "better endowed" (Tsang 2017, 2018, 2019). This term also applies to the long-term packages from their big-fish clients. The insights gathered from the interviews with the MSWs verify the information. MSWs are primarily "bottoms" ("0"), and clients are rarely concerned about the MSW's penis size as they are always on the "top" ("1"). While there is literature noting that some BDSM clients can choose to be bottoms, none of the clients interviewed in this research ever considered paying to service the sex worker. The clients asserted that they were paying to be in control. They opted to dominate the worker and maximize their sexual gratification. Moreover, these racialized tropes also shaped the nature of how clients and sex workers negotiated money.

Client Jie (thirty-eight) complained about a time when he lost an apartment to an MSW who took advantage of his good nature and sensitivity. He had gone to another club in a different city and hooked up with an MSW. He felt that there was chemistry between them, and after a marathon night of sex, he found that he had developed feelings for this young man. He reframed the context of the relationship and decided to make a dramatic gesture to reward his newfound lover. Jie said this MSW came from an impoverished family and claimed that his parents had health problems and needed money. According to Jie, this MSW used attentive listening, appreciative laughter, and verbal affirmations, which made him feel respected and loved. Therefore, he used his considerable wealth to draw up documents signing over an apartment he owned in Beijing to the MSW. Three days later, that MSW vanished. He found out weeks later that the boy had returned to an ex-boyfriend in town:

> I was cheated. He used my fantasy and intimacy with him. He is a liar and user! I admit I had a crush on him. . . . I paid for that and learned a precious lesson. That boy revealed his true character after I gave him the apartment. Once he received the legal documents that verified the apartment belonged to him, he vanished. I was angry at myself. I had not even put in my name as co-owner! I was willing to give him my love after paying for sex. But such fantasy about intimacy can only give me wrinkles and sadness.

King (54), another client, described his own experience of romantic attachment to an MSW:

> I once fell in love with an MSW. . . . He persuaded me to play S&M and burned me putting melted wax all over my body; I had to stay in the hospital for one week. Later, I found out he had a record of violence and criminal behavior involving drug dealers, addicts, and even human traffickers! After this experience, I needed to back off and set boundaries with MSWs. . . . I have to be careful not to trust them.

Kimmel (1994, 125) asserted that "the hegemonic definition of masculinity is a man in power, a man with power, and a man of power." The clients knew they could not find heteronormativity when they bought commercial sex from the MSWs. This literature raises essential questions regarding how and to what extent these paid sexual encounters offer opportunities for the clients to be serviced, served, or controlled (if that is the service requested). The commercial sex trade is a goods-for-service exchange, and the client uses the payment aspect to wield the power that determines what service will be rendered. Clients control the experience, even if they choose to be the giver of pleasure. Financial power is the structural antecedent to the encounter, which explains why buying commercial sex does not generally involve romance, desire, and intimacy unless the client chooses. Many clients I spoke with said they approached Pistachio as a private playground where they felt free to unleash their LGBTQ+ identity. Some accounts, noted here, show that the playground also teaches them things about themselves.

But creating this safe space for clients may reinforce the compartmentalization of heteronormativity of their clients. The environment enables the client to live one role in the club, then safely flip the switch back when they leave and return to their wife, family, and heteronormative existence. While clients did not explicitly use queer terminology, they expressed a desire for complete control in these sexual transactional encounters. As the paying party, clients asserted authority, power, and control. Healthy relationships included the notion of equality, where partners share the experience and relinquish control, but at least in the initial encounters, the prevailing ideal aligned clients with a heterosexual top role, and the MSWs were expected to assume a feminized bottom position.

Women Buying Sex from Male Sex Workers

I met twenty-seven women buying commercial sex in Pistachio and other places. More than half—seventeen—were married but felt profoundly ignored by their husbands. The other ten were single. Most female clients tended to be middle-aged, between thirty and sixty, and financially either upper middle class or upper class. Those women were entrepreneurs and wives of tycoons. Their children were teenagers or young adults, which resulted in even more free time. These women were financially comfortable but lonely, at least when they first began going to the club. Some initially came to Pistachio to drink and kill time; some were looking for sex. They were looking for companionship and thought that if the mood were right, they might have sex with one of the young men there.

Women, when sexually emancipated, exhibit agency in fulfilling their desires. Their ability to seek out opportunities to satisfy sexual needs reflects their autonomy. The phenomenon of women purchasing commercial sex from male sex workers is evolutionary in its challenge to patriarchal norms. Many of these women may have been ambivalent or uncertain initially about buying commercial sex services. But over time and with experience, they became empowered, confident, and assertive. This finding about female clients challenges prevailing assumptions about sex work and sheds light on the complexities of female sexuality.

Researchers have mostly ignored women who buy sex because, as Minichiello and Scott (2014) have suggested, women's sexual appetites have been traditionally stereotyped as deviant and problematic. Women buying sex do not fit traditional views about female sexuality, and society frowns on such behavior. Three possible reasons why more studies have not been published may be a lack of funding for research that has no obvious population health benefits (e.g., HIV research), a reluctance to engage with stigmatized subject matter, and some evidence of very low prevalence of women buying sex in studies with other foci.

Seeking Companionship and Love

I met one female client named Fanfan (forty-five) in the summer of 2017. She said she came to Pistachio out of loneliness and looking for companionship. She sat at the bar and played with her Apple smartphone for much of the evening. She seemed like she was waiting for friends to arrive. Dressed in designer clothes and sporting a fashionably short bob, her delicate skin made her look much younger than her actual age. Her Chanel bag suggested she was stylish, trendy, and rich. I asked her if she wanted a drink, and she shook her head and sighed. Then we started talking, and she told me her story. Her husband had several mistresses and seldom came home. That had been going on for more than ten years, and she could not remember the last time they had sex. Fanfan heard about the club and began coming with her girlfriends to drink and dance with each other. Over time, she met the young men there and soon talked freely about her background and her husband. She flirted with one of the boys and felt something long dormant. She felt younger, bolder, and more confident. Between the drinks and the flirting, she felt desire rising and realized that she was hungry to be touched. Although she knew that a woman buying sex is deeply frowned upon, she shrugged and said, "Sometimes, you just get tired of being alone":

> Some of the MSWs I meet here are open to sex with women. I guess they prefer men, but if they are willing, why not? I am called the "old ox who chews young grass" [*laonu chi nencao* 老牛吃嫩草, an old person who wants to fall in love with a young person]. Moreover, it is true; sometimes, I hope one of these boys will fall in love with me. I really want to do things—not just sex, but shop, drink tea, and take walks—with a handsome young guy. There is one here I am fond of, but even though I give generous tips, he never treats me the way I want. He is always in a hurry to leave after we have sex. I guess I am just daydreaming and fooling myself, but honestly, I do not want to wake up!

The world is fragile, and modernity is liquid (Baumann 1999); people need love and affection, despite their financial status. Fanfan said that the stereotype that only men purchase sex is unfair to women and needs to change. She said that it is natural to look for companionship. Her favorite MSW, Anderson (twenty-nine), later told me that he considered Fanfan a sugar momma, a big fish. When they first met, Anderson told Fanfan that he was skilled at "healing the heart of men" and "stealing the heart of women." Although he confided in me that he was not interested in women, he knew how to get a reaction from them.

> In the beginning, she was not looking for sex. She enjoyed my company, and we talked a lot. Eventually, she started calling me dear husband [*laogon* 老公], and I called her sweetheart [*tianxin* 甜心]. I attended to her and pampered her with massages, treating her like a princess [*gongzhu* 公主] or queen [*nühuang* 女皇]. My relationship with Fanfan lasted for two months. I never wanted her to divorce her husband, and I never wanted her to have fantasies of intimacy with me. I only wanted to get paid for my time. I would prefer she find another old Chinese woman to dance with and kiss. Finally, I had to delete her from WeChat and cut ties with her.

When I returned several months later, Anderson had moved on and said he was living with a tycoon in Tianjin.

Flora (forty-five) was another one of the twenty-seven female clients buying commercial sex in Pistachio. Flora's husband was a director of a publicly traded company and married Flora when she was only eighteen.

After she gave birth to their second child, her husband came home less often. Her husband attributed his absence to his job; as a company director, he often had to stay late entertaining business partners and spend evenings in downtown hotels. However, Flora hired a private detective and twice caught him in hotels with mistresses. She began taking drugs, drinking excessively, and having flings with young men. One lover from Pakistan took nude photos of her and blackmailed her for one million yuan (US$120,000). Afterward, he demanded a second million, and she gave it to him. To her relief, she said he disappeared after the second payment and had not threatened her since.

Like FanFan, Flora first came to Pistachio with friends to drink, chat, and have fun. She met one MSW, Jiayan (twenty-four), who treated her noticeably well. Jiayan was tall, muscular, sweet, and caring. One year later, Flora wanted to divorce her husband and marry Jiayan. She said she was even willing to give up custody of her children if she could marry him. However, her friends warned her that the only thing Jiayan wanted was her money.

Flora later updated me about her situation. She had continued her relationship with Jiayan and increasingly saw that he only wanted her money. Finally, she became bored with him and stopped using his services. She remained unhappily married and a regular patron of the club. Since Flora could not get a divorce, she accepted the fact that she was in a dead-end marriage. To cope, she decided to spend all her husband's money having sex with young men as often as she could. Flora was aware that the men at Pistachio treated her like a cash cow (*tikuanji* 提款机). After her betrayal by the MSW Jiayan, she learned to be more realistic about her visits to Pistachio; the only thing she wanted there was sex. "I know this is just a playground," she said. "My money buys romantic thrills, like a roller-coaster ride. Buying sex makes me sky-high! But at some point, you know you still have to go home."

Finding Pleasure through Control

Another female client was Lian (forty-nine), a middle-aged entrepreneur who never married. Lian came from an impoverished family in Chaozhou, Guangdong. Through hard work, she attended a top university in Guangzhou. Then, she worked as an accounting manager in a garment factory before running her own business at twenty-eight. She has managed her garment factory since 2002 and became quite wealthy. She was independent and self-confident. She told me that now that she was successful, she could indulge her desire for physical and sexual pleasure with a man. Lian said she is neither sexually subtle nor passive:

> Sweetie, if I am hungry for sex at that moment, I can be more vigorous, aggressive, and proactive than the Peoples Liberation Army [*nüge bi jiefangjun hai jiefang* 女客比解放军还解放]. I love S&M and role-playing. Sometimes, I go to the forest for sex and dress in camouflage. I do not know why I love such a game. When the boy finishes with sex, I will toss 1,000 yuan [US$150] onto the ground to watch him scamper around to pick it up. I like to watch that because I know these young guys make fun of me at the club and do not love me. They only love my money. I can see their reluctance to have sex with an older woman. I totally understand, but I use my money to buy me happiness!

Lian enjoyed the freedom afforded by her wealth but had no pretensions about love or intimacy. She was purchasing sex services for her enjoyment. In China, she might be called a golden leftover lady (a wealthy, unmarried woman over thirty years old).

Tianli (fifty-one) was another female client who bought sex from queer men. She was the executive director of a vast, upscale ten-story beauty parlor. In her early twenties, she had been mistreated and abused by her boyfriend and still carried on the memory as she remained single:

> Believe it or not. Someone called me an evil boss [*molaoban* 魔老板]. Oh yes! I am. I am also an evil sex client, no kidding. I do not trust any man or believe what one says. They are abusive. Men are always destroying women. I would rather believe that ghosts exist in the world, but I would never trust a word from a man! [*ning kexiang xinzhenshi shangyouguibu yaoxiang xinnan rennazhangpozui* 宁可相信这世上有鬼, 不要相信男人那张破嘴]. If I am still so naive to believe in love at my age, I am an idiot. Those young boys are such terrible actors. I tell them to kiss me, and I can tell they are reluctant; I know those boys want to vomit in the washroom after I leave, and they only do it for the money. . . . However, when those

young boys cannot arouse me or leave me unsatisfied, I complain to their boss and get a night for free!

Tianli met me in Pistachio on a warm, overcast, and cloudy evening. She had her wild look with a low-cut top, super-short skirt, and two-inch-high heels. She had a bourbon with her. She told me she could be very horny and aggressive if she could find some fresh meat (young and handsome MSW) in Pistachio:,

> Do not feel bad for those boys; they are just acting. They tell lies and make fun of me because I am old and not pretty. Sometimes, those young boys cannot satisfy me. I ask them to kiss me; they will, but only because of money. I know those boys felt they needed to spit in the washroom after I left. I am neither loved nor aroused. They are such horrible actors, sometimes their acting is so bad I have to complain to their *mamasan*!

Tianli told me about her buying commercial sex from the MSW in Pistachio. She concluded that it was so difficult to find a man who had "studied a woman like a book" [*kan nuren deshu* 看女人的书], was familiar with a woman's body [*shuxin nuren shenti* 熟悉女人身体], knew a woman's body by heart [*you shenti qufan* 用身体去翻], and could use their soul to read a woman [*you linghun qudu* 用灵魂去读]. Tianli's insights were philosophical and profound.

Female Clients and Condom Use

One night in the summer of 2019, I saw Nessa (thirty-seven) in Pistachio. I invited her to sit next to me and gave her a glass of wine. We talked about her experiences and why she had come to the club. She was unashamed and spoke with confidence about the tactics used by the MSWs to seduce women clients. She said most of the MSWs use "consciously applied tactics" such as rehearsed sweet-talk and flirtatious banter, all following traditional gendered "mating" roles as one hears in the courtship stage. For female clients, the MSWs will use a discourse of romance or try to give a good impression of caring and attention to her. However, this superficial approach is not always effective. Nessa confirmed that when she became bored and stopped responding, the MSWs would quickly vanish:

> Some of the MSWs know how to fool me. They pretend to love me, and of course, it is not true. I really need a good man to pamper and spoil me. Why is it so difficult? I have money, but money cannot buy marriage, family, youthfulness, or true love.

At an NGO, I met another female client, Yunfei (forty-one), who told me something new. Yunfei, a single woman, said that she had "passed her prime." She had remained single on purpose, but she was still eager to become a mother. Yunfei said that because of this, she sometimes insisted that the MSW she bought should not use a condom because she felt she would never get pregnant at her age. She said she did not worry about HIV because the chance for her to get infected was very low. Besides, she said, she only engaged in regular sex with those boys, never anal sex. So why bother with a condom? She commented that it would be great if she could get pregnant. She wanted to become a mother. It would save her money and time compared to flying to Thailand for IVF. Buying sex is like buying a Chanel or Hermes bag. It made her happy. She knew the blunt truth that those boys would sleep with any woman who could provide money for them.

Pleasure, Manipulation, and Control

The women who came to Pistachio for sex wanted control back in their lives. They felt they did not need a man in their lives except for the act of sex. Since these female clients were exceptionally wealthy, they said they wanted a man who would do what they said and give them sexual satisfaction. They were not interested in traditional male patriarchy telling them what to do and how to do it in bed.

Another female client, Xuan (twenty-eight), appeared stereotypically feminine with her stylish dress, makeup, high heels, and name-brand handbag. Despite her prim and proper appearance, Xuan was a consummate party girl. She admitted that she regularly went to Pistachio or other bars with a group of friends where they would take drugs (*liubing* 溜冰) such as ecstasy, cocaine, and whatever else was available and dance all night. Sometimes, they arranged three-day sex parties with MSWs, where they alternated between sex, drugs, and dancing until they passed out from exhaustion. Xuan revealed a pervasive ignorance about condoms and sexually transmitted diseases. Like many of these women, she said the men did not need condoms because there was little chance of her becoming pregnant. She said the men also felt they only needed to use condoms to avoid unwanted pregnancy. More education is needed here and a discussion of safer sex and access to AIDS prevention methods (e.g., condoms and pre-exposure prophylaxis).

When I chatted with *mamasan* Yang (thirty), he said that those women had a strong sexual appetite and that manipulation tactics were common in Pistachio. Most of the MSWs came from rural China, and they focused on making more money to escape their poverty. They believed they needed Viagra to feel high and maintain their stamina to deal with demanding female clients. Most of the female clients likewise wanted the MSWs to have rock-hard penises. Some MSWs admitted that they took various Chinese medicines, like deer cartilage, and ate particular foods like oysters to maintain peak performance. The MSWs commonly referred to women in their thirties as tigers (*nuren sanshi ruhu* 女人三十如虎) and women over forty as wolves (*nuren sishi ruling* 女人四十如狼). The female clients were older, confident, rich, and horny. Some female clients had lots of energy and played until midnight; others insisted on going until the morning. Some MSWs complained that they were tired and needed Viagra to stay up all night. Yang told me he once received a call from a young MSW who had fainted from a Viagra overdose, which decreased his blood pressure to a critical level, and had to be taken to the hospital, for a short stay.

Conclusion

The lived experiences of the MSWs and their clients reflect how MSWs interact with clients in China's gay sex industry. Their stories identify some common themes regarding the motivation for entering sex work. Broad categories of motivations include money and sexual thrills, but more complex factors involve family upbringing, job opportunities, and the search for intimacy, acceptance, and love. There is a constellation of motivations that are frequently interrelated. Some MSWs seek the security of a wealthy partner and strive for stable relationships so they can help their parents or family back home. Others are driven to hustle to acquire as much money and material goods as possible. Some love the stimulation of dressing up and performing; they embrace the hedonism and sensuality this life offers. Still, others have found that it is where they feel good about themselves and about the pleasure they provide. For those MSWs, money brings variable conditions that level out and rationalize every social relationship it enters. It embeds and changes social life and is a many-splendored instrument with cultural and economic significance.

This chapter examined some of the stories from clients of MSWs. The chapter also focused on the experiences of a subset of clients who are neither male nor gay. Middle-aged women constitute a small but significant group of patrons of MSWs. These women are typically financially well-off, educated, self-confident, and familiar with abuse at the hands of boyfriends, husbands, and lovers. As such, they patronized Pistachio to satisfy their physical desire for sex. Money can buy love in the form of MSWs servicing them and fulfilling their physical and emotional needs without ever challenging them or talking back.

6

Male Sex Workers and Stigma

The Queer Body, Necropolitics, and the Medical System

Huaqi, a twenty-seven-year-old from Shandong Province, candidly remarked that he started working at Pistachio as a full-time sex worker after breaking up with his boyfriend of four years. He said that, at the time, there was really nowhere else for him to go. He still had to pay the owner of the bathhouse a commission every time he serviced a client there. Before sex work, Huaqi had come out to his family that he was gay. His parents had forced him to marry a village girl, which ended in divorce. His parents had little education, and his mother could not even read, yet she insisted that he go to a local clinic for infertility. The doctor there prescribed an expensive aphrodisiac costing 5,000 yuan (US$750):

> My mom wanted me to find a better hospital. . . . but where could I go? We ended up seeing a urologist, and the doctor told me to remove my trousers. I asked why—he asked why not. I told him I was gay, and he said that is not a disease. I told him I knew, but my parents were forcing me to get married, and I just wanted them to talk some sense into my parents. So the doctor called my parents in, and they talked for a while. When my parents emerged from the office, they were crying and said they would sell their house and land because they were too ashamed even to live there. The doctor was bewildered and asked why my parents wanted me to seek treatment for a mental illness in his hospital. My parents were in tears, asking what the neighbors would think about us when they discovered I was gay; I was their only child. I have not returned to see my parents for three years, not even for Chinese New Year.

Huaqi's experience of coming out to his parents in their rural village in North China was similar to others in the gay community at large, as well as the subgroup of MSWs. Huaqi said he faced rejection and exclusion from his parents, who held traditional patriarchal values. In China, gay men face homophobia and sociocultural discrimination regarding their self-identity, resulting in marginalization and loneliness (Lowe and Tsang 2018). In China, the closest English word that translates to same-sex attraction is *queer* (*kuer* 酷儿). This is a marked improvement from the previous word used before it was decriminalized in 2011, *sickness* (*bing* 病), referring to types of mental illness.

The *Hukou*, HIV, and China's Medical System

In China's highly structured medical system, only certain hospitals are allowed to treat individuals with HIV. When I was in Tianjin in the summer of 2018, an NGO director connected me with a doctor working at an HIV-designated hospital in North China. We arranged an interview, and when I arrived, Dr. Paul (forty-nine) openly referred to the social problem of MSWs living with HIV:

> Most of us doctors fighting HIV are members of the Chinese Communist Party. I must comply with what the Party wants us to do. One day, I told my supervisor, "Doctors should rescue HIV patients. We should forget the risk of infection or government order. As an infectious disease doctor, I pledged to serve HIV patients regardless of race, gender, class, wealth, occupation, and nation." But afterward, I was accused of "insubordination and disobeying the party's order." My supervisor said, "I solemnly warn you: If you keep being stubborn and continue treating those HIV patients, you will be dismissed immediately and reported to the Central Government." I was speechless. After this unhappy episode, I believed most HIV doctors, including myself, became reluctant to help HIV patients . . . there was nothing I could do but obey. . . . The less you do, the fewer mistakes you will make. Therefore, I have to say that our society, government, medical doctors, and general citizens do not like HIV patients. It is not only gay sex workers living with HIV; it includes all HIV carriers.

The conversation with Dr. Paul reflected the struggle of China's MSWs. It illustrated how the multilayered stigma they experience acts as a form of necropolitical power, an instrument of the state's discrimination against MSWs living with HIV. One unintended side effect of this state power is the subsequent reluctance by medical professionals to care for MSWs living with HIV and the discrimination that comes from government officers.

One sunny afternoon in August 2018, Lennon took me to visit one of the NGOs in North China. There, we spoke with a director:

> The Chinese government does not care about MSWs unless they become infected with HIV or have AIDS. The government or police turn a blind eye to the MSWs as they are neither legal nor criminal. So far, the Chinese government has provided different medications and tests for those MSWs living with HIV. However, the resources are very uneven, and it is not fair to those MSWs with a rural *hukou*. Urban *hukou* is better for receiving good medications as most large-scale hospitals have better facilities and equipment. The best hospitals are located in urban China.

Data collected from twenty-five MSWs living with HIV, fifteen HIV medical doctors, and twelve NGO directors provided evidence that the necropower of stigma was routinely exercised on the bodies of MSWs. This chapter targets this unique subset of MSWs and notes how the necropolitics of social death and state-sanctioned stigma have permeated China's health-care system, discouraging MSWs from receiving the help they need. The concept of necropolitics helps us understand the predicaments of men with HIV who sell sex to other men in China. China's *hukou* system requires them to go to their birth village for any state services. Within this context, MSWs who have a rural *hukou* cannot access the highly active antiretroviral therapy (HAART) and PrEP (pre-exposure prophylaxis), powerful HIV prevention tools. Since the *hukou* requires MSWs living with HIV to return to their rural village for medical treatment, the national health system has imposed a way to "out" them, resulting in stigma that celebrates the deaths of MSWs as a form of biopolitical power. Health-care workers have justified their stigmatized reactions by focusing on the danger to themselves and wider society from MSWs who are living with HIV. Therefore, once MSWs contract HIV, they enter a recursive loop of stress and declining health.

MSWs engage in high-risk behaviors resulting in health problems and then face discriminatory reactions from family and state institutions when seeking treatment.

The Reality of the Four Free One Care Policy

In 2011, China's premier, Wen Jiabao, visited the Centers for Disease Control and Prevention (CDC) in Beijing and vowed to provide funding and policy support to research drugs and vaccines guaranteed to improve care for HIV patients. He confirmed that the Chinese government would provide more funding and strong policy support to ensure improvements in patient care and research into drugs and vaccines. He also promised to fight poverty in areas where HIV was prevalent, to provide more substantial societal support for AIDS prevention, and to fully implement the Four Free One Care policy (Shao and Zhong 2012). The Four Free One Care policy provided free HIV treatment, free voluntary counseling and testing, free prevention of mother-child transmission, free schooling for AIDS orphans, and provision of social relief for HIV patients (Shao and Zhong 2012).

According to the Chinese Constitution Article 55, medical doctors who refuse to provide treatment or conduct surgery on someone who is living with HIV would be subject to penalties such as medical license disqualification and even jail time (Goldwin 2013). In addition, Constitution Article 41 stated that designated hospitals should provide counseling, diagnosis, and treatment services. Those hospitals cannot refuse treatment for people who are living with HIV or AIDS (Goldwin 2013, 71). Nevertheless, stigma against gay males, lesbians, bisexuals, transgender, and those living with HIV has persisted, aided by ambiguities in the wording of the law (Tsang et al. 2019).

The reality is that MSWs living with HIV face different situations from that which has been stipulated by Chinese law. Round and Kuznetsova (2016) argued that untold numbers of migrants who enter these illegal spaces are subjected to discrimination and social death, ushered into conditions that deny them autonomy, and face social ostracism that denies them access to services as if they do not exist. Anecdotally, MSWs with HIV said that hospital doctors and staff noticeably avoid initiating conversation, asking questions, or even making eye contact with them.

Likewise, government officers and even police often do not try to help or assist. Most troubling is that family members and even those in the gay community do not accept or even acknowledge them.

Stigma and the Necropolitics of Social Death

The marginalized communities of MSWs living with HIV have faced significant hardship yet found ways to survive in the state-sanctioned medical care system. Davies, Isakjee, and Dhesi (2017) argued that stigma-based political inaction toward migrants can result in death. When institutional policies, medical care, and the general attitude of the government lead to little or no help being given, such death can result. In China, MSWs who migrate to the city for work have been subject to conditions that prevent them from flourishing. MSWs learn to survive in their underground trade by, for example, paying bribes to the police to stay out of jail.

In bringing TSWs into the necropolitical discussion, Haritaworn, Knuntsman, and Pocosso (2017) argued that the queer community is generally ignored by the government, particularly those who have been patients living with HIV and trying to access health care. When urban MSWs with a rural *hukou* returned to their hometown health facility, they were forced to disclose details of their HIV-positive status, with obvious ramifications for their family and the local village. There has been much said about multilayered stigma and how ignorance about LGBTQ+ patients on the part of medical professionals has raised mortality rates (Mayblin and Kazemi 2018; Tsang 2019a, 2019b).

This perspective helps extend the emerging literature on HIV-infected MSWs by differentiating how social death is not living death. It grapples with stigmas in three ways: (1) the individual must cope with a host of actual discriminatory behaviors as well as perceived slights; (2) the individual becomes outed by the system for lacking an urban *hukou*; and (3) once out, the individual becomes a formally marginalized citizen under China's medical care system.

Necropolitics helps explain the impact of stigma within the context of MSWs in today's China. Stigma is generally defined as a social process of "othering, blaming, and shaming," leading to status loss and discrimination (Deacon 2006; McKinnon 2016). Stigmatized groups are devalued by exercising social, cultural, economic, and political power (Link and Phelan 2006). From a socio-medical perspective, Scambler situated stigma within sociocultural structural contexts and the interaction between stigma, class, capital, and power. He noted the critical difference between "felt stigma" and "enacted stigma." Felt stigma (internal stigma or self-stigmatization) is the "fear of encountering discrimination and an internalized sense of shame" on the grounds of "socially unacceptable difference" (Scambler 1998, 1054). It refers to the expectation of discrimination which prevents people from talking about their experiences or proactively seeking help. Enacted stigma (actual discrimination and unacceptability) refers to the experience of unfair treatment by others. Enacted stigma, as "structural or institutional discrimination," is embedded in social, economic, and political power (Scambler 2018). Both stigmas—felt and enacted—are damaging when they lead to withdrawal and restriction of social support. Smit et al. (2001) found that HIV-positive gay men who experienced higher levels of stigma were more likely to use illicit drugs. Where the prescription of PrEP is concerned, Goparaju et al. (2017) noted that stigma from family members and the medical profession in the United States discourages women who are HIV-negative from taking PrEP. The necropolitical power of fear from discrimination (felt stigma) is a significant factor to consider.

In the case of the MSWs living with HIV, the public designation of their situation, where their bodies are marked as vessels of HIV infection, subjugates their status to that of a social death. Both felt stigmas and enacted stigmas restrict access to health care, facilitating necropolitical outcomes for being a carrier of HIV. This study begins by acknowledging that the death worlds of MSWs who are living with HIV, which propagate both enacted and felt stigma, cannot be separated from the spatial codes that create death conditions.

The Necropolitics of Hukou

In China, this global pattern of gendered sex-work migration has manifested a rural/urban *hukou* divide. The *hukou* has exacerbated the marginalization and rural/urban segregation faced by MSWs (Kong 2012a). In the city, having a rural *hukou* can lead to alienation because it marks one as being a villager and, colloquially, a rube or country bumpkin. Male migrant workers in the city are typically underpaid (Mayblin et al. 2019) and afraid of their precarious access to local social services (Shi 2019). In addition to institutionalized exclusion, the second-class citizenship of MSWs has been endorsed by the state's neoliberal development discourses. Rural MSWs are often labeled as "low-*suzhi* [quality]," "uncouth," and "provincial" and blamed for damaging the social image of the city.

In the peasant migrant workers' struggles against the lack of social security, Shi (2019) argued that "workers' bodies created a site for claim-making within the disciplinary space and had the potential of redeploying that space for their own ends. . . . The workers had to subvert the physical boundaries that inscribed disciplinary power over their bodies." The situation of China's rural MSWs appears even worse than that of the factory workers. The necropolis created by felt and enacted stigmas, drug use, and health abandonment clearly resists the spaces of urban homonormativity and heteronormativity in China.

In his ethnography of MSWs in urban China who lack urban *hukou*, Kong (2012) noted that MSWs were often seen as "failed" gay citizens: "bad" gays who mix sex with money, corrupting the image of middle-class gay men. Scholars think *hukou* (Kong 2015; Mayblin et al. 2019), cadres (government officers), and others, both in-system and out-system (Xie and Wu 2008), are the three major fault lines by which to analyze social stratification in China. Scholars must address the gap in the international literature on the biopolitical and necropolitical conditions faced each year by hundreds—perhaps thousands—of gay rural-to-urban migrants in China.

The Legal Context of Male Sex Work and HIV

Government estimates in 2018 suggested that there were around eight million MSWs in China (China Health and Family Planning Commission, 2018). Many were migrants who moved to the city, away from their hometown. That same report estimated that more than 10 percent of those—approximately 850,000—were living with HIV. The migrants who moved to the city for work were often subject to discriminatory conditions due to a lack of skills or connections. Desperate to survive, many migrants became part of the underground trade of illegal activities to at least pay the bills. Sex work, drugs, and organized crime enabled them to live but kept them beholden to others. For them, it was common to pay bribes to various persons because they were not legally entitled to *hukou*-related services in the city, which became a form of biopolitical control of these rural poor.

For those who ended up with HIV, there is a multilayered stigma and ignorance about LGBTQ+ patients on the part of medical professionals (Kong 2012a). Stigma and discrimination are expressed indirectly through institutional and social policies. The *hukou* system requires these patients to return to their hometowns for medical treatment even though the quality of that care is dramatically inferior to health-care in the city. Without an urban hukou, a migrant would have to pay much higher fees to be treated at a city hospital. Since migrants tend to be poor, they cannot afford city treatment. But when MSWs show up at a rural hospital for HIV treatment, they face stigma and discrimination from the medical personnel who disapprove of the MSWs lifestyle and also fear being accidentally infected.

Living with HIV: Male Sex Workers and Felt Stigma

The MSW interviewees living with HIV were acutely aware of the felt stigma. As I spoke with them, they explicitly lamented their situations and criticized themselves for being a sex worker, contracting HIV, and even being gay, often pejoratively referring to themselves as money boys, using slang—*xiaodi (小弟)*—that directly translates as "little penis." Most of the felt stigma was expressed as shame and regret. In addition, the fear generated from felt stigma prevented all the patients from disclosing their occupation as sex workers to their families (Qiao et al. 2019) Most admitted that they took drugs regularly to escape even thinking about it.

The twenty-five MSWs described feelings of anxiety and mixed emotions about themselves, which lasted at least half a year. Mafan (thirty-two) said:

> For a long time, I could not let my parents or my partners know I had HIV. I hated myself. . . . I hated HIV. I was so afraid inside. One day, I could not tolerate it anymore and told my parents that I was gay and a sex worker. They stayed calm even as they kicked me out of our village. . . . I

take methamphetamine quite often; I work with some drug dealers and smugglers in Yunnan. . . . There is always a strong demand for drugs from communities like ours. Sometimes, I do not care enough to use condoms after taking drugs.

Xijiang (20) said:

I took methamphetamine whenever my parents pushed me to marry and give them grandchildren. Come on, I have HIV; how can I give them kids? Since my father found out, he has not allowed me to go to the ancestral hall. He said I have betrayed our village and our tradition of marriage. So I have given up. Now, I just focus on sex without worrying about the consequences. Death is just a matter of time for me. Why worry? The drugs allow me to live for myself. I know it is risky, but the harm to my body does not come to mind. At least it keeps me from caring.

A powerful sociocultural norm repeatedly brought up was the persistence of parents urging them to make them grandparents. Shuo (twenty-two) said:

My parents wanted me to get married and have a kid. I felt like I failed them. Failing to get married is a disgrace and a sign of disrespect to parents. Who is going to inherit the bloodline, particularly in rural China? I lost face before my relatives and family members during the Spring Festival. My neighbors even thought my parents did something wrong since I still do not have kids. My mom said she would even be happy if I "rented" a bride once to show the neighbors just to shut them up. Some days, she still calls almost once an hour, urging me to get married.

MSWs who return to their village to come out in front of their parents invariably suffer abandonment. They may then turn to drugs to console themselves and help them endure the conflict that followed. Mang (nineteen) said:

I had contracted HIV and had to return to my village for treatment. My boyfriend came with me and we stayed at my parents' home. They were happy to see us at first, but I had to tell them the truth. When I told them

I was being treated for HIV, they were confused. The more I talked, the angrier they became. My mother cried and begged me to reconsider, that I should marry a girl and have a kid. But since I am gay and have HIV that is not possible! My father told us to leave immediately and we did. Therefore, I take drugs to forget my troubles. Drugs help me feel good and make the sex fantastic. Then, I do not need to think about how unwanted I am at home.

The consequences of coming out show why MSWs keep their sexuality and occupation a secret from family members and turn to drugs to help them cope with the harsh realities of their life situation.

Living with HIV: Male Sex Workers and Enacted Stigma

Majian, a thirty-six-year-old MSW living with HIV for two years, described the stigma coming from government officials:

I do not have any sympathy from my parents because I contracted HIV from my ex-partner. Most people blame us for our risky behavior. . . . If they know I have HIV, they will stare and keep a distance from me. Therefore, I do not dare let them know. Some government officials consider me as "scum" [*feiwu* 廢物] and say we do not deserve to receive proper treatment. The Department of Health and Department of Security [police] think we are troublesome because we have increased their workload.

Menrui (twenty-eight) had been living with HIV for five years and worked in an HIV-NGO as a volunteer for two years. He said that he discovered that every December 1, only the provincial CDC will publish HIV data reported by the Health Department. He said that the government was playing tricks with the numbers. For example, it might be reported that only two people were infected and died of HIV even though many bodies were dumped in a landfill. Alternatively, they might attribute several deaths to tuberculosis or general pneumonia to avoid letting the public know HIV cases have increased. Menrui said:

The government does not really want to see us. They want us to be quiet and hide that we even exist. We cannot afford medical care in the city. But they think we make the city look bad and dirty. We are a liability—the stumbling stone of China's modernity! The discrimination against those of us with HIV comes from the government, medical doctors, and cadres. I can tell the government wants to dump us into a landfill, ship us to an outlying island, and let us die and be forgotten. The government does not care about us.

Mao (twenty-eight), who had been living with HIV for two years, said the government needed clear guiding principles on how to treat people with HIV. Most of the money spent on NGOs goes for HIV testing. However, testing is not treating, and how best to heal HIV patients remains uncertain and lacks clear guidelines:

> The hospital I visited in my hometown was highly decentralized, and how they chose to act depended upon their needs, not mine. I saw hospital staff use a mattress to roll up dead bodies and send them to be burned in the landfill. I am sure the families were not informed because HIV is so sensitive in China. They usually report the patients died of something like skin allergy or cancer rather than HIV. I know they do not treat HIV patients as humans.

The Chinese authorities have treated HIV more as a medical and law-enforcement issue than a social issue. National policies protect the rights of the people living with the disease, but enforcement often fails at the local level, where it is usually reduced to binary thinking. Local government officials tend to simply divide the population into those who have HIV (e.g., sex workers, drug users, and MSMs) and those who do not, then work to isolate them from each other to contain the disease. Thus, it is no surprise that HIV continues to be a public health problem as it spreads through unprotected sex. MSWs are a high-risk group, but the government considers their HIV infection rate only in terms of how it affects stability and harmony in Chinese society. Treatment, medication, and counseling services have been woefully underdeveloped in urban China, and the situation is worse in rural areas. Deeply ingrained traditions and values result in near-universal social avoidance, reflecting enacted stigmatizing of MSWs living with HIV. The MSWs often initially struggle with felt stigma but then adapt and accept their situation over time. Social forces declare that since they do not embody the stereotypical ideal portrayed in state-sanctioned notions of masculinity, they must be pushed to the fringes of society.

Although medical and allied health-care professionals in China are required by law to treat patients who are living with HIV, enacted stigma permeates the health-care system. The relationship between underprivileged MSWs and the Communist medical system's use of necropolitical power to destine queer bodies to death—particularly those who are living with HIV—can now be better understood.

Jianhui (thirty-one) had contracted HIV and saw doctors regularly to get his PrEP and other medication. He explained how humiliating the experience could be:

> To get the PrEP, I had to beg the CDC to prescribe the medicine to me repeatedly. If I did not beg the doctor, he would not give it to me. The doctors refused to prescribe it. They said I looked fine. I am in good shape, and there is no need to take medication. But it is evident that my skin still has a rash, and my lungs are bad. How am I to get better? Begging the doctor was no fun.

According to Jianhui, during his ten years of HIV treatment in China, he observed that hospitals discourage health workers from using gloves and masks to save money. Occupational exposure to blood (and thus blood-borne viruses) is high, while compliance with standard precautions among health workers is relatively low. There are few public reports about incidents, creating an environment where health workers in non-designated hospitals are fearful and often refuse to accept HIV or AIDS patients.

Chen (twenty-four) was an MSW who moved back to his hometown to treat his HIV. The discrimination he received from the doctors and government officers left him hurt and vengeful:

> Discrimination from those doctors and officials hurt a lot. I felt so numb. Although I was HIV positive, I still solicited clients for some income. Condom use is still not a habit for me. At this point, I really do not care. I had one client who put something in my drink, which knocked me out. I did not have the chance to let him know I was HIV positive. When I

woke up, he was still fucking me. I did not tell him he was probably getting HIV from me. Too bad for him (smiling).

MSWs living with HIV face further risks besides discrimination from health workers. In China, MSWs must cope with multilayered forms of enacted and felt stigma toward queers working as prostitutes. The participants in this study grappled with chronic felt stigma as they hid their sexual orientation from family members for fear of reprisal and persecution. To cope with their mental anguish, they often resorted to drug use, which in turn fed enacted stigma. Enacted stigma towards MSWs with HIV in China comes from several sectors, including government policies that promote traditional binary sexual orientations and police and security who monitor and periodically make arrests. Together, felt and enacted stigmas create necropolitics—the message to MSWs that they are a danger to medical professionals and society itself. Since governments often justify sacrificing the few to protect the many, the biopolitical control of this group becomes an inevitable part of a more comprehensive necropolitical project.

Getting Treated Using Rural *Hukou*

The politics of health care puts MSWs outside of China's medical care system. Having a rural *hukou* demotes MSWs living with HIV to the status of marginalized urban citizens and socially dead. As a permanent identification number, the *hukou* can be used to alienate HIV-positive MSWs from their family home or village. This is a testament to the fact that MSWs are placed in a state of precarious social death. The stigma attached to HIV is also felt through pressure from China's medical services, which discriminate against rural MSWs. In the absence of state support or policies to alleviate their suffering and hardship, the abandonment of MSWs living with HIV will undoubtedly continue.

Yanquan (thirty-eight) had been HIV positive for approximately one month and described the differences in treatment:

> In the city, people with HIV can get the Triumeq [an antiretroviral drug used in China], which contains three ingredients in a pill. A monthly prescription of Triumeq costs around 450 yuan [US$73]. But I had to go

to the hospital near my village. That medicine is cheap, but it does not do anything. I think it is to keep my life going a little bit longer. I will instead try some traditional Chinese medicine to ease my symptoms.

Wingzhong (twenty-eight) also had to push with great effort to get treatment because of his rural *hukou*:

I heard some middle-class gay communities receive better medication for HIV and find it easier to heal in the USA. This is not my case. To pick up my medication each month, I have to take the high-speed train, but it takes thirteen hours to get to my hometown and back. Once I am there, it takes an additional five hours of consulting with the doctor and waiting for the medicine. It is incredibly inconvenient. But what else can I do? I do not have an urban *hukou*.

Rui (twenty-nine) also lamented his rural *hukou*:

There is nothing I can do in the city. I do not have an urban *hukou*. I am not allowed to get HIV medicine from those urban hospitals or clinics. Instead, I had to ride on the high-speed railway for more than ten hours because I live in a remote village in North China. I feel like the HIV medications in my hometown are not enough; they do not seem to do anything. I feel like those hospitals in the city would provide better services and medication. I know some of my friends get a higher medical allowance than I do in my hometown. I guess this is because of my rural *hukou*.

Sheng (thirty-four) had a rural *hukou*, was kicked out of a relatively comprehensive medical system in urban China, and was sent back to his hometown. He was eligible to live and work in the city but could not access medical care. Sheng found himself very sick and needed PEP (post-exposure prophylaxis) to treat his HIV infection. PEP is supposed to be taken within seventy-two hours of being exposed to HIV to stop the infection:

It takes seventeen hours to travel from my village to the nearest hospital to get the PEP. I was so sick I could not take the high-speed train to see the doctor. So I stayed in the city. I spent 9,300 yuan [US$1,500] to buy the PEP from the drug stores. Those thirty days of taking PEP and waiting were a dark side for me. I lost thirty pounds and refused to see anyone. I put myself under quarantine while I took the PEP. However, all my money and effort proved futile. The result was positive. So then, I have two options. One is returning to receive mediocre medical service in my rural hometown. The other option is to spend all my money to get better treatment in the city. I am desperate, and honestly, I am not optimistic.

The fear of discrimination is universal; it is found in conservative and collectivist countries like China, as well as in Western democracies known for tolerance and more liberal attitudes. The data reported here confirmed that deeply ingrained structures of enacted stigma result in a reluctance to seek medical help from doctors and staff.

Being Marginalized by China's Medical System

Health-care professionals and nurses in dependency wards face a high risk of being infected by patients. Such was the case in 2003 when the SARS virus erupted in Hong Kong and Southeast Asia. In the broader international literature on stigma, Hafeez et al. (2017) noted that although the United States is tolerant of nonconforming sexualities, health-care providers nevertheless can stigmatize the LGBTQ+ community by a lack of awareness about the challenges faced by those who need treatment. Therefore, even inadvertent stigma from medical professionals can lead to mental and physical health disparities suffered by LGBTQ+ communities.

In China, there is a notable lack of awareness among police and medical officers regarding the causes of HIV infection. The problem is further compounded by depersonalization; infected people are discussed only as statistics, which prevents urgent and specific changes from being proposed. For example, shortages of medical supplies such as masks and gloves are debated by administrators and policymakers as a general funding issue. However, without masks and gloves, doctors might refuse to touch infected patients. The government's focus on aggregate numbers removes the human aspect, which is the focus of patients and medical workers.

Kang, twenty-eight, experienced the problem firsthand:

> When I visited my doctor every month, he told me they were broke and did not receive enough funding from the government. There is a shortage of protective equipment, so my treatment is quite mediocre. The medication will not heal AIDS, but it will not let me die either. All they can do is prescribe mediocre medications which neither heal nor help. The doctors scolded me for being so naïve about what they could do to help me. Government missteps and administrative failures put me at risk; if I need emergency surgery, most of the doctors will refuse to help. One doctor laughed at me and said, "We have to reuse goggles, surgical gowns, and even shoe covers. I even have to reuse my N95 surgery mask. I am on the front line fighting the HIV epidemic."

Stigma from medical professionals is partly influenced, as Kang explained, by how the Chinese government treats HIV-positive and gay and lesbian individuals. When people are treated as case numbers—mere digits—it reflects the non-humanness of the gay body. Referring to people in the aggregate provides the authorities with a mechanism to exercise biopolitical control. Acknowledging this aspect of stigma, some HIV-positive MSWs agreed that medical professionals should look after themselves and their families first.

Maya (thirty-four) had been living with HIV for five years and wanted the recommended cocktail therapy combining zidovudine, lamivudine, and efavirenz. But he said that the cost—approximately 200,000 yuan (US$29,411) a year—puts it out of his reach. "I only have the rural *hukou* and cannot afford the cocktail therapy," he said. "For my treatment, the government monthly allowance is about 50 yuan [US$7.5]. It is not much, but it is better than nothing."

The stigmatizing of MSWs who are pathogenically diseased has been conditioned by the attitude and funding of the government; the attitude toward MSWs living with HIV frames them as deserving of stigma and being left to die. The intersection between the living death of the physical body and the enacted stigma directed at MSWs from the medical profession is the manifestation of necropolitical power. From their perspective, the body of the MSW is a potential (or actual) carrier of HIV and, therefore, is assigned the status of what Mbembe (2003) has called the "living dead." By extension, this view holds that MSW deaths will not constitute moral or financial loss to society. In this worldview, medical doctors caring for HIV patients may deny care due to a lack of safety equipment because they—the doctors—are deemed more worthy of life (Threadcraft 2017; Tsang et al. 2018; Tsang et al. 2020).

Narratives from Medical Doctors

I met Katy (twenty-seven) in a North China café through one of the NGOs. She had been a doctor treating HIV patients until she became infected and had to leave. Katy had become infected while helping a patient during surgery. That patient had a respiratory disease and diabetes, as well as HIV. She described the moment she accidentally cut herself during the procedure and the fear she felt when it was confirmed that she was HIV-positive. Hospital regulations required that she resign, so she left and worked as a secretary in a trading company. Her parents did not know of her condition. Her fiancé found out and broke up with her, leaving her single. Katy said that she took her medication regularly, and that her HIV was under control. Katy described her final days at the hospital:

> I was so scared because I am a doctor too. I procrastinated getting treatment for a month. I felt shocked and broken. I could not accept the reality. I felt robbed—I have not seen the world yet, and now I am so afraid of death. When it was confirmed, I was forced to resign from the hospital without compensation. They said that since I had a health issue, I was no longer qualified to be an infectious disease doctor. I was crushed and could not tell my parents. Then my boyfriend found out, and he broke up with me. I am still single and try to hide my HIV status.

Hua (thirty-seven) was a medical doctor who had also accidentally contracted HIV at his hospital and had to undergo PEP until he recovered:

> The last surgery I did on an HIV patient was a horrible experience. I was helping with injections and checking his body. I had an open wound on one of my fingers, which suddenly came into contact with his blood.

I did not realize I had an open wound; of course, I wore gloves. However, I was still infected. I immediately washed my hands, but it was too late. I took PEP and went home to see what would happen. The next day, I had symptoms of fever, diarrhea, and a skin rash. My immune system felt very weak, and soon after, I had additional symptoms of bronchitis, coughing, and the rash moved to my mouth. I locked myself inside my apartment for two weeks and refused to see my girlfriend. . . . Around the end of the fourth week of taking the HIV medicines, the side effects disappeared. It was a miracle! I no longer had the coughing, and my immune system seemed to be getting back to normal. My fever was gone. I retook the blood test, and it was negative. . . . From now on, I will think about myself and my family first.

Zhong (forty-five) was another HIV doctor who had an incident where he thought he contracted HIV from a patient. But Zhong was tested and found to be HIV-negative:

Those thirty days of waiting after taking PEP were very dark for me. I lost fifty pounds. I avoided seeing anyone, and I placed myself under quarantine while I took PEP. I was so scared that I might be infected. I was relieved when the test came up negative. I think I was lucky this time. I may not be so fortunate next time.

I met an experienced HIV doctor, Dong (fifty-five), who admitted that the local government did not give him much choice at the hospital:

I am unsure how the funding is allocated, but our hospital has not received enough funding from the local government. There is a shortage of protective equipment, and we either run out of goggles or the goggles are not up to standard. The sad fact is that even if I promise a patient to do surgery, the surgery only prolongs their deteriorating condition. Therefore, I will advise HIV patients to take their medication regularly instead of opting for surgery.

Another doctor, Fangji (forty-three), confirmed the view of the hospital administration. Fangji admitted that helping HIV patients was not his priority, even though the hospital was designated as such:

I love my patients, but I love myself and my family even more. I am not proactive about helping the patients. This is not the order and guiding principles of our "big" boss. Also, my hospital is always short on supplies. We lack goggles, surgical gowns, and even shoe covers. Sometimes, I must re-use my surgery mask. The shortage of medical supplies prevents me from helping HIV patients because I am at risk of infection.... What doctor dares to help HIV patients under these conditions?

Another HIV doctor, Sija (twenty-nine), described her own experience:

When I contracted HIV, my hospital asked me to take unpaid leave and stay home until my situation improved. However, I know I will never be allowed to come back as a doctor again. Later, when I was almost recovered, the hospital asked me to resign. There was no compensation and no subsidies for my medication. I felt abandoned by my supervisor and top management. I almost dried up my savings and did not dare to ask my parents for help. There was not any public anger or grief after I was infected with HIV from my patient.... My sacrifice did not trigger any show of support. My former colleagues did not want to be seen with me. They kept away from me and left me alone. They remain silent. If one day I pass away, probably my hospital will only respond by saying, "saddened with grief."

Another doctor, Hua (thirty-seven), accidentally contracted HIV at the hospital and had to undergo PEP until he recovered. Hua said it makes him crazy that the occupational safety of healthcare workers in China is almost nonexistent. Hospitals generally discourage health workers from using too many gloves and masks due to cost concerns. He told me that his salary would be deducted if they found him using any new personal protective equipment.

Narratives from NGO Directors

Due to a shortage of funding, most of the NGOs working with queers try to maintain a harmonious relationship with their "big boss," the Chinese government. Zhidong (forty-five) said that each side tries to treat the other with respect:

I had a hostile relationship with the CDC before, and the government followed me and forced me to stay quiet. I was beaten up by both gangsters and police and spent four months in a hospital. Afterward, I saw how to deal with the CDC, and our relationship improved. Now, our NGOs can get more funding from the local government and CDC. The Chinese authorities have treated HIV more as a medical and law enforcement issue than a social issue.

I met Tiejie (fifty-two), one of the NGO founders, in the summer of 2019. Tiejie said the government needed clear guiding principles on how to treat people with HIV. Currently, most of the money spent on NGOs goes for HIV testing, but how best to assist and treat HIV patients remains uncertain because the guidelines are unclear.

Therefore, most of the doctors interviewed unanimously agreed that the government money allocated to help those with HIV in gay communities was not enough. HIV services and treatment vary in each province. In Beijing, for example, infected persons can obtain a higher medical allowance than those living in Chengdu. Infected people need to be treated in hospitals. But so far, these expenses cannot be reimbursed. The gap between the urban and the rural is enormous, especially the infected gay communities who only possess a rural *hukou* and live in rural areas.

COVID-19 and China

During data collection and writing this book, the COVID-19 pandemic turned the world upside down. Millions of lives were lost worldwide, and countless others were affected. In China, the initial response was marked by strict control over information, including infection rates and case numbers. However, skepticism about the accuracy of China's reported numbers persisted throughout the crisis. China's official tally of COVID-19 cases and deaths faced scrutiny due to several factors. First, the overwhelmed health-care system in Wuhan, where most of China's victims died, made it challenging to obtain a complete picture. Hospitals were overflowing, and testing capacity was limited. As a result, the reported numbers likely underestimated the true extent of infections and fatalities.

Furthermore, some deaths occurred before individuals could be tested, and suspected cases were not always included in the official count. The situation was particularly dire during the peak of the outbreak. Anecdotal reports and social media posts raised questions about the accuracy of the death toll, but such discussions were often censored. China has been criticized by other countries for lacking transparency because it has not shared critical data with international organizations investigating the origins of COVID-19. The high threshold for determining whether a person died from COVID-19 or due to preexisting conditions has also raised concerns. Every country now considers contingency plans for the next outbreak.

In the West, there is ongoing debate about China's reporting accuracy. It is essential to approach this issue cautiously and to recognize that obtaining precise numbers during a crisis is difficult in any country. Understanding the limitations of reported data is crucial for informed decision-making and global cooperation (BBC 2021). The management and reporting of HIV/AIDS cases in China have also been subject to complex dynamics, influenced by both public health considerations and broader political and social factors. In this context, the Chinese government's approach to handling HIV data warrants examination, particularly in light of the COVID-19 pandemic. The COVID-19 pandemic disrupted health systems worldwide, affecting various aspects of health-care delivery, including HIV testing and reporting. In China, where information control has been a longstanding practice, the pandemic further complicated the accurate identification and reporting of HIV/AIDS cases.

China's historical approach to sensitive public health data, including HIV/AIDS figures, has been characterized by tight control and limited transparency. The taboo surrounding HIV/AIDS discussions has contributed to the underreporting of cases (Tsang 2020). On World AIDS Day, when global attention is focused on the epidemic, the Chinese government typically announces an unbelievably low number of new HIV cases, often as few as two or three. This apparent suppression of data raises questions about the true prevalence of HIV in the country (Tsang 2019a). China's exceptionalism—its belief in its unique path to development and governance—plays a significant role in shaping its approach to public health reporting. With a vast landmass and a population of 1.4 billion, the Chinese government perceives itself as vulnerable to social movements. The fear is that even a single dissenter in each city could trigger a chain reaction of dissent, potentially destabilizing state control (Zhao et al. 2023).

Conclusion

Data were obtained through interviews with twenty-five MSWs living with HIV, fifteen medical doctors, and twelve NGO directors. This chapter argued that necropolitical mechanisms are responsible for negatively impacting the palliative outcomes or imminent death of MSWs, those with HIV, or individuals who are potential HIV carriers. However, the data also confirmed that even medical professionals can be unintended victims of the biopolitical control of MSWs. In the context described, MSWs frequently encounter biopolitical exclusion and are vulnerable to necropolitical brutality. To elucidate, these individuals face systemic discrimination in accessing medical care due to their rural household registration status, which denies them the privileges associated with urban household registration. The pervasive stigma perpetuated by both the public and the Chinese government further exacerbates their marginalization. This discriminatory environment persists throughout China. Enacted stigma in urban China is inflicted on these rural-to-urban migrants who are also gay. This discrimination subjects MSWs to biopolitical retaliation. In the words of Davies, Isakjee, and Dhesi (2017), "The permanent wounding of individuals, rather than their direct and active killing, can be used as a means of control." Thus, stigmatization of MSWs living with HIV and denying them health access form a cruel apparatus where they are "kept alive but in a state of injury" (Mbembe 2003).

The data show how stigma fuels biopolitical modes of governing queers and peasants and is intrinsically linked to instances of leaving them to die. The findings also demonstrate how biopolitical measures can negatively affect collateral groups—medical workers—who are also at risk (Tsang 2019d). Mbembe's notion of necropolitics provides critical insight into contemporary conditions in China's health-care system, where all involved may be exposed to death. Gay and other gender-nonconforming forms of behavior expose MSWs to state-sanctioned stigma that supports biopolitical control and punishing them for being HIV-positive (Wright 2011). Although the sexual activity of MSWs is consensual, they are fully conscious of the necropolitical power that treats them as the living dead for failing to uphold the ideals of traditional masculine Chinese citizenship. As bodies constituting the "necessary other" among heterosexual hegemony, LGBTQ+ communities in China are vanquished to the private and embodied domain.

Necropower of state-sanctioned biopolitical control is an effective tool for managing MSWs and those infected with HIV. It also helps secure the state's future by controlling peasant male migrants who enjoy the benefits of urban China. The political dynamics of the Chinese healthcare system examined here include the voices of medical doctors, MSWs living with HIV, and NGO directors. The politics of death assigned to the gay body are invariably indistinguishable from the enacted stigma that is institutionalized in the medical system. To this end, the distinctions drawn by Scambler (2018) reveal that enacted stigma is an integral part of necropolitical power, which creates multiple death worlds through psychological trauma and anxiety through felt stigma. Queers are discouraged from accessing public health-care services because they expect to encounter discrimination from medical professionals and family members. But by doing so, they internalize chronic stress, which further increases their susceptibility to death through other pathologies.

Further research should operationalize the necropolitics arising from stigma in health services as well as in sociology and cultural studies of nonconforming gender and sexuality in China. Gendered notions of citizenship in China have produced a set of biopolitical conditions that insulate the population from perceived threats from stereotyped groups such as MSWs, MSM, lesbians, and transgender people. As such, members of the LGBTQ+ community are subject to social death as nonhuman and nonliving entities. Enacted and felt stigma function as biopolitical measures protecting Chinese society's moral order and future. However, this stigma can backfire and create necropolitical conditions for medical doctors who must treat patients with HIV infections. The medical system is part of a much broader biopolitical and necropolitical environment, whereby effeminate boys are excluded from the Chinese Dream. The mechanisms of necropower confirm why reducing stigmatization in China's health services—and the broader society—of these excluded groups is a necessary first step to becoming a more inclusive, progressive society.

The non-stigmatization of vulnerable groups is a human rights issue in China. The felt and enacted stigmas experienced by the rural MSWs make them precarious citizens, marginalized as socially dead. The government's position seems to be that since nobody is directly killed or murdered, no one should be held responsible. However, the experience of MSWs living with HIV reflects a social death, outsourced to penal colonies, an "extraordinary rendition" that becomes ordinary, obfuscated by the state bureaucracy, and covered up by one media spectacle after another (Murray 2008; Puar 2007). International organizations can amplify the voice of the NGO community, urging public policy changes in China. However, it is not easy to attract global attention when public opinion is muzzled. Public health and infectious disease management require multidimensional policies and voices instead of relying on official voices from the state apparatus. State-controlled health care in China reflects the government's message that justice is less important than control, and control is the key to reducing the number of infections of a contagious disease such as HIV. Our humanity demands that we keep raising awareness about the exclusion of HIV-infected MSWs from the health-care systems in China.

The culturally ingrained practice of expressing enacted stigma toward gay communities and subgroups like MSWs prevents these individuals from coming out (Tsang et al. 2019). They will continue to hide their orientation and occupation from their family members. For MSWs who are living with HIV and struggling with social necropolitics, NGOs, state actors, and other social service providers can consider how to reduce the social stigma associated with gays and lesbians as well as address the cultural expectation for adult children to give their parents a grandchild.

The necropolitics of social death should open debates among policymakers, for example, how sovereignty and state power assign bodies without bio-value to necropolises, as examples where deaths do not matter and are of no concern to even the urban gentrified gay communities. The notion of the necropolitics of social death helps socio-medical researchers understand how the loss of political rights and the denial of appropriate health care create death worlds where individuals are left to die. Some MSWs even hide their HIV history and still have sex with their clients. Therefore, MSWs urgently need more counseling services, workshops, and education to avoid spreading HIV to their clients and sex partners.

7

A Sisterhood of Hope

How China's Transgender Sex Workers Cope with Intimate Partner Violence

I met Meiha (forty-eight) in summer 2018. For six years, she had been a TSW who also performed Chinese opera in a theatre, wearing heavy makeup. She was tall, slim, and delicate, even fragile. She was a popular performer, often receiving generous tips of 1,000 yuan (US$150) or more. She was older than most TSWs but kept herself physically fit, her skin youthful and unblemished. As we spoke after her opera performance that night, she suggested we go for a drink nearby.

We sat for over an hour, and she told me her story. Despite being assigned and raised a boy, she knew she was a woman at age fifteen. Nevertheless, when she was twenty-two, Meiha fulfilled the filial obligation in China, marrying a woman and having one son and one daughter. With only a primary school education, Meiha had to work in a village factory. After twenty years as a husband and father, as the children were adults and the elder son finished college, Meiha declared to her family that "he" was "she." They did not respond well. They called her a monster and told her to leave the village.

Meiha moved to the city, and in early 2014, she transitioned via breast implantation surgery. Meiha said her only path then was to become a freelance TSW. She installed the gay dating app Blued onto her phone and began meeting interested men. She soon met her partner, whom she described as strong and tall, and in December 2014, they moved in together. Meiha said that as a woman, her partner was the only one she ever kissed in public. They would walk hand in hand despite hearing derogatory comments from people around them. But Meiha did not care. However, she soon discovered that her partner was also very controlling, and the relationship began a downward spiral. That is when she discovered her partner's true character and encountered intimate partner violence (IPV):

He always wanted more money to buy drugs and alcohol. But when he had them, he was frantic and unstable. Once, he demanded that I find more clients to make more money, and I refused. He erupted like a volcano. He yelled at me, scolded me, then began beating me. I fought back, but the more I fought, the angrier he became. He damaged my apartment, smashed my lamps, my TV, and the furniture, and he even threatened me with a knife. Usually, when we fought, I would tolerate him. Finding a boyfriend, much less a life partner has been difficult. But that night, I was fed up and had enough; I told him to move out. He was angry, but he left without incident. The next day, I was going to change the lock, but he came to my apartment and said he was there to pack his belongings. I did not know he had brought a small knife. I was not paying attention when he walked up to me in our kitchen, and I suddenly felt pain in my arm. He had stabbed me! I screamed and pushed him, then ran away. I left the building and hid in an alley. I called a friend to take me to the hospital. I did not dare to call the police. They would just make fun of me.

When Meihua arrived at the hospital, the issue of the rural *hukou* once again emerged as a significant factor:

> I had to pay for treatment from my own pocket because I had no health insurance from the government. I admitted that my partner attacked me, and the hospital insisted I report it to the police. But I refused. Being transgender, my identity is not approved. . . . Therefore, I stayed silent. The hospital finally let me go, and I moved to another city and changed my name, address, and even my mobile phone number. Hah! He still found me using that damn dating app. At least he is in another city and mostly leaves me alone. I still do not have medical insurance to support my therapy and medication, and I still have to pay from my pocket to see a doctor regularly. Therefore, I write a journal and talk to my sisters online. . . . I am glad they listen to me.

I asked Meihua why she had not left him sooner. Her answer was telling:. "I liked him, she confessed. "I hoped he would change and did not want to drive him away. In the beginning, I tolerated him and sacrificed a lot. It is not easy for someone like me to find a partner."

Meihua lived a precarious lifestyle. When faced with threats of physical violence, TSWs cannot rely on the police. They turn to themselves and the sisterhood when they need help:

> I avoid attention from the Chinese police and government. Calling the police brings more trouble. I was once caught having sex in the park, and they put me in a detention center. I do not want the police to bother me. They just make fun of me. I rely on my sisters when I need help. I use WeChat with one particular sister to talk about problems with my partner. With the police, sometimes, I get tired of playing the arrest game with them. They catch me in the park or a street alley. I then called other sisters nearby on WeChat to come rescue me. Sometimes, the sisters go get the gangsters, and for some extra money they come to help me. We will all go to the police station together, so we have more bargaining power. Sometimes, we even call a journalist to try and draw more attention. The police do not bully us as much when there is a lot of attention.

Meiha's case revealed the conflicted professional life of many TSWs. Against professional stigma and fighting with police, all twenty-five TSWs interviewed admitted that they regularly also struggled at home with IPV. TSWs face considerable challenges that affect their mental health and make their situations more vulnerable and precarious. TSWs often experience violence from clients, police, and others, but it is estimated that 50 percent of these acts of violence are at the hands of their intimate partners (Asia Catalyst 2015). The marginalization of TSWs is fueled by abuse through isolation and shaming, which prevents them from seeking help through formal channels like police or counseling services. There is limited research on IPV involving TSWs who are biologically male at birth and transition to women, and their partners, who are typically heterosexual or bisexual men. In China, stigmatization, homophobia, heterosexism, and transphobia structurally disadvantage TSWs, and this power structure tacitly supports violence and abuse against them. To survive, TSWs rely on informal networks with their sisters—other transgender, nonbinary, gender nonconforming peers— for advice and emotional support. This network is more effective than criminal justice or social policy efforts at combatting IPV. Ethnographic data from in-depth interviews with twenty-five TSWs provided insight into IPV and how informal social support has been a protective factor that helped them cope with routine acts of violence. The findings identified the importance of sisterhood and how it protects TSWs and helps them manage their physical and mental health.

Transgender Women in China

The struggles faced by transgender remain a significant social issue in China, having been pushed to the margins of society. They are shunned and rarely discussed or even acknowledged to exist, marginalized even more than their counterparts in the West. The term *transgender* is applied to persons whose identity has been mismatched with their biological sex, leading to gender-reassignment procedures. While mismatches may occur with either gender, this chapter focuses on those assigned male at birth, whose identity emerges to be different regardless of genitalia, behavior, or plans to alter their bodies (Nichols 2010). People who identify outside of the gender binary are often referred to as nonbinary. Nonbinary gender identity can include identifying as neither male nor female, both male and female, or as different genders at different times (Richards et al. 2016). Some who are transgender also identify as nonbinary.

Globally, the number of transgender people is increasing. It is estimated that 9.2 percent out of every hundred thousand have received or requested gender affirmation surgery or transgender hormone therapy; 6.8 percent out of every hundred thousand have received transgender-specific diagnoses; and 355 out of every hundred thousand identify themselves as transgender (Collin et al. 2016). The number of people experiencing abuse and violence is also increasing. A study from Massachusetts in the US surveyed 1,600 people and found transgender individuals reported lifetime physical abuse rates by a partner of 34.6 percent versus 14.0 percent for gay or lesbian individuals (Landers and Gilsanz 2009). Another study reported that up to 50 percent of violence experienced by transgender individuals comes from their intimate sex partners (Courvant et al. 2001).

Transgender Sex Workers

The overall number of TSWs seems to be rising along with a variety of concomitant public health issues. For example, among sex workers,

TSWs are forty-nine times more likely to acquire HIV than all adults of reproductive age, and the rate of HIV infection among TSWs is 27.3 percent, nine times higher than FSWs and three times higher than MSWs (Asia Catalyst 2015; Tsang 2020). Compared to the overall transgender population, TSWs are particularly vulnerable regarding the vastly under-researched area of IPV.

There are no official estimates regarding how many transgender individuals exist in China, but one rough estimate is four hundred thousand (Jiang et al. 2014). Indeed, transgender-specific data collection, HIV programming, and outreach are almost nonexistent in China. Globally, transgender populations disproportionately experience human rights violations in the form of stigma, discrimination, and violence (Chiang 2012; Liu and Wilkinson 2017; Lyons et al. 2017; Tang et al. 2016). IPV must be addressed because of the relationship between issues of employment, infection with HIV, and emotional stability. Rates of self-harm, suicide, violence, and bullying are high and linked with IPV (Asia Catalyst 2015).

TSWs are perhaps the most precarious and vulnerable group in China's commercial sexscapes, not least because of the difficulty in finding compatible sex partners who treat them with compassion, love, and acceptance. Like TSWs in many other countries, Chinese law does not recognize transgender identity; the term does not even appear in any law or policy, which implies that the category does not even exist. The Chinese language does not indicate gender other than traditional character designations of male (男) or female (女). As such, issues like IPV among nonbinary groups remain largely unexplored, undeveloped, and unmentioned in today's China (McClennen 2002).

This chapter argues that TSWs need added protections to safeguard and improve the living conditions of that vulnerable community. As such, informal networks appear to be better mechanisms for fighting IPV than the policymaking and criminal justice systems. In this study, twenty-five TSWs were interviewed about the growing stigma attached to IPV, health risks such as contracting STIs, and occupational hazards such as being arrested and given detention. All TSWs interviewed experienced at least one form of IPV, including sexual assaults, physical violence, verbal assaults, financial exploitation, stalking, and extortion. This chapter has three objectives: to fill a research gap in queer criminology by noting the importance of emotional support for TSWs which come from other TSWs; to examine TSWs self-reliance strategies, comparing the perceived effectiveness of those efforts with formal state-sanctioned migrant assistance programs; and to expand Western scholarship on IPV and provide empirical data from a non-Western country.

Intimate Partner Violence among Transgender Individuals

Studies of IPV typically identify how men use violence against female victims as an extension of patriarchy (Choi et al. 2019). Studies of IPV have been extended to include examining violence against transgender people (Dennison-Hunt 2007; Dozier 2005; Farley and Barkan 1998; Girschick 2008; Hines 2006; Rubin 2004; Schilt 2006). The literature on transgender individuals in China has also examined HIV transmission and sexual and mental health issues (Best et al. 2015; Cai et al. 2016; Chen et al., 2019). Much of the literature notes that the primary agents of aggression and victimizing behaviors against women are heterosexual men. Men still routinely enact hegemonic masculinity (Connell 2005), and those who are transgender are frequent targets of patriarchy (Connell 1995; Connell and Wood 2005). Various groups represented by LGBTQ+ often find themselves at the bottom of the gender hierarchy, perpetuating perceptions of straight male privilege. This in turn disadvantages transgender people who do not perform gender heteronormativity, depriving them of political, social, and cultural power.

Some literature also uses the Foucauldian perspective to assert that power is not just structural or held by a group of individuals. Instead, power emerges from the discourse between individuals (Foucault 1972). For transgender individuals, this power lies behind the cisgendered discourse that shapes structural responses to IPV (Guadalupe-Diaz 2017). Therefore, IPV is not solely a result of a patriarchal power structure but rather a consequence of structurally informed discourses that not only marginalize transgender people but also create distinct realities across race, class, sexual orientation, and gender identity. However, the literature on IPV may not strictly apply to the phenomenon of IPV toward TSWs. TSWs are not within the logical framework of heterosexuality, heterosexism, and the normalization of heterosexuality or heteronormativity.

Queer criminology has been used to explain IPV against transgender individuals in Western countries like the United States (Connell 2005). Queer criminology refers to "exploring the manifestations of transphobia and homophobia in the realm of crime and criminal justice" (Buist and Lenning 2015; Friedrichs 2009). However, while Western queer criminology relies on the criminal legal system to improve the precarious situation of transgender people, China's criminal justice and social policies are under no compunction to help. In China, TSWs must rely on informal support networks to help them cope with IPV.

Queer Criminology and Informal Sectors of Help

Queer criminology treats transgender as a fluid, dynamic, and nonbinary category. In China, the criminal justice system and social policies alone cannot eliminate the stigma faced by TSWs. Instead, there is evidence that self-help programs provide structure and agency for TSWs to resolve their problems. Guadalupe-Diaz (2017) noted that self-help programs encouraging transgender individuals to seek help from their friends or NGOs helped them solve IPV-related trauma related to depression and emotional frustration. Studies of female sex workers in Brazil (Kerrigan et al. 2008), Turkey (Guler 2020), India (Blankenship 2008), and Swaziland (Fonner et al. 2014) show that trust, solidarity, and social cohesion within the FSW community increased condom negotiation with sex partners resulting in higher rates of condom use. In China, Zheng (2008) found that bar hostess support networks in China were enabled by blood relationships, common background or birthplace, and activities or behaviors that were mutually beneficial.

Likewise, for TSWs, informal social support coming from sisterhood and social cohesion seems to moderate the relationship between IPV and symptoms of depression, even though the TSWs also suffered from police harassment and different forms of IPV from their sex partners (Nichols 2010). Informal networks have been the most helpful for TSWs in coping with IPV in China. In the face of health-care barriers, TSWs turned to their peers for social support and assistance to address that unmet need. The twenty-five TSWs interviewed reported that their sisterhood—other TSWs—provided emotional support, physical safety, and protection against their partner and even against the police.

Forms of Intimate Partner Violence
Sexual Assaults

Among the TSWs I interviewed, sexual assaults were the most commonly mentioned form of IPV, and they spoke at length about the ways their partners assaulted them. For example, Yee was a twenty-four-year-old TSW who had lived with her partner for one year before they broke up. When interviewed in the conference room of an NGO, Yee wore no makeup and dressed in modest jeans and a T-shirt. She said that at first, her partner often spoke of his infatuation with her breasts and his curious excitement that they both had male organs. For a while, they seemed compatible living with each other, and she willingly accommodated her partner's sex drive. But after the first month, he began collecting sex toys and fantasy costumes. The sex became progressively more extreme and less pleasurable. Yee did not know exactly when it turned abusive:

> His favorite thing became using a dildo on me that pulses and throbs to music. Even now, he inserts it, and then I have to do a striptease dance for him. He says it helps arouse him, and he masturbates as I dance. In bed, he treats me like I am a toy for his pleasure. Sometimes he has me blow into his anus with a straw, and sometimes he wants me to urinate as I give him a blowjob. Once, I ended up vomiting from the filth and had to go to the hospital. I told him many times that I do not like these things, but he does not listen to me.... One night, I refused his requests, and he shouted at me, "Who do you think you are? You are only a she-male, a monster! You are acting like a princess—What a joke!" He then beat me with the dildo and put it inside me again.

Although they broke up, the IPV has continued, and she remains conflicted about resolving the relationship. Her ex-partner worked in a nearby mobile phone factory and still regularly visited her apartment, where he forced himself sexually on her. Yee did not recognize that she was being serially raped. Instead, she dismissed the assaults with a shrug, saying, "He is always hungry for sex." Remarkably, Yee shifted in mid-sentence from how he still bullied her and pushed her to get vaginoplasty to the neutral topic of the procedure itself. Yee went on at great length about how the procedure was too expensive and that if she could raise the money, she would prefer to have it done in Thailand, because although the procedure is cheaper in China, she worried if it would be done correctly.

Another TSW, Lily (twenty-eight) shared her experiences with "chem fun parties" (*bunfun paidui* 缤纷派对), where as many as thirty people of all genders and persuasions come together for sex coupled with drugs, alcohol, and food. These parties are hosted at private houses or luxury hotel suites and may last for days. She said her partner joined her that weekend and took it even further:

> We were in a private room, and he beat me and slapped me because he said I loved to play S&M. He tied me to the ceiling with a red rope and dripped candle wax on my shoulders, my breasts, and my thighs. He called another man in, and together, they used a little whip that left marks on my ass. It hurt some, but when I resisted, he did what he always does; he just playfully hit me and slapped me some more. . . . They both finished on my face and hair and left the room laughing to get something to eat. I cleaned up and took a shower.

Ruijia (thirty-nine) reported that her partner repeatedly found ways to demean her and undermine her confidence:

> He liked to act like he was a stranger, a doctor, playing with my sexual organs like he was studying them and taking measurements. He would poke, prod, and squeeze both my breasts and my penis. There was no emotion on his face, and I felt hurt and humiliated. Later on, he would often suggest we should invite girls to our apartment for group sex— and even wanted to bring in a big dog if I would allow it! In the end, he backed down, but I don't know. . . . My partner also liked to mix *maotai* with drugs, but it often made him abusive. He would get loud and start saying whatever he wanted, like calling me a filthy dirty whore.

Non-Sexual Physical Assaults

Fan (twenty-four) was a TSW who had been living with her boyfriend for over two years. They met each other through a gay dating app. Her partner was a factory worker who hated his work, kept changing jobs, and finally stopped working altogether. He said he wanted to be a "kept man," financially supported by Fan:

> After taking drugs, my partner could be brutal. We fought intensely when he was like that, yelling and cursing each other. He was so critical of what I do and who I am. It really hurt me. Occasionally, our fighting would get so heated that he would hit me in the face or slap my breasts. Finally, we broke up, and he had to move out. However, his stuff is still in my apartment, and he always wants to come over to try again. I need to see a doctor regularly for my depression.

I met Juan (thirty-two) in a high-end bar. She wore an elegant, tight dress (*qipao*) that accentuated her slim figure and highlighted her long black hair—the picture of traditional Chinese femininity. As we spoke, Juan talked about her stage performance and love of music and dancing. Her notable dancing skills have landed her regular appearances on nationally televised variety shows. Officials routinely invited her to perform for audiences in rural and poor areas. She fondly recounted stories about how her dancing captivated ethnic minority audiences in Xinjiang and Tibet. Her typical outfit included elaborate makeup and full-length traditional Chinese costumes that show no skin from the neck down.

Juan said that China was still very conservative, despite having "bid farewell to the concubine." She said it was still frowned on for men to hold hands, let alone kiss, in public. She and her partner, a DiDi driver (taxi driver), had a seven-day honeymoon period when they first came together, holding hands and kissing in secret whenever they could. Soon afterward, practical aspects replaced romance, and conflicts emerged:

> One day, we argued over finances, like who paid for rent and who paid for food. I had been paying the rent and all the other monthly bills. He said his slim salary could not even buy him lunch and keep gas in his car. He thought my salary was so easy to make and so much higher. Our argument became a fight, and he ended up cutting me with a knife. I still have not forgiven him, and our hostility is still unresolved.

Faho (thirty-five) had been living with her intimate partner for two years, and he put her in the hospital as well. When she talked to me, she still felt the pain. She said her partner hid a fruit knife in his sleeves and that he had suddenly and without warning stabbed and punched her, breaking her ribs. Faho was hospitalized for six months. The attack that day resulted from a series of fights they were having. Still, she forgave him and never reported the attack to the police, who likely would not have provided sufficiently meaningful help to justify the effort and the public record that would have resulted. When I visited Faho in December 2019, she said she still tolerated her partner's violence and had no intention of leaving him. Loneliness can be a powerful justification.

Verbal Assaults

The twenty-five TSWs generally agreed that most of the verbal assaults occurred within the context of body shaming. Partners openly disparaged the bodies of TSWs, mocking, teasing, and even laughing openly at them. Not surprisingly, verbal assaults would escalate into physical attacks when drugs or alcohol were a factor.

Yoyo was a forty-four-year-old transgender woman who completed gender reassignment breast surgery. Yoyo had married a woman several years ago, and they had two sons. The sons, now eighteen and twenty years old, studied at a university in China. Yoyo said her wife knew she preferred men but was ignorant about her identity as a transgender woman.

When Yoyo came to Tianjin in 2015, she initially engaged in cross-dressing. She bought wigs, dresses, and high heels and learned to use makeup. She met her first partner at the club where she performed, a bartender who worked there. She then met another man in 2017 through an online app, and they conversed for two days before she had the courage to meet him in a bar. They quickly moved in together. Her partner immediately began complaining that his working hours were too long and his income was too low. Although passion disappeared after the first two months, they stayed together for four years. Yoyo admitted that they stopped having sex a long time before they eventually broke up:

> We grew bored with each other pretty quickly. He asked for sex occasionally after our honeymoon period, but I steadfastly refused him because he kept insisting I get vagina surgery. Each time I declined, he would push and argue to the point that he would become mean and laugh at

me.... One day, we had a huge fight that ended everything. He was very depressed that night and started drinking heavily. He was soon touching me and then started undressing me. When I told him to stop, he instead pulled out his phone, pointed at my sexual organs, and laughed as he took photos. I was so shocked and speechless that I could not move. I told him that he was a scoundrel.... Later that night, he said I was so desperate, but no man would ever want me. When I said he was a bully, he replied that I should be grateful to him because only he was interested enough to conquer me. He said that since I was transgender, I was a double loser, neither man nor woman. He called me a monster.... I am glad that we are over. I still hate him.

Jackie (thirty-two) had been a TSW for four years and had been living with her partner, who used a wheelchair, for six months. Jackie found that after the third month, they were not compatible, as they fought almost every day. Back in 2010, her partner had been in a car accident and, despite therapy and rehabilitation, needed her help to get around. Jackie said her partner was hot tempered, but she loved him and tried to care for him. Over time, Jackie discovered that her partner was emotionally and psychologically controlling through overt verbal attacks and subtle judging comments:

He did not like my job as a TSW. I think it made him jealous. Sometimes, he would yell at me, calling me a "cheap duck, a chimpanzee" [*pingya* 平鸭, a cheap male prostitute] because I sold my body for sex. The yelling and insults happened all the time. Still, I did not want to leave him because it is not easy to find a partner in the transgender community. He often called me an indecent slut. He said he did not want me to be a sex worker. However, he cannot provide for us financially. Therefore, he keeps calling me a sissy and an ass worker. I get tired of it and would love to find a man who wants and accepts me for who I am.

Pan (thirty-eight) also had to deal with control issues and bullying from her partner:

My partner said I was unattractive and looked like a giant chimpanzee. He says I look unnatural. His words really hurt. I found myself looking in the mirror and wondering, "Do I really look like a giant she-male chimpanzee?" He constantly criticizes me for being such a dirty woman while he prides himself on his neatness. I do not know if I should leave him; I do not even know how to begin. I have been trying to make our relationship work, but lately, I have suffered from anxiety and insomnia. I lie awake in bed worrying about the housework I forgot to finish. . . . A dirty house really irritates him.

Jiating (twenty-four) experienced hate from neighbors where she lived and worked:

In the summer of 2018, I bumped into a neighbor, and she yelled in my face: "Get out of here, you freak! You are a stain on our good city. Pack your bags and leave our neighborhood. Now! We do not want you here." She then spit on me and quickly walked away. I felt assaulted by hate every day. Because my Adam's apple and body hair gave me away, the residents saw me as a man. The hate I felt in their eyes made me depressed. It affected my mental health, my self-esteem, and my self-confidence.

Jiating told me that her femininity allowed her to express herself and let her emotions out. If she felt sad after bumping into troublemakers or bad clients, she channeled her femininity into a song. She has also learned to keep a low profile and avoid neighbors.

Financial Exploitation

Shenshen (forty-two) was a TSW who had worked in the field for three years. She was so passionate about the topic that she brought her photo album to the interview. As she displayed the images of her boyfriend, she admitted that, at first, she enjoyed a sweet and intimate life with him. But three months later, the honeymoon was over. Shenshen said the memory was her only fantasy about romance. The reality was that this man wanted only her money:

We had fights, and he would beat me. Afterward, he would beg me to forgive him. He never had money for rent and bills, not even for drugs.

I supplied everything! He asked me for a six-month allowance of 10,000 yuan [US $1,400]. I thought hard about it and finally decided to give it to him. I hoped that if he could appreciate what I did, we could return to being a regular couple. But I was wrong. He took the money and forgot about me. Now, I just want him out of my life.

Wen (forty-five) shared another story of deceit:

My partner tried every excuse for money. He said his parents needed money for surgery, or he needed money for his new business, or his brother needed money to go to college, or his relatives needed money to repair their house. I knew they were all lies. If I had any spare money, I would have given it to him. But I thought it was unhealthy and unfair to me, so finally, I yelled at him and asked him to leave. It was a painful decision. Living with him was one rip-off after another. He keeps calling me though, and I am still struggling with him.

Qiang (thirty-three) finally saw the truth when she recorded her boyfriend's drunken taunts one night and played them back for me. His words were abusive and designed to inflict pain, emblematic of the exploitation suffered by TSWs from partners whose demands are as crude as they are wholly self-serving: food, shelter, expense money, and sex.

Don't you dare think you are a virgin or a princess! Of course, I just live with you for the money. Do you think someone else will love you? A monster? Hello! Wake up, monster! I found out you are broke and ugly. So, I am leaving you to find another big fish—I always wanted to dump you anyway! Do you think you are easy to live with? Ugly Slut! You should be grateful I have not stabbed you in your sleep. . . . I only wanted your money!

Stalking and Extortion

While the interviewees confirmed they had broken up with the partners described throughout this chapter, many of these relationships remained unresolved. Stalking and extortion were still things they had to deal with. Fafa (twenty-nine) said her partner continued to harass her for an entire year after they broke up:

> I would get weekly deliveries to my apartment of packages containing urine, shit, or semen. I moved four times to escape him. He also threatened to send naked pictures of me to my mother and post them on WeChat, TikTok, and Weibo. Once, I gave him 10,000 yuan [US$1,538] to leave me alone, and he agreed. However, three months later, he demanded more money for drugs, and I gave him another 10,000 yuan. Then he returned a third time, demanding 50,000 yuan [US$7,692]. This much, I could not afford.

In the summer of 2019, I arranged to meet with Hui (thirty-eight), a TSW, at a nearby clubhouse where she found her clients online. She had lived with her present partner for three years. She had recently found that her intimate partner behaved very aggressively to her and disrespected her as a TSW. She also experienced public humiliation from a vindictive ex-lover she had broken up with back in 2018. For revenge, her partner sent naked photos of her to her sister and mother, complete with her genitalia in full view. That ex-lover also sent pictures by mail to the village mayor in her hometown, letting it be known she was transgender and worked in the bushes selling sex in Tianjin. She said her family cut all ties with her and that they had been banned from the ancestral halls as she was now considered dirty, sinful, and accursed.

Sisterhood and Informal Social Networks

The interviewees agreed that they could not rely on the police or social policymakers for help. They said that TSWs learned to first seek help from other TSWs. This informal network was described as their sisterhood of support. For example, Xing (thirty-one) said she had once asked for police help, but they said the problem was of her own making:

> After we broke up, my ex-boyfriend continued stalking me on WeChat and TikTok. I called the police and complained to them. They came to my apartment and said, "You know your (assigned) identity, right? Did

you ever have your new identification card made with your new gender? Please do not waste our time if you cannot provide this evidence. You people really hurt our city's image. This is not police business. Find your own way to clean up your mess." Around 3:00 a.m. I was so depressed that I was going crazy and thought about committing suicide. I called my sister and talked to her about what happened. She was so kind and nice. She talked to me for nearly three hours. As the sun rose and we finished, I realized her words were like the dawn of the new day.

Fan (twenty-four) said her sisters helped her feel like a typical girl living an ordinary life:

My sister from Beijing visits me regularly, sometimes twice monthly; she usually brings my favorite desserts, and we go shopping for cosmetic products. Sometimes, we went to a salon or beauty parlor just to pamper ourselves. Shopping is like therapy; her visits help me find meaning and enjoy life. Sometimes, we organize a little party and invite other sisters to join us. The last time was Christmas, and we had a great time. Her support has been so important to me. It is not easy finding someone you can trust and with whom you can be yourself.

The conversations with the TSWs showed that advice and support came from their sisterhood. However, this tight circle of friends takes time and effort to form, and the nature of relationship-building makes it difficult for lone wolves or a new TSW with trust issues. The sisterhood ideally is a group of friends who hang out together and are available to each other for help and personal counseling. The sisters may be coworkers, colleagues, friends, and sometimes even lovers. From their shared experience as TSWs and similar struggles, they lean on one another for advice, support, and the occasional escapist fun. Juan (thirty-two) said she found strength just by talking to her sisters about her experiences:

When I am alone and feel depressed or after I feel my partner has bullied me, I can text my sister, and she will stop by for a chat. When she is with me, I feel like I finally have a shoulder to cry on. She does not judge, and I can trust her. I can talk to her about my partner, and she will listen before giving advice. Sometimes, she says I should be patient or forgiving.

Sometimes she says my partner is taking advantage of me and I should leave the jerk immediately.

Like Meiha, Yoyo (forty-four) affirmed the power of the sisterhood:

I cannot ask the police to protect me if my partner keeps harassing or stalking me. The only ones I will talk to for help are my sister or someone at the NGO. I remember my sisters and I once vowed to help each other improve our lives. For example, when I sell sex in a public park, I will ask the sisters nearby to keep watch for me. If the police show up, they can quickly call a gangster to our location to interrupt the arrest . . . or even go with me in solidarity to the police station . . . . My sisters are my shelter.

The other informal sector helping the TSWs is the transgender NGOs in Tianjin. Those TSW NGOs are common in the Tianjin area as the government spent money to provide HIV testing or counseling services. Yee (twenty-four) said that the NGOs provide shelter and, if needed, a place for her to heal. Especially if a staff member was also transgender, it could be a safe space to talk when she felt unhappy:

The NGOs that understand me the best are gay or trans. I hope they will one day provide a qualified counselor or social worker to help us. Since I came out to my family, I have had a horrible relationship with them. I do not have many close friends and sometimes I feel the whole world hates me.

Perhaps the most vital function of sisterhood is to provide TSWs with support and affirmation. This support system helps them feel connected to their humanity. The TSW community is relatively small and vulnerable; they do not easily make friends with outsiders as they have encountered many people who look down on them for who they are and what they do. Since intimate partner relationships have been fraught with verbal and physical violence, TSWs have to rely on each other to be able to let down their guard. They actively arrange time with other sisters to accompany them for running errands, shopping, and enjoying the little pleasures in life, even just going out for dessert. The sisters might gossip and criticize each other, but in a life full of danger, struggle, and betrayal, they have learned to trust each other, knowing they are each on the same trans-journey in life.

The Path for Reform in China
Support from Sisterhood/Informal Network

The home environment for TSWs may be as unsafe as the work environment. The twenty-five TSWs I interviewed offered evidence of their partners routinely attacking them with a steady barrage of homophobic, sexist, and derogatory comments. When the home environment is full of intimidation and fear, the TSWs become silenced because their identity is not recognized in China. Government and media outlets have long discriminated against LGBTQ+ groups. These include the representatives of SAPPRFT (State Administration of Press, Publication, Radio, Film and Television of the People's Republic of China), local TV stations, newspapers, and even internet platforms like Sina Online. The Chinese government strategically represses transgender communities to keep them silent and invisible. Among the interviewees, fourteen out of twenty-five TSWs had experience being sent to detention centers after they were caught publicly engaging in sexual activity for money. The twenty-five TSWs in this study reported having been judged to be unworthy victims because they stand accused of transgressing cultural norms by acting seductively, being manipulative and provocative, and having ambiguous relationships with men. Therefore, police routinely target TSWs in public parks after they receive complaints from nearby residents.

In response, the informal sisterhood network learns to stay hidden and safe from the public's judging, criminalizing, and stigmatizing gaze. They use mobile phones and chat functions to help develop a sense of intimacy and trust among themselves. The sisters offer assistance, support, and care, which helps them exist in a hostile environment. In addition, due to the complexities of shame, isolation, and the stigma associated with gender identity, which was categorized by the government as mental illness, TSWs rely heavily on the internet to access resources in a safe, nonjudgmental environment. TSWs have also learned to mobilize their communities and work together when dealing with the police.

Being in groups is the best way to bolster the confidence of the TSWs in advocating for themselves and minimizing the effects of stigma, violence, and incarceration.

The help from their sisterhood seldom involves money or political lobbying. Mostly, they go to each other for psychological and emotional comfort. These links are relational more than transactional. The perspective of queer criminology argues that criminal justice and social policies can help solve some of the problems faced by TSWs. However, for today's TSWs in China, this will not become a reality anytime soon. For example, several members of the Chinese LGBTQ+ community held an online protest against Sina Weibo on April 13, 2018, when Sina Weibo banned online content "related to gay." The success of the Chinese LGBTQ+ group made an unprecedented step in the battle against widespread discrimination, which further forced the Chinese authorities to react to guarantee de-criminalization and de-stigmatization of gays in Chinese society (Lowe and Tsang 2018). This shows the importance of an informal network and how TSWs can also develop online communities to build cohesion and trust.

The Need for Legal Protection and Criminal Justice

As noted throughout this work, Chinese society and language remain primarily binary. Most policies and laws are written from a worldview that labels one as either a man or a woman. For example, according to Chinese law, the archetypical definition of sexual violence is "forced penetration of a victim through violence or intimidation" (World Health Organization 2002). The law was envisioned to protect women who experience sexual harassment and violence by men. Although sexual harassment was included in the Law to Protect Women's Rights in 2005, it provided no legal definition of, or punishment for, the act, only stipulating the nature of sexual harassment as a civil affair rather than a criminal violation (An et al. 2002). In China, the legal framework concerning transgender rights is intricate and often inadequate in providing comprehensive protection. While there have been notable advancements, significant challenges persist for transgender. Legally, explicit safeguards against discrimination based on gender identity or sexual orientation are absent. Although the decriminalization of LGBTQ+

communities occurred in 1997, the rights of transgender individuals remain ambiguously defined. Official policies frequently fail to encompass transgender men and women because trans men/women are not seen as men/women. Those seeking legal gender recognition encounter rigorous prerequisites, including familial consent and workplace approvals. For TSWs in China, the law does not extend to transgender men or women. There is no written character for transgender in the Chinese language. The Chinese government policies and documents still broadly define TSWs using mental health terminology but otherwise remain silent, "not encouraging, not discouraging and not promoting" (Mountford 2010).

Conclusion

The twenty-five participants in this study have struggled with several types of IPV. Sometimes, the IPV was emotionally damaging and manipulative; sometimes, it was life-threatening. All of them experienced some form of sexual violence and recognized times they had to deal with the other types of IPV mentioned in this chapter. Although the queer criminology position asserts that gender can be both binary and nonbinary, transgender people must engage with a criminal justice and legal system in China that neither recognizes nor supports their fundamental rights. TSWs are at an even more significant disadvantage because their occupation puts them in direct conflict with norms and laws prohibiting sex work.

The psychological impact of IPV is marked by depression, anxiety, post-traumatic stress disorder, and even physiological effects like migraines (Tsang et al. 2018, 2019). The participants in this study doubted any groundbreaking government policy to protect TSWs was forthcoming. While countries like the United States have enacted laws to protect transgender people from workplace discrimination, those laws do not extend to the illegal activity of the commercial sex industry.

The first step for reform in China would be to formally acknowledge the existence of transgender people as a subgroup of the nation's citizenry and that notwithstanding their marginalization, they deserve the same protections afforded every Chinese citizen. An essential second step might be to at least decriminalize sex work or provide amnesty to then help train them to enter other occupations. TSWs have tried to find informal networks like talking to their sisters, meeting friends on the internet, and looking for help through NGOs. Some NGOs provide counseling and safe spaces for TSWs experiencing IPV. These informal networks constitute a challenge to the Chinese government because they are discrete and private.

It is vital to link these issues faced by TSWs within the greater context of MSWs and the LGBTQ+ community. The government, as well as the dominant culture, seems to view TSWs as oddities, as objects—not humans—because they do not fit into any traditional category. The accounts provided demonstrate some ways this traditional thinking about gender is simply impractical. TSWs should not have to rely solely on informal networks for help. It would be more helpful if the Chinese government and police developed proactive ways to protect and serve this marginalized subgroup, perhaps offering professional counseling services, job opportunities, and retraining schemes as they do for other groups. TSWs should have the same fundamental rights enjoyed by everyone else in China. It is time for China to listen.

This chapter helps us understand TSWs in at least three ways. First, various and specific forms of IPV have been described. Second, these IPV episodes are presented against sociocultural structures that frame the interactions between TSWs and their partners. Third, an informal network among TSWs enables them to help each other when in need. TSWs are socially, economically, politically, and legally marginalized, and they struggle financially and emotionally in the face of persistent harassment and sexual violence. Still, the TSWs who described their experiences with IPV have provided insights regarding psychological stress, coping effectiveness, and the efficacy of self-help programs. Their experiences should inspire us because, despite the struggles and pain, their stories reveal how they faced the headwinds of life and overcame their situations through pluck, resourcefulness, and loving support from the sisterhood.

As an experienced ethnographer, I have sought to interpret, reinterpret, and present the data I have collected honestly and meaningfully. I have reported what the informants told me, and I have presented that information so readers can understand the context of what is being studied. Ethnography is not a license to compete with imaginative storytelling, using literary devices to keep the reader's attention. To portray these accounts of TSW experiences as "a bit like trauma porn" unfairly likens the accounts to a pulp romance novel. My informants lived this experience, and I have used their words—translated into English—to convey their reality. I can understand that some may find these accounts too descriptive or too graphic. This is appropriate for such a sensitive topic. However, the language reflects the words these TSWs used to describe what they have gone through and continue to experience. What they said was fact-checked and confirmed in follow-up conversations to ensure that I had conveyed their preferred interpretation. Princeton ethnographer Mitch Duneier (2011), among others, has confirmed the importance of this approach. When I met the TSWs presented in this book, it quickly became clear that the thing they mostly wanted to talk about was their daily struggle with the ways their intimate partners bullied them.

For context, these transgender women in China were all in their late thirties and had experienced years of stigma and pain. They had all been driven out of their hometown villages and had fallen out with all their immediate family members. They said they felt lonely and were longing for love and companionship. However, in traditional patriarchal and conservative China, there is nothing the Chinese government is doing to educate the general population not to discriminate against transgender individuals in general, let alone the TSWs. TSWs are tough and resilient in the face of overwhelming odds. I respect them and their tenacity to survive. My hope is that we might all learn to respect them in this way.

Conclusion

Life after Sex Work: Work Trajectories in China's Political Economy

I returned to Tianjian in January 2020 before the outbreak of COVID-19. My friend Herman was still running his high-end gay bar, and both Yang and Fei were still *mamasans* at Pistachio. Unsurprisingly, there was high turnover among the workers; very few of the MSWs I had interviewed were still there. However, what surprised me was discovering that some of those who left had changed careers and were capitalizing on their emotional labor skills, trying to make it in China's rapidly growing online sales industry. As an online show host or livestreamer (literally "internet celebrity"), they could sell products like clothing or cosmetics or services like modern dance lessons, yoga, or even massage techniques. This career shift enables aging MSWs to shift from sex work to more mainstream product sales careers and possibly leave sex work for good.

Senft (2008) defined livestreamers as individuals who build online popularity in a particular niche using new information technologies like short videos, blogs, and social networking sites. Unlike traditional celebrities, who may gain fame through acting or singing and often maintain distance from their fans (Senft 2008), livestreamers maintain relatable online personas and present their content without overt audience manipulation (Liu et al. 2021). Livestreaming in China has evolved into a popular and multifaceted industry. Influencers, often showcasing their daily lives, performances, or gaming skills, attract viewers who reciprocate with virtual gifts as remuneration. This trend has permeated e-commerce, with platforms like Alibaba incorporating livestreaming to augment sales of diverse products, including groceries, branded items, cosmetics, and apparel. Approximately half of China's internet users have interacted with livestreaming. Unlike Western countries, where social media platforms have lagged in integrating e-commerce functionalities, livestreaming in China is a significant conduit for online shopping. Chinese livestreamers, while enjoying extensive opportunities with numerous platforms vying for top talent, are also subject to stringent regulations and actions with their followers in on- and off-platform revenue streams in China.

In 2020, China's livestreaming industry boasted 587 million users and generated an estimated 961 billion yuan (Zixun 2021). While livestreamers in Western countries tend to focus on building fame rather than selling products, livestreamers in China are generally more driven by profits. Social media and e-commerce in China have enabled livestreamers to generate significant revenue through online retail activities. The shift to online commerce has created an environment conducive to the growth of livestreaming as a profession, providing young rural and marginalized people with new career opportunities. In Western countries, influencers build a following to attract advertisers and sponsorships. Livestreamers in China are focused on immediate profits from daily product sales. In China, livestreamers convert their onscreen practices and interactions with their followers into on- and off-platform revenue streams (Tan and Shi 2021; Tan and Xu 2020).

Clients have always favored young men (and women) for sex. As they age, many MSWs see that their time is running out and eagerly look for ways to move into another career. There is therefore great appeal for them to sell products on social media platforms like Weibo (微博), WeChat (微信), Weiduan (微店), Douyin (抖音), Kuaishou (快手), and Xiaohongshu (小红书). Inspired by some initial success stories, I pursued some old contacts and tried to catch up with those trying to make it as livestreamer sales hosts.

I spoke with Mingchi (thirty-seven), who was working as a livestreamer in Tianjin. He said that the hours were long and the pay was low, but he felt that this was a good move for him:

> Am I still attractive? I am not as glamorous as I was ten years ago. But sex work is competitive, and I am just getting too old.... At least as a livestreamer, I feel the work is more stable, and I do not have to pretend I am young. I mostly talk to people about products. I can be funny and chatty and let my personality shine. In my other life, all the conversations eventually came back to sex and a price. Now, it is different. I can still flirt, but there is no sex involved unless I want it to be. I have to say, this change is welcome.

Another success story is Yian (forty-two), a former MSW who gracefully transitioned out of the commercial sex industry in January 2019. He was a taxi driver before he moved to become a livestreamer. I visited him at his Shanghai studio in January 2020 before the outbreak of COVID-19. At 2 p.m., Yian began his livestream program, talking to his audience and selling cosmetics like lipsticks, creams, and face masks through Taobao. For twelve hours, Yian interacted with the steady stream of scrolling texts, alternating between questions about the products and compliments on his performance. Once finished, Yian removed his headset, stepped away from the microphone, and relaxed in front of the enormous beauty lamp in his home studio. He picked up each of the three iPhones on his table to respond to fans in the WeChat groups. Three assistants raced around him, cleaning up the room. Yian beamed with pride:

> The salary is much better than I earned before [as an MSW]. I am thankful to have found another career in my mid-life. My skills work well here. Some days, I am lucky; my yearly earnings can be over one million yuan [US$154,000]. This is amazing to me. . . . I never expected that I could do this.

Yian was one of the few mega-success stories. His experience going from rags to riches is inspiring to other rural migrants as well. Yian said that after the interview, he picked up his birthday gift, a new high-end Mercedes-Benz costing 2.8 million yuan [US$400,000]. Yian has used his time as an MSW to brand himself a "bad boy" who dances outside the lines. He does not openly talk about his past, opting to let the rumors circulate among his followers because it confirms his street cred and builds his reputation. I had met him in 2017 at Pistachio. Even then, he had talked to me about losing his competitive edge as he grew older. "It is so difficult to find a long-term partner or a rich guy to give me full package services [*baoyang* 包养]. This job is so unstable, and others look down on us. I do not know how long I can last." As a livestreamer, Yian said he would never look back.

Another former MSW, Dingrui (thirty-eight), left the club in 2019 and relocated to a retail sales position at a Guangzhou fashion boutique. Before sex work, he worked in a garment factory and developed extensive fabric knowledge. He was muscled and good-looking, but the pay cut forced him to keep looking for ways to earn cash. He devoted his efforts to developing an online and social media persona. He used his love of Japanese manga and punk fashion to dye his hair and style it into dramatic tall spikes. He posted selfies to his public account on WeChat and Douyin (抖音 China's version of TikTok). His stylish, handsome boy photos soon attracted a substantial online following. The following year, he focused on selling clothing online through livestreaming.

Intrigued by the success of Yian and Dingrui, follow-up conversations revealed that their stories are not uncommon. A significant number of MSWs interviewed in that earlier study—at least 40 of the 201—had transitioned to the e-commerce phenomenon of livestreamers. Although the average income of livestreamers is a modest 4,000 yuan (US$570) per month (Arcbering 2017), those interviewed said they could make a living selling different products on social media platforms like Weibo, WeChat, Weidian, Douyin, Kuaishou, and Xiaohongshu.

Before the internet, sex workers had limited mobility or opportunities for employment. Now, migrants, sex workers, edgeworkers, and other marginalized groups see a way to escape poverty and attain heretofore unimaginable wealth if they can be a hugely successful livestreamer (Lin and de Kloet 2019; Tan et al. 2020; Wang 2020a). Lele Tao (BBC Trending 2017), MC Tianyou (Hernández 2017), and Papi Jiang (Li 2019) are examples of ordinary livestreamers who have become famous and wealthy. For example, the "King of Lipstick," Li Jiaqi, sold fifteen thousand lipstick tubes in just five minutes (*Global Times* 2018). In 2020, Douyin estimated that Li had over forty-two million fans and that his 2019 estimated income was 200 million yuan (US$29 million) (Huang 2020). Besides selling products, livestreamer post photos and videos of their livestreamed shows on apps like Douyin, Kuaishou, and Blued.

Career Trajectories: Turning Street Smarts to E-Smarts

Many of the former MSWs working as livestreamers use interpersonal skills and street smarts, which helped them survive in the commercial sex industry. The pretty faces, muscled bodies, and quick smiles that helped them grab clients in the gay bars now help them build a following, attracting and keeping viewers through their ready-built, attractive, and engaging personas. The competitive high-risk sex industry forced them to be quick-witted and to think on their feet, negotiating with gangsters and police. These street-smart skills now help them manage and protect themselves online as they take risks and speak extemporaneously for hours at a time. Through their past experiences, they know the value of looking their best for the camera and their new-found fans.

Technologies of Embodiment

Most MSWs worked meticulously to optimize their physical appearance, particularly the face. Taiyi (twenty-four) worked in a high-end bar in Tianjin in 2015, but five years later, the perennially upbeat hypertalkative personality was a popular livestreamer on both Taobao and Douyin. During his interview, he bragged about the cosmetic surgeries that keep him looking his best, particularly his hair transplant, liposuction, and Botox injections. Taiyi has a daily regimen of skincare, supplements, and physical exercise. In 2019, he went to Thailand for a nose job, Botox injections, and a "face-slimming needle." He has been meticulous about his on-camera appearance, modeling clothes while answering questions from followers.

Mengfei (thirty-two) said he now called himself a "cosmopolite with a smartphone, skincare products, and fashionable clothing." The former MSW saw online fame would bring more business. His Taobao shop generated around 300,000 yuan (about US$41,000) per month, with peak sales during festivals like Singles Day (November 11), Valentine's Day, and Lunar New Year. He signed a contract with Tophot, an incubator aimed at nurturing livestreamers to help them improve. Tophot recommended surgery to give him the livestreamer face—doe eyes, pointy chin, high nose, and fair skin—although Mengfei pointed out that his face was already well-kept from years of attention and needed no further improvements.

Sensuous Attachment to the City

Affective sensuous attachment to the city helps these individuals work as livestreamers. Kingchi (twenty-four) said that he found Shanghai to be dynamic and full of positive energy, the perfect environment for him to sell his yoga and massage skills online. Working, as he says, "with heart and care," the yoga coach talks and demonstrates his skills to roughly eight hundred thousand followers on how to use yoga to relax and reduce stress:

> I am a big fan of yoga. In Shanghai, it is popular with young adult men and women. The special breathing and focus techniques quiet the soul, enhance mindfulness, and give you a non-judgmental temperament. Viewers ask questions about the benefits and safety of yoga. I even advise you on how to change your body shape. My heart brought me to be a livestreamer. . . . The Shanghai gay community has been accepting, and my friends and I feel safe and secure here.

Kingchi earned less money as a livestreamer than as a sex worker. He told me that he earned about 5,000 yuan (US$735) per month in Shanghai. Shanghai is an expensive city. However, his efforts are typical of many who use livestreaming to promote their business. He brands himself by posting selfies on social media and live streaming on Taobao and Douyou. Kingchi admitted that the hours were long and the money barely enough. But he enjoyed setting his own hours and appreciated the work's focus on his own self-promotion. He said it cannot compare to the harsh life—thrilling, but harsh—at the club in Tianjin. His life as a sex worker has become a fading memory.

Another case was that of Zhilan (twenty-eight), who left Tianjin, where he was an MSW and moved to Chengdu because of its reputation as a gay-friendly city. Zhilan said the city inspired him; even the architecture seemed gay-friendly. There was an openness in the public parks, shopping malls, cafés, and unisex public washrooms in Chengdu. Zhilan said this environment inspired him to focus on reaching his dream of livestream dancing. In 2020, Zhilan said he had over five million followers:

> Some days, I dance in front of the camera for more than twelve hours with only a few breaks. Once, I hurt my ankle and had to take it easy for the final two hours. For the rest of that program, I was clever. I told them I was showing them slow versions of my moves so they could practice them at home.

Zhilan's attachment to Chengdu captured the power of sensuous disposition, anchoring him and giving him hope. All the former MSW agreed that urban life is superior to rural life, giving them hope, security, and inspiration to chase their dreams.

Livestreamers and Their Audiences

As livestreamers engage with their audiences, their fame is facilitated through a community of interested internet viewers (Abidin 2018). Livestreamers are expected to be authentic, transparent, and willing to interact directly with viewers. Successful livestreamers project intimacy, bridging the distance between themselves and their followers. Peijun (twenty-two) was a talented dancer and a former MSW in Tianjin:

> I do dances like "The Renegade" with "Lottery (Renegade)," "WAP Dance," "Cannibal," and "Vibe (If I back It Up)." I also love performing Chinese opera and have ready my hairnet, outfits, and manicured nails. I can grab my foundation and wig and transform into a Chinese opera figure in seconds. Whatever the audience wants me to be, I do it fast—like magic. That is why I have more than two hundred thousand followers.

Peijun said that he considered his fans like family members and tried to make each one feel unique. Many livestreamers were grateful for loyal followers (*laotie* 老铁) who jumped in to help them promote products.

Ziyi (twenty-eight) followed the path forged by Li Jiaqi, who sold lipstick from Taobao. Ziyi said that his knowledge of cosmetics and spontaneous behavior helped his popularity online. For example, instead of applying lipstick to his arm like many beauty bloggers, he applied the lipstick directly to his lips during the show, giving the performance indisputable authenticity. During one noteworthy livestream on Taobao, he once tried on three hundred different lipsticks and creams in a ten-hour show. Since 2020, he has been said to have more than one million followers. While most of them are women, the number of men is noticeably increasing:

> When I speak, I use my soothing voice to touch my audience. I am like the boy next door, the good friend who shows you a great product I just

found. However, I do not let on that I am gay. The hardest thing to do is persuade people that the products are authentic because, in China, everything can be counterfeit, even lipstick. I signed with some designer brands and at first, I lost money. However, I made it back in 2020 by giving people incisive comments, like how to identify genuine quality lipstick or cream.

His experience as an MSW made him an excellent communicator. Social media platforms enable livestreamers to build their brand by promoting themselves and the products that appeal to their followers. This intimate livestreamer-follower relationship builds consumption (Wang 2020), helping the livestreamer establish their distinctive and "authentic" character setting (Marwick 2013; Senft 2008). Their ability to visually hold an audience's attention and build rapport to strengthen their personal brand attracts advertising clients, resulting in greater bargaining power and financial success.

Transferrable Risk-Taking Skills

To maintain people's attention, livestreamers—like entertainers—have learned that they must sometimes take risks to surprise and delight the audience. Performances are built upon trial and error, and sometimes, comments intended to be humorous can misfire and become major missteps in front of the live-streamed audience. Weiji (twenty-nine) encountered this lesson:

> I lost all my savings when I first started live-streaming on Taobao. Once, the police literally grabbed me as the 1:1 designer clothes arrived at my warehouse. Technically, the bags were not designer brands, but the quality was very close (1:1). Then the Customs Office confiscated all my products and shut me down. . . . After two years, I had only one hundred followers. Even worse, I was indebted to my parents for borrowing 250,000 yuan [US$38,800]. This challenging time lasted 6 months. Then, I changed my strategies and started selling counterfeit designer handbags on WeChat. There was a huge demand, and finally, I gained my money back .

Xibin (twenty-six) had consecutive disastrous sessions selling cosmetics:

> One day, I decided to experiment with a new look to grab attention. I appeared in my S&M leather harness and spiked collar. Apparently, some followers thought my new look was too bizarre because I lost ten thousand followers that day. . . . The next day was worse. I was trying to tell some jokes, and suddenly, this customer complained, saying, "Do not buy cosmetic products from him. He sells expired cosmetic products!" She said my cream aggravated her skin allergy. She bothered me throughout the session, texting everyone, "Do not believe him; he is a liar selling counterfeit cosmetic products." My business was gone. After a few days, I pulled myself together, repacked, and restarted the business on another platform. I am still fighting to rebuild my brand.

Sometimes things do not work out. Dandan (twenty-four) left sex work and contracted with an agency to be a livestreamer. He said that they coerced him to undergo plastic surgery, then charged him exorbitantly high interest:

> I went to Chengdu in 2019. There, I met people at the agency [*jingjiren* 经纪人] who had me sign a contract so I could begin as a livestreamer. They assured me I would be famous. At first, I sold lipstick and face cream through live streaming, but I could not get more than one thousand followers. The agency convinced me I needed a nose job. Since I was broke, the agency gave me a loan but charged me the highest interest rate [*luodai* 裸贷]. Unfortunately, the nose job failed . . . . My face looks horrible, and no one watches me. I cannot even go back to being a sex worker.

I was told that Dandan had returned to his rural village and was back living with his parents, deciding what his next move would be. All the MSWs have learned to be resilient, relying on themselves to be self-sufficient. Livestreaming has been just one path affording the opportunity to discretely escape the necropolitics faced by MSWs in China.

Unlocking the Closet behind the Velvet Red Door

The undergirding conceptual framework throughout has been that necropolitics creates highly disciplined biopolitical conditions for MSWs and former MSWs who changed careers to livestreamers yet remained members of the LGBTQ+ community. They were placed at risk of social death, facing stigma and placing their bodies precariously into biopolitical conditions marked by surveillance and control. These forces create the biopolis in the countryside and necropolis in the city, whereby the subjugation of non-conforming sexuality to death worlds is part of an ambitious reproductive social order. This social order allows rural gay men to be disregarded, erased from political representation, and treated as the dead.

As bodies constituting the "necessary outside" of heterosexual hegemony, lesbians, gays, and transgender people in China have been essentially vanquished to the private and embodied domain, negatively impacting their citizenship status. In the context of Xi Jinping's China Dream, there have been orchestrated attempts to deter public expressions of men appearing weak and effeminate. Male singers and entertainers have consciously avoided any signs of androgyny, which might attract rebuke from the government and the wider society (Song and Hird 2014).

The China Dream masculinizes boys and men because gay men and effeminate men are seen as weakening the national character—they are a stumbling block to China's geopolitical ambitions and state-building. LGBTQ+ communities are therefore a key concept. Only certain forms of masculine gayness are allowed, and those tend to be reflected by wealthy, urban, middle-class gay men. The associated stigma drives rural lesbians and gays to seek nominal marriages with each other to fit in with the political developments of Xi's China Dream and the post-Chinese Cultural Revolution.

The rights of LGBTQ+ people rests at the heart of the nation's concerns about China's international identity. In China, stigma in the form of blaming and shaming those in the LGBTQ+ communities is a means to conceal the inability of the modern state (whether due to corruption or lack of expertise) to deliver freedom for the people. Thus, the phenomenon of *tongqi*, as well as gays and lesbians who seek nominal performative marriages, has resulted in the Chinese state creating a series of necropolitical conditions. These conditions have had a latent effect of increased HIV rates—a liability for taxpayers and health-care service providers—in post-reform China.

Mbembe (2003, 39) proposed that "contemporary forms of subjugation of life to the power of death (necropolitics) profoundly reconfigure the relations among resistance, sacrifice, and terror." For example, MSWs must stop marrying village girls via arranged marriages to avoid the stigma associated with being single and childless. The pressure to conform has led to drug use as a coping mechanism to deal with the harsh necropolitical and biopolitical conditions. For *tongqi*, their options are either to maintain the facade of their marriage or terminate the union and suffer the consequences. In either case, a third outcome may be contracting HIV.

Using necropolitics of social death as a frame of reference helps us understand the stigma directed toward LGBTQ+ communities in China and how the state uses biopolitical measures to control the bodies of the citizenry. Homophobia and violence are destructive forces impacting the lives of young gay migrants. However, the concept of homonormativity is also significant. It refers to the internalization and replication of heterosexual norms within the gay community, which can lead to the marginalization and exclusion of those who do not conform to these norms. While it can be a survival strategy or a way to pass in a heteronormative society, it can also perpetuate harmful stereotypes and expectations, thereby contributing to the challenges faced by these individuals. It is not a contradiction; rather, homonormativity and homophobia can coexist, and both can be detrimental to the wellbeing of young gay migrants. However, the concept of social death also includes the possibility that they can resist and overcome those difficulties. Thus, the necropolitics of social death is the central conceptual framework for this book. MSWs are subject to being "kept alive but in a state of injury" (Mbembe 2003, 21), which reflects social death rather than physical death.

Masculinities, femininities, and understandings of the treatment of dissident sexualities are always relational to idealized or archetypical norms (Butler 1993). Thus, this book helps us understand how citizenship in China is gendered. Both enacted and felt stigma are explicitly and implicitly expressed toward lesbians and gay men. Whether they marry each other for transactional purposes or a gay man marries a hapless *tongqi*, the consensus is that each of them is excluded from the Chinese Dream.

Significance of These Findings

This book sheds light on the sociology of sex work and also migration studies. It provides insights into the transformation of the commodification of affective labor and technologies of embodiments to survive in urban China without an urban *hukou*. There is a significant stigma to being a gay sex worker in China. Although the activity is illegal in China, it has been impossible to abolish, and sex workers remain abundant and common, working in the city's underground venues (Tsang 2019a). A bigger question is whether rural male migrants working in the sex industry are able to inspire other uneducated men to move into a mainstream service industry like livestreaming.

In terms of migration studies, this work has focused on the experiences of rural males who move to urban centers and find that their sexual orientation defines their career. They must cope with negative attitudes and a range of psycho-social outcomes, which include depression and drug abuse. Migration and sex work allow the men to re-situate themselves into the center of the dominant urban social milieu in a manner previously unattainable. The commercial sex industry provides them the financial means to engage in the consumption of luxury accouterments, markers of cosmopolitan success.

Destigmatizing Gay Male Rural Migrants

In today's China, society generally displays a spectrum of attitudes to the fundamental issues explored in this study. Matters of gender and sexual diversity, urban vs. rural *hukou*, heteronormative national-cultural expectations of family, gender, and marriage, and LGBTQ+ discrimination and stigmatization are generally met with ambivalence at best and hostility at worst. China's rural LGBTQ+ community has expressed concern that they are treated as adjuncts of the country, with their rural background and sexuality conscripted into fulfilling the nation's longstanding ideal to project social harmony. For example, gay men complain that they have been denied political, social, and economic opportunities. They work in gay bars, making strategic investments to accumulate social capital that in turn can increase their desirability. They consider emigration to bridge conflicting duties to family and self and to access employment and opportunities (Zheng 2015). China's ambivalence toward managing social differences has resulted in an economically progressive but socially conservative society, polarized between the highly valued urban *hukou* and the less-valued non-urban *hukou*. It is essential to destigmatize gay citizens and provide all sex workers with fundamental rights and protections. Furthermore, male sex work is fraught with high-risk outcomes, from sexually transmitted diseases to assault or even suicide. This book recommends that policymakers improve counseling and emotional support services for this at-risk group.

Initiate Self-Help Programs

As the male migrants capitalize on emotional labor and technologies of embodiment in the gay commercial sex industry, they gain access to urban social hierarchies. The migrants consider activities like plastic surgery along with fine dining and buying luxury goods as the aspired ideal, which takes its cue from their temperate counterparts. The urban imaginary constructs queer peasants as exploitable subjects who must conform to urban expectations. Male migrants embark on their migratory journeys to the city with the dream of enjoying the lifestyle of their urban middle-class counterparts. However, first they must gain acceptance, and cosmetic or surgical enhancements must be enacted to mask their rural masculinity. This allows them to learn that they can initiate their retraining rather than relying on government institutional policies to help them. As these men teach themselves to capitalize on affective labor and technologies of embodiment, they learn self-efficacy. They rely on their own initiative, using affective labor as sex workers to resolve their situation. A self-help program for male migrants may inspire others who want to work in urban settings but find themselves ill-equipped with few marketable skills.

For MSWs, probably the most pressing problem that needs to be dealt with is the practice of entering marriages of convenience and engaging in marriage fraud which is a symptom of the traditional concept of heteronormativity. The LGBTQ+ communities I spoke to did not come out to their parents because they did not want to lose face or make their parents lose face. Losing face involves shame and embarrassment, and once committed, does not quickly heal. To avoid losing face, financially independent male migrant sex workers find it expedient to either commit marriage fraud with a *tongqi* or enter a marriage of convenience with a *lala*. Marriage gives them social protection and a facade that they conform to traditional values and familial ideals (Choi and Luo 2016; Engebretsen 2014, 2017). To solve the problem of marriage fraud, marriage of convenience, and the stigmatization of LGBTQ+ individuals, there must be an extensive awakening to respect the choices about identity that people have made. Parents need some education or counseling to be more realistic, accepting, and loving when they learn that a son is gay or a daughter is lesbian.

The issue of extending the bloodline through children and then grandchildren is a matter of choices, and their input decreases over time. There are several options via technology to fulfill their bloodline-extension wishes, like employing a surrogate or using in vitro fertilization with a partner. Thus, gay or other queer couples can extend their bloodline without using the marriage of convenience or marriage fraud. It is clichéd to think that technology can save us or fix social problems. However, assisted reproductive technologies such as surrogacy have led to a global rethinking and more openness about what it means to be a family, family membership, relationships, expectations, and obligations. In countless families worldwide, sexual orientation is neither suppressed nor discriminated against. Gay couples start families and have children. While not without its critics, commercial surrogacy is a common pathway for LGBTQ+ couples to start their own families with biogenetically related children. However, in the context of China, surrogacy is prohibited, and the law related to surrogacy is insufficient (Ding 2015). Although some gay couples can travel abroad for surrogacy, transnational surrogacies are not available for all. Critical studies on surrogacy and gay men indicate that the typical beneficiaries of transnational or domestic surrogacy are white and upper middle class (Bergman et al. 2010; Berkowitz 2018). Similarly, most of the wealthier MSWs in this book told me they were encouraged to consider international surrogacy.

Another important finding is that a significant number of the MSWs interviewed initially have been able to change to other service industries, such as becoming livestream hosts. As they age, MSWs actively look for ways to grow and use their skills beyond sex work. Initially, the poor, young, often low-educated migrants decide to capitalize on their opportunities to escape poverty by becoming an MSW. But over time, they discover that they are getting too old to be competitive in the commercial sex industries and can no longer negotiate the packages and perks they could when they were younger. However, their experience has made them streetwise, and they find they can use social media and affective labor to alter their career trajectories. As online hosts and entrepreneurs, they can leave sex work and finally be able to tell family and friends what they do for a living.

The MSWs I interviewed did not want sex work to be made legal. If that happened, they would be forced to declare income, pay taxes, and, worst of all, openly declare their occupation. As mentioned throughout, this last aspect is probably the most significant deterrent. None of the individuals interviewed here wanted to tell their parents and family that they perform sex services for money. However, legalization combined with current registration practices could enable employers to find out themselves or lead to the unlikely but possible scenario that it is included on an applicant's resume. Because of these reasons, Chinese society is not ready to embrace the fact that the principles of affective labor and technology of embodiment quickly transfer from sex work to other service industries in the digital era.

Whether sex work could ever be regulated such that it could become mainstream is beyond the scope of this work; simply as a matter of public health, it is deeply problematic because of the high-risk behaviors associated with it. In practical terms, there is no sign that the Chinese government or policymakers will consider legalizing sex work in China, regardless of sex or sexual orientation. The commercial sexscapes will always be regarded as the world's oldest profession, but in China, the government's approach has been to hide it inside a locked closet.

In Western societies, there exists a pervasive sentiment that China may not be fully transparent in its reporting of COVID-19 numbers. This perception, whether grounded in fact or fueled by geopolitical tensions, significantly influences how China's health data, including HIV/AIDS statistics, are interpreted globally. Amid the COVID-19 pandemic, this skepticism has been amplified, adding another layer of complexity to the understanding of China's health landscape. The COVID-19 pandemic disrupted health systems worldwide, affecting various aspects of healthcare delivery, including HIV testing and reporting. In China, a country where information control has been a longstanding practice, the pandemic further complicated the accurate identification and reporting of HIV/AIDS cases. Therefore, when examining China's approach to health data management, it is crucial to consider these Western perceptions. They shape the global discourse on China's public health practices and can potentially impact international collaborations and policies. Trust and transparency in public health communication at the international level are of utmost importance. While it is essential to strive for accuracy in health data, it is equally important to understand the broader sociopolitical context in which this data is interpreted. This understanding is critical to fostering a more nuanced and constructive dialogue on global public health.

My research journey pauses here, but I am confident that new and exciting paths will be blazed in the future.

ACKNOWLEDGMENTS

This has been perhaps the most fascinating segment of my lifelong research journey in China. It is my account of interviews with male sex workers (MSWs), transgender sex workers (TSWs), male sex workers living with HIV, male and female clients of MSWs and TSWs, medical doctors, and a particularly unique subgroup called *tongqi*. *Tongqi* (同妻, literally "homowives") are women who have unwittingly married gay men hiding their sexual orientation. Each interviewee was part of a hard-to-find sample, and I cherished the chance to meet them and learn their stories. Although we began as strangers, we ended as friends. As I earned their trust and confidence, many of the MSWs and TSWs I met stated that they felt comfortable and safe talking to me. As a result, they shared their struggles, their stories, and even their secrets. My demeanor and professionalism facilitated the process of forming these friendships. Neither party ever engaged in flirting or inappropriate behavior. Our interactions were focused, honest, and mutually supportive.

I want to thank all those who helped bring this book to fruition. First and foremost, my deepest thanks go to the interviewees, whose courage and willingness to speak frankly and openly about their struggles have been inspiring. Their recollections provide remarkable insights about their lives beyond their occupation. We can better understand their journeys by examining their history, upbringing, social pressures, and occupational hazards, which in turn influence the stresses in their work, marriage relationships, and experiences with HIV. Those interviewed numbered 151 male sex workers, 57 male clients (bisexual/gay men), 27 female clients (heterosexual, single, married), 59 *tongqi*, 25 male sex workers living with HIV, 15 HIV doctors, 12 directors of NGOs, and 25 TSWs. The interviewees in this book provided fascinating and deeply precious insights about their lives, which helped carry me forward as an ethnographer, researcher, and writer. I am pleased to have maintained some friendships through WeChat and TikTok. Without their trust and help, this book would not have been possible. Their exciting stories vividly present life in the gay commercial sexscapes of China, which keeps my research journey rocking and forward looking.

An outstanding debt of thanks goes to my university classmates Herman and Lennon for their professional contacts and access to these communities. Herman allowed me to collect data as an unpaid bartender in his club. He facilitated meetings with a wide range of influential people across China, enabling me to complete the necessary fieldwork with access to a high-end bar. The long hours can sometimes take a toll emotionally, and I'm grateful that Herman provided a listening ear and much-needed emotional support. Thanks to his friendship and familiarity with both underground people and cadres, the fieldwork went smoothly and generally without incident. I owe him a great deal and am forever indebted to him.

I am grateful to Lennon, my research friend who is always there for me when I need his personal and professional knowledge to recommend some gay communities, *tongqi*, NGO directors, and medical doctors. I extend my heartfelt gratitude for his help in making this book possible.

I am also forever indebted to my friend Peter, who provided financial support for my doctoral studies when I was in England. As I was writing this book, he was my consultant, providing invaluable information and insights for me to finish this project. Peter updated me about practices, jargon, and terminology unique to gay communities. His knowledge and information indeed have been beneficial and constructive.

I would also like to thank my husband, Jeff, who spent many hours discussing my research and academic career trajectory. He also made sacrifices so I could chase after my dreams to write this book. He had to accept being without me for weekends, holidays, and vacation breaks during and throughout this effort. His help and editorial support have been precious and significant. I owe him for his support, comfort, laughter, and encouragement, particularly through the final stages of writing this book.

Finally, I am indebted to my parents for their support and forbearance. They also have endured my absences during weekends, holidays, and vacation breaks. I could not have completed this without everyone's contribution, care, and love. Thank you.

BIBLIOGRAPHY

Abidin, Crystal. 2018. "Internet Celebrity: Understanding Fame Online." Emerald Publishing.
An, Ti. 2005. "Xingsaorao Lifa Weihe Jie Funv Baohu Zhike" [Why the law of sexual harassment is placed under women's protection]. *Nanfang dushi bao* [South metropolitan newspaper], June 29, 1–11.
Asia Catalyst. 2015. "'My Life Is Too Dark to See the Light.' A Survey of the Living Conditions of Transgender Female Sex Workers in Beijing and Shanghai." asiacatalyst.org.
Baumann, Zygmunt. 1999. *Liquid Modernity*. Polity Press.
BBC. 2017. "Lele Tao: China's 'Online Goddess' on $450K a Year." www.bbc.co.uk.
———. 2021. "Covid-19 Pandemic: China 'Refused to Give Data' to WHO Team." www.bbc.com.
Berg, Rigmore C., Soll-Brit Molin, and Julie Nanavati. 2019. "Women Who Trade Sexual Services from Men: A Systematic Mapping Review." *Journal of Sex Research* 57 (1): 104–18.
Bergman, Kim, Richie J. Rubio, Robert-Jay Green, and Elena Padrón. 2010. "Gay Men Who Become Fathers via Surrogacy: The Transition to Parenthood." *Journal of GLBT Family Studies* 6 (2): 111–41.
Berkowitz, Dana. 2008. "A Sociohistorical Analysis of Gay Men's Procreative Consciousness." *Journal of GLBT Family Studies* 3 (2–3): 157–90.
Bernard, H. Russell. 2011. "Research Methods in Anthropology Qualitative and Quantitative Approaches." AltaMira.
Bernstein, Elizabeth. 2007. *Temporarily Yours: Intimacy, Authenticity and the Commerce of Sex*. University of Chicago Press.
Best, John, Weiming Tang, Ye Zhang, Larry Han, Fenying Liu, Shujie Huang, Bin Yang, Chongyi Wei, and Joseph D. Tucker. 2015. "Sexual Behaviors and HIV/Syphilis Testing among Transgender Individuals in China: Implications for Expanding HIV Testing Services." *Sexually Transmitted Diseases* 42 (5): 281–85.
Bie, Biejie, and Lu Tang. 2016. "Chinese Gay Men's Coming Out Narratives: Connecting Social Relationship to Co-cultural Theory." *Journal of International and Intercultural Communication* 9 (4): 351–67.
Blankenship, Kim M., Brooke S. West, Trace S. Kershaw, and Monica R. Biradavolu. 2008. "Power, Community Mobilization, and Condom Use Practices among Female Sex Workers in Andhra Pradesh, India." *AIDS* 22: S109–S16.

Bourdieu, Pierre. 1978. "Sport and Social Class." *Social Science Information* 17 (6): 819–40.
Brainer, Amy. 2019. *Queer Kinship and Family Change in Taiwan*. Rutgers University Press.
Brandth, Berit, and Marit S. Haugen. 2005. "Doing Rural Masculinity—From Logging to Outfield Tourism." *Journal of Gender Studies* 14 (1): 13–22.
Brents, Barbara G. 2016. "Neoliberalism's Market Morality and Heteroflexibility: Protectionist and Free Market Discourses in Debates for Legal Prostitution." *Sexuality Research and Social Policy* 13 (4): 402–16.
Bridges, Tristan, and Cheri J. Pasco. 2014. "Hybrid Masculinities: New Directions in the Sociology of Men and Masculinity." *Sociology Compass* 8 (3): 246–58.
Bryant, Antony, and Kathy Charmaz. 2007. *The SAGE Handbook of Grounded Theory*. Sage.
Buist, Carrie L., and Emily Lenning. 2015. *Queer Criminology*. Routledge.
Butler, Judith. 1990. "Gender Trouble. Feminism and the Subversion of Identity." Routledge.
———. 1993. *Bodies That Matter*. Routledge.
———. 2017. "Bodies That Matter." In *Feminist Theory and the Body*, edited by Janet Price and Margrit Shildrick. Routledge.
Cai, Yong, Zixin Wang, Joseph T. F. Lau, Jinghua Li, and Tiecheng Ma. 2016. "Prevalence and Associated Factors of Condomless Receptive Anal Intercourse with Male Clients among Transgender Women Sex Workers in Shenyang, China." *Journal of the International AIDS Society*, suppl. 3S2 (July): 1–11.
Cao, Wei, Evelyn Hsieh, and Taisheng Li. 2020. "Optimizing Treatment for Adults with HIV/AIDS in China: Successes over Two Decades and Remaining Challenges." *Current HIV/AIDS Reports* 17 (1): 26–34.
Chen, Bo-Wei, and Martin Mac An Ghaill. 2015. "Exploring Detraditionalisation through Gender Reflexivity in Late Modernity: The Negotiation of Family/Filial Responsibilities among Taiwanese (Younger) Professional Men." *Families, Relations and Societies* 4:449–64.
Chen, Runsen, Xuequan Zhu, Lucy Wright, Jack Drescher, Yue Gao, Lijuan Wu, Xin Ying, Ji Qi, Chen Chen, Yingjun Xi, Lanxin Ji, Huichun Zhao, Jianjun Ou, and Matthew R. Broome. 2019. "Suicidal Ideation and Attempted Suicide amongst Chinese Transgender Persons: National Population Study." *Journal of Affective Disorders* 245 (15): 1126–34.
Cheng, Fung Kei. 2016. "I Want to Come Forward." *Cogent Social Sciences* 2:1–8.
Chiang, Howard, ed. 2012. *Transgender China*. Springer.
Chiang, Howard, and Alvin K. Wong, eds. 2020. *Keywords in Queer Sinophone Studies*. Routledge.
China's Health and Family Planning Commission. 2018. Accessed July 31, 2020. www.avert.org/professionals/hiv-around-world/asia-pacific/china.
Choi, Susanne Y. P., and Ming Luo. 2016. "Performative Family: Homosexuality, Marriage and Intergenerational Dynamics in China." *British Journal of Sociology* 67 (2): 260–80.

Choi, Anna Wai-Man, Barbara Chuen-Yee Lo, Ruby Tsz-Fung Lo, Peter Yee-Lap To, and Janet Yuen-Ha Wong. 2019. "Intimate Partner Violence Victimization, Social Support, and Resilience: Effects on the Anxiety Levels of Young Mothers." *Journal of Interpersonal Violence* 36 (21/22): NP12299–NP12323.

Chou, Wah-Shan. 2000. *Tongzhi: Politics of Same-Sex Eroticism in Chinese Societies*. Haworth

———. 2003. "Homosexuality and the Cultural Politics of Tongzhi in Chinese Societies." *Journal of Homosexuality* 40 (3/4): 27–46.

Collin, Lindsay, Sari Reisner, Vin Tangpricha, and Michael Goodman. 2016. "Prevalence of Transgender Depends on the 'Case' Definition: A Systematic Review." *Journal of Sexual Medicine* 13 (4): 613–26.

Connell, Raewyn. 1995. *Masculinities*. Allen and Unwin.

———. "Masculinities and Globalization." 1998. *Men and Masculinities* 1 (1): 3–23.

Connell, Raewyn, and James W. Messerschmidt. 2005. "Hegemonic Masculinity: Rethinking the Concept." *Gender & Society* 19 (6): 829–59.

Connell, Raewyn, and Julian Wood. 2005. "Globalization and Business Masculinities." *Men and Masculinities* 7 (4): 347–64.

Corbin, Juliet, and Anselm Strauss. 1990. "Grounded Theory Research: Procedures, Canons, and Evaluative Criteria." *Qualitative Sociology* 13 (1): 3–21.

Courvant, Diana, and Loree Cook-Daniels. N.d. "Trans and Intersex Survivors of Domestic Violence: Defining Terms, Barriers and Responsibilities." Academia.edu. Accessed November 12, 2024. www.academia.edu.

Davies, Thom, Arshad Isakjee, and Surindar Dhesi. 2017. "Violent Inaction: The Necropolitical Experience of Refugees in Europe." *Antipode* 49:1263–84.

Deacon, Harriet J. 2006. "Towards a Sustainable Theory of Health-Related Stigma: Lessons from the HIV/AIDS Literature." *Journal of Community and Applied Psychology* 16 (6): 418–25.

Debrix, Francois. 2017. "Horror beyond Death: Geopolitics and the Pulverisation of the Human." *New Formations* 89/90:85–100.

Dennison-Hunt, S. 2007. "The SW5 Project. London, UK: UK Network of Sex Work Projects." *Journal of Interpersonal Violence* 20, no. 3 (March): 320–42.

Ding, Chunyan. 2015. "Surrogacy Litigation in China and Beyond." *Journal of Law and the Biosciences* 2 (1): 33–55.

Dozier, Raine. 2005. "Beards, Breasts, and Bodies." *Gender & Society* 19 (3): 297–316.

Driver, Felix, and Brenda S. Yeoh. 2000. "Constructing the Tropics." Special Issue. *Singapore Journal of Tropical Geography* 21 (1): 1–5.

Duggan, Lisa. 2002. "The Sexual Politics of Neoliberalism." In *Materializing Democracy: Toward a Revitalized Cultural Politics*, edited by R. Castronovo and D. Nelson. Duke University Press.

Duncan, Duane. 2010. "Embodying the Gay Self: Body Image, Reflexivity, and Embodied Identity." *Health Sociological Review* 19 (4): 437–50.

Duncan, James, S. 2000. "The Struggle to be Temperate: Climate and 'Moral Masculinity' in Mid-nineteenth Century Ceylon." *Singapore Journal of Tropical Geography* 21 (1): 34–47.

Duneier, Mitchell. 2011. "How Not to Lie with Ethnography." *Sociological Methodology* 41 (1): 1–11.
Economist. 2019. "Reported Cases of HIV in China are Rising Rapidly." www.economist.com.
Engebretsen, Elisabeth. 2014. "Queer Women in Urban China: An Ethnography." Routledge.
———. 2017. "Under Pressure: Lesbian-Gay Contract Marriages and Their Patriarchal Bargains." In *Transforming Patriarchy: Chinese Families in the Twenty-First Century*, edited by Gonçalo Santos and Stevan Harrell. University of Washington Press.
Farley, Melissa, and Howard B. Barkan. "Prostitution, Violence, and Posttraumatic Stress Disorder." *Women Health* 27, no. 3 (1998): 37–49.
Farley, Melissa, Jacqueline M. Golding, Emily S. Matthews, Neil. M. Malamuth, and Laura Jarrett. 2017. "Comparing Sex Buyers with Men Who Do Not Buy Sex: New Data on Prostitution and Trafficking." *Journal of Interpersonal Violence* 32 (23): 3601–25.
Farquh Choi, S., and M. Luo. 2016. "Performative Family: Homosexuality, Marriage and Intergenerational Dynamics in China." *British Journal of Sociology* 67 (2): 260–81.
Fonner, Virginia A., Deanna Kerrigan, Zandile Mnisi, Sosthenes Ketende, Caitlin E. Kennedy, and Stefan Baral. 2014. "Social Cohesion, Social Participation, and HIV Related Risk among Female Sex Workers in Swaziland." *PloS One* 9 (1): e87527.
Foucault, Michel. 1972. "The Discourse on Language." In *Truth: Engagements across Philosophical Traditions*, edited by Jose Medina and David Wood. Blackwell.
Friedrichs, David O. 2009. "Critical Criminology." *In 21st Century Criminology: A Reference Handbook*, edited by Mitchell, J. Miller. Sage.
Gao, Ming. "Unsettled 'Structure of Feeling' of Chinese Migrant Workers—Cases from the Service Sector of Shanghai." 2017. *Inter-Asia Cultural Studies* 18 (2): 281–301.
Gezinski, Lindsay B., Sharvari Karandikar, Alexis Levitt, and R. Ghaffarian. 2016. "'Total Girlfriend Experience': Examining Marketplace Mythologies on Sex Tourism Websites." *Culture, Health & Sexuality* 18 (7): 785–98.
Ghaziani, Amin. 2014. *There Goes the Gayborhood? An In-depth Look at America's Changing Gay Neighborhoods.* Princeton University Press.
Gilbert, Nigel, ed. 1993. *Research Social Life.* Sage.
Gill, R., K. Henwood, and C. Mclean. 2005. "Body Projects and the Regulation of Normative Masculinity." *Body and Society* 11 (1): 37–62.
Girschick, Lori. B. 2009. *Transgender Voices: Beyond Women and Men.* University Press of New England.
Glaser, Barney G., and Anselm L. Strauss. 2017. *Discovery of Grounded Theory: Strategies for Qualitative Research.* Routledge.
Global Times. 2018. "Lipstick King: The Man Who Sells Most Lipsticks in China." www.globaltimes.cn.

Goldwin, John. 2013. "Legal Protections against HIV-Related Human Rights Violations Experiences and Lessons Learned from National HIV Laws in Asia and the Pacific." United Nations Development Program, Bangkok, Thailand.

Gong, Jing, and Tingting Liu. 2022. "Decadence and Relational Freedom among China's Gay Migrants: Subverting Heteronormativity by 'Lying Flat.'" *China Information* 36 (2): 200–20.

Goparaju, Lakshmi, Nathan C. Praschan, Lari W. Jeanpiere, Laura S. Experton, Mary A. Young, and Seble Kassaye. 2017. "Stigma, Partners, Providers and Costs: Potential Barriers to PrEP Uptake among US Women." *Journal of AIDS Clinical Research* 8 (9): 730.

Guadalupe-Diaz, Xavier L. 2019. *Transgressed: Intimate Partner Violence in Transgender Lives*. New York University Press.

Guadalupe-Diaz, Xavier L., and Jana Jasinski. 2017. "'I Wasn't a Priority, I Wasn't a Victim': Challenges in Help Seeking for Transgender Survivors of Intimate Partner Violence." *Violence against Women* 23 (6): 772–92.

Guler, Ezgi. 2020. "Divided Sisterhood: Support Networks of Trans Sex Workers in Urban Turkey." *Annals of the American Academy*, no. 689 (May): 149–67.

Hafeez, Hudaisa, Muhammad Zeshan, Muhammad Tahir, Nusrat Jahan, and Sadiq Naveed. 2017. "Health Care Disparities among Lesbian, Gay, Bisexual, and Transgender Youth: A Literature Review." *Cureus* 9: e1184. doi:10.7759/cureus.1184.

Haritaworn, Jin, Adi Kuntsman, and Silvia Posocco, eds. 2014. *Introduction to Queer Necropolitics*. Routledge.

Hernández, Javier. 2017. "Ranting and Rapping Online in China and Raking in Millions." *New York Times*, September 15. www.nytimes.com.

Hines, Sally. 2006. "Intimate Transitions: Transgender Experiences of Partnering and Parenting." *Sociology* 40 (2): 353–71.

Ho, Loretta W. 2009. *Gay and Lesbian Subculture in Urban China*. Routledge.

Hoang, Kimberley K. 2010. "Economies of Emotion, Familiarity, Fantasy, and Desire: Emotional Labor in Ho Chi Minh City's Sex Industry." *Sexualities* 13 (2): 255–72.

———. 2015. *Dealing in Desire: Asian Ascendancy, Western Decline, and the Hidden Currencies of Global Sex Work*. University of California Press.

Hochschild, Arlie R. 2012. *The Managed Heart: Commercialization of Human Feeling*. University of California Press.

Hu, Lingshu. 2018. "Is Masculinity 'Deteriorating' in China? Change of Masculinity Representation in Chinese Film Posters from 1951 to 2016." *Journal of Gender Studies* 27 (3): 335–46.

Huang, Alice. 2020. "Who Is Millionaire Li Jiaqi, China's 'Lipstick King' Who Raised More Than US$145 Million in Sales on Singles' Day?" *Style*, March 9. www.scmp.com.

Huang Shuzhen and D. C. Brouwer. 2018. "Negotiating Performances of 'Real' Marriage in Chinese Queer Xinghun." *Women's Studies in Communication* 41 (2): 140–58.

Jagose, Annamarie. 1996. *Queer Theory: An Introduction*. New York University Press.

Jazeel, Tariq. 2014. "Subaltern Geographies: Geographical Knowledge and Postcolonial Strategy." *Singapore Journal of Tropical Geography* 35 (1): 88–103.

Jeffreys, Elaine. 2016. *Sex and Sexuality in China*. Routledge.

Jiang, Hua, Xian Wei, Xiaohai H. Zhu, Hui Wang, and Qing Feng Li. 2014. "Transgender Patients Need Better Protection in China." *Lancet* 384 (13–19): 2109–10.

Jin, Xiaoyi, Qiuju Guo, and Marcus W. Feldman. 2015. "Marriage Squeeze and Intergenerational Support in Contemporary Rural China: Evidence from X County of Anhui Province." *International Journal of Aging and Human Development* 80 (2): 115–39.

Johnson, Andrew A. 2007. "Authenticity Tourism, and Self-Discovery in Thailand: Self-Creation and the Discerning Gaze of Trekkers and Old Hands." *Journal of Social Issues in Southeast Asia* 22 (2): 153–78.

Jones, Angela. 2020. *Camming: Money, Power, and Pleasure in the Sex Work Industry*. New York University Press.

Jones, Julie. 2005. "Ageing Gay Men: Lessons from the Sociology of Embodiment." *Men and Masculinities* 7 (3): 248–60.

Joseph, Laura. J., and Pamela Black. 2012. "Who's the Man? Fragile Masculinities, Consumer Masculinities, and the Profiles of Sex Work Clients." *Men and Masculinities* 15 (5): 486–506.

Jung, Sun. 2011. *Korean Masculinities and Transcultural Consumption*. Hong Kong University Press.

Katsulis, Yasmina, and Alesha Durfee. 2012. "Prevalence and Correlates of Sexual Risk among Male and Female Sex Workers in Tijuana, Mexico." *Global Public Health* 7 (4): 367–83.

Kempadoo, Kamala. 2001. "Freelancers, Temporary Wives, and Beach-Boys: Researching Sex Work in the Caribbean." *Feminist Review*, no. 67 (March): 39–62.

Kerrigan, Deanna, Paulo Telles, Helena Torres, Cheryl Overs, and Christopher Castle. 2008. "Community Development and HIV/STI-Related Vulnerability among Female Sex Workers in Rio de Janeiro, Brazil." *Health Education Research* 23 (1): 137–45.

Kimmel, Michael S. 1994. "Masculinity as Homophobia: Fear, Shame and Silence in the Construction of Gender Identity." In *Theorizing Masculinities*, edited by H. Brod and M. Kaufman. Sage.

Kingston, Sarah, Natalie Hammond, and Scarlett Redman. 2020. *Women Who Buy Sex: Converging Sexualities?* Routledge.

Kipnis, Andrew. 2007. "Neoliberalism Reified: Suzhi Discourse and Tropes of Neoliberalism in the People's Republic of China." *Journal of the Royal Anthropological Institute* 13 (2): 383–400.

Kleinman, Arthur, Yunxiang Yan, Jing Jun, Sing Lee, Everett Zhang, Pan Tianshu, Wu Fei, and Guo Jinhua. 2011. *Deep China: The Moral Life of the Person*. Stanford University Press.

Kong, Travis S. K. 2009. *Chinese Male Homosexualities: Memba, Tongzhi and Golden Boy*. Routledge.

———. 2012a. "Reinventing the Self under Socialism: Migrant Male Sex Workers (Money Boys) in China." *Critical Asian Studies* 44 (2): 283–308.
———. 2912b. "Sex Entrepreneurs in the New China." *Contexts* 11 (3): 28–33.
———. 2017. "Sex and Work on the Move: Money Boys in Post-Socialist China." *Urban Studies* 54 (3): 678–94.
Landers, S., and P. Gilsanz. 2009. "The Health of Lesbian, Gay, Bisexual, and Transgender (LGBT) Persons in Massachusetts." Massachusetts Department of Public Health. www.mass.gov.
Lanzieri, Nicholas, and Tom Hildebrandt. 2011. "Using Hegemonic Masculinity to Explain Gay Male Attraction to Muscular and Athletic Men." *Journal of Homosexuality* 58 (2): 275–93.
Li, Anglia K. 2019. "Papi Jiang and Microcelebrity in China: A Multilevel Analysis." *International Journal of Communication* 13:3016–34.
Li, Ke. 2015. "What He Did Was Lawful: Divorce Litigation and Gender Inequality in China." *Law and Policy* 37 (3): 153–79.
Li, Ke, and Sara Friedman. 2016. "Wedding Marriage to the Nation-State in Modern China, Legal Consequences for Divorce, Property, and Women's Rights in Domestic Tensions." In *National Anxieties: Global Perspectives on Marriage, Crisis, and Nation*, edited by Kristin Celello and Hanan Kholoussy. Oxford University Press.
Li, Yinhe. 2006. "Regulating Male Same-Sex Relationships in the People's Republic of China." In *Sex and Sexuality in China*, edited by E. Jeffreys. Routledge.
Lin, Xiaoding. 2014. "'Filial Son,' the Family, and Identity Formation Among Male Migrant Workers in Urban China. *Gender, Place and Culture* 21 (6): 717–32.
Lin, Xiaodong, and M. Ghaill. 2017. "(Re)-Masculinizing 'Suzhi Jiaoyu' (Education for Quality): Aspirational Values of Modernity in Neoliberal China." In *Masculinity and Aspiration: International Perspectives in the Era of Neoliberal Education*, edited by Garth Stahl, Joseph Nelson, and Derron Wallace. Routledge.
Link, Bruce G., and Jo C. Phelan. 2006. "Stigma and Its Public Health Implications." *Lancet* 367 (9509): 528–29. doi:10.1016/s0140–6736(06)68184–1.
Liu, Hui, and Lindsey Wilkinson. 2017. "Marital Status and Perceived Discrimination among Transgender People." *Journal of Marriage and Family* 79 (5): 1295–1313.
Liu, Min. 2013. "Two Gay Men Seeking Two Lesbians: An Analysis of Xinghun (Formality Marriage) Ads on China's Tianya.cn." *Sexuality & Culture* 17:494–511.
Liu, Tingting, and Chris K. Tan. 2020. "On the Transactionalisation of Conjugal Bonds: A Feminist Materialist Analysis of Chinese Xinghun Marriages." *Anthropological Forum* 30 (4): 443–63.
Liu, Tingting, Chris K. Tan, and Miao Li. 2021. "Zhibo Gonghui China's 'Live Streaming Guilds' of Manipulation Experts." *Information, Communication and Society* 26 (6): 1210–25.
Lo, Iris P. 2020. "Family Formation among Lalas (Lesbians) in Urban China: Strategies for Forming Families and Navigating Relationships with Families of Origin." *Journal of Sociology* 56 (4): 629–45.

Louie, Kam. 2012. "Popular Culture and Masculinity Ideals in East Asia, with Special Reference to China." *Journal of Asian Studies* 71, no. 4 (November): 929–43.
———. 2014. *Chinese Masculinity in a Globalizing World*. Routledge.
Lowe, John, and Eileen Y. Tsang. 2018. "Securing Hong Kong's Identity in the Colonial Past: Strategic Essentialism and the Umbrella Movement." *Critical Asian Studies* 50 (4): 556–71.
Lyons, Tara, Andrea Krusi, Leslie Pierre, Thomas Kerr, Will Small, and Kate Shannon. 2017. "Negotiating Violence in the Context of Transphobia and Criminalization: The Experiences of Trans Sex Workers in Vancouver, Canada." *Qualitative Health Research* 27 (2): 182–90.
Mac an Ghaill, Martin, and Chris Haywood. 2007. *Gender, Culture and Society: Contemporary Masculinities and Femininities*. Palgrave Macmillan.
Mai, Nicola. 2017. "Mobile Orientations: An Autoethnography of Tunisian Professional Boyfriends." *Sexualities* 20 (4): 482–96.
Marwick, Alice E. 2013. *Status Update: Celebrity, Publicity, and Branding in the Social Media Age*. Yale University Press.
Mayblin, Lucy, Mustafa Wake, and Mohsen Kazemi. 2019. "Necropolitics and the Slow Violence of the Everyday: Asylum Seeker Welfare in the Postcolonial Present." *Sociology* 54:107–23.
Mbembe, Achille. 2003. "Necropolitics." *Public Culture* 15 (1): 11–40.
McClennen, Joan C., Anne. B. Summers, and Charles Vaughan. 2002. "Gay Men's Domestic Violence: Dynamics, Helpseeking Behaviors, and Correlates." *Journal of Gay and Lesbian Social Services* 14 (1): 23–49.
McKinnon, Sara L. 2016. "Necropolitical Voices and Bodies in the Rhetorical Reception of Iranian Women's Asylum Claims." *Communication and Critical/Cultural Studies* 13 (3): 215–31.
Messerschmidt, James W., Michael A. Messner, Raewyn Connell, and Patricia. Y. Martin. 2018. *Gender Reckonings*. New York University Press.
Milrod, Christine, and Ronald Weitzer. 2002. "The Intimacy Prism: Emotion Management among the Clients of Escorts." *Men and Masculinities* 15 (5): 447–67.
Minichiello, Victor, and John Scott, eds. 2014. *Male Sex Work and Society*. Harrington Park.
Minichiello, Victor, Jone Scott, and Denton Callander. 2013. "New Pleasures and Old Dangers: Reinventing Male Sex Work." *Journal of Sex Research* 50 (3/4): 263–75.
Monto, Martin A., and Norma Hoteling. 2001. "Predictors of Rape Myth Acceptance among Male Clients of Female Street Prostitutes." *Violence against Women* 7 (3): 275–93.
Monto, Martin A., and Christine Milrod. 2014. "Ordinary or Peculiar Men? Comparing the Customers of Prostitutes with a Nationally Representative Sample of Men." *International Journal of Offender Therapy and Comparative Criminology* 58 (7): 802–20.
Mountford, Tom. 2010. "The Legal Status and Position of Lesbian, Gay, Bisexual, and Transgender People in the People's Republic of China." International Gay and Lesbian Human Rights Commission. https://outrightinternational.org.

Murray, Stuart J. 2008. "Thanatopolitics: Reading in Agamben a Rejoinder to Biopolitical Life." *Communication and Critical/Cultural Studies* 5 (2): 203–7.
National Bureau of Statistics of China. 2017–19. *China Statistical Year Book*. www.stats.gov.cn.
Niccolai, Linda M., Elizabeth J. King, Ksenia U. Eritsyan, Liliya Safiullina, and Maria M. Rusakova. 2013. "'In Different Situations, in Different Ways': Male Sex Work in St. Petersburg, Russia." *Culture, Health and Sexuality* 15 (4): 480–93.
Nichols, Andrea. 2010. "Dance Ponnaya, Dance! Police Abuses against Transgender Sex Workers in Sri Lanka." *Feminist Criminology* 5 (2): 195–222.
Okanlawon, Kehinde, Ayo S. Adebowale, and Ayotunde Titilayo. 2013. "Sexual Hazards, Life Experiences and Social Circumstances among Male Sex Workers in Nigeria." *Culture, Health and Sexuality* 15 (suppl. 1): 22–33.
Pan, Suiming. 2006. "Transformations in the Primary Life Cycle: The Origins and Nature of China's Sexual Revolution." In *Sex and Sexuality in China*, edited by E. Jeffrey. Routledge.
Pan, Suiming, and Aili Wang. 2004. *Dangdai Zhongguoren de xingxingwei yu xingguanxi* [Sexual behavior and relation in contemporary China]. Social Sciences Documentation Publishing House.
Pan, Suiming, and Rui Yang. 2004. *Xing'ai shinian: Quanguo daxuesheng xingxingwei de zhuizong diaocha* [Sexuality of Chinese college students: A ten-year longitudinal nationwide random study]. Social Sciences Documentation Publishing House.
Peng, Yen Wen. 2007. "Buying Sex: Domination and Difference in the Discourses of Taiwanese Piao-ke." *Men and Masculinities* 9 (3): 315–36.
Pettinger, Lynne. 2013. "Market Moralities in the Field of Commercial Sex." *Journal of Cultural Economy* 6 (2): 184–99.
Puar, Jasbir. 2007. *Terrorist Assemblages: Homonationalism in Queer Times*. Duke University Press, 2007.
———. 2013. "Rethinking Homonationalism." *International Journal of Middle East Studies* 45:336–52.
Qian, Yue., and Zhenchao Qian. 2014. "The Gender Divide in Urban China: Single-Hood and Assortative Mating by Age and Education." *Demographic Research* 31:art. 45.
Qiao, Shan, Eileen Y. Tsang, Jeffrey S. Wilkinson, and Freddy Lipeleke. 2019. "'In Zimbabwe There Is Nothing for Us': Sex Work and Vulnerability of HIV Infection among Male Sex Workers in Zimbabwe." *AIDS Care Psychological and Socio-Medical Aspects of AIDS/HIV* 31(9): 1124–30.
Rabinow, Paul. 2007. *Marking Time: On the Anthropology of the Contemporary*. Princeton University Press.
Ren, Zhengjia, Catherine Q. Howe, and Wei Zhang. 2019. "Maintaining 'Mianzi' and 'Lizi': Understanding the Reasons for Formality Marriages between Gay Men and Lesbians in China." *Transcultural Psychiatry* 56 (19): 213–32.
Rich, Adrienne. 1980. "Compulsory Heterosexuality and Lesbian Existence." *Signs* 5 (4): 631–60.

Richards, Christina., Walter P. Bouman, L. Seal, M. J. Barker, T. O. Nieder, and G. T'Sjoen. 2016. "Non-binary or Genderqueer Genders." *International Review of Psychiatry* 28 (1): 95–102.

Riessman, Catherine K. 1993. *Narrative Analysis*. Sage.

Rivers-Moore, Megan. 2012. "Almighty Gringos: Masculinity and Value in Sex Tourism." *Sexualities* 15 (7): 850–70.

———. 2016. *Gringo Gulch Sex, Tourism, and Social Mobility in Costa Rica*. University of Chicago Press.

Rofel, Lisa. 2007. *Desiring China: Experiments in Neoliberalism, Sexuality and Public Culture*. Duke University Press.

———. 2010. "The Traffic in Money Boys." *Positions* 18 (2): 425–58.

Round, John, and Irina Kuznetsova. 2016. "Necropolitics and the Migrant as a Political Subject of Disgust: The Precarious Everyday of Russia's Labour Migrants." *Critical Sociology* 42 (7–8): 1017–34.

Rubin, Henry. 2004. *Self-Made Men: Identity and Embodiment Among Transsexual Men*. Vanderbilt University Press.

Sanders, Teela. 2008. "Male Sexual Scripts: Intimacy, Sexuality and Pleasure in the Purchase of Commercial Sex." *Sociology* 42 (3): 400–17.

Sassatelli, Roberta. 2000. "From Value to Consumption. A Social-Theoretical Perspective on Simmel's Philosophie des Geldes." *Acta Sociologica* 43 (3): 207–18.

Scambler, Graham. 1009. "Stigma and Disease: Changing Paradigms." *Lancet* 352 (9133): 1054–55. doi:10.1016/s0140-6736(98)08068-4.

———. 2018. "Heaping Blame on Shame: 'Weaponising Stigma' for Neoliberal Times." *Sociological Review Monographs* 66 (4): 766–82.

Schilt, Kristen. 2006. "Just One of the Guys: How Transmen Make Gender Visible at Work." *Gender & Society* 20 (4): 465–90.

Senft, Theresa. 2008. *Camgirls: Celebrity and Community in the Age of Social Media*. Peter Lang.

Shao Yiming and Zhong Weijia. 2012. "Challenges and Opportunities for HIV/AIDS Control in China." *Lancet* 379 (9818): 803–4.

Shi, Wei. 1993. "Fear As Political Dynamics." *Inter-Asia Cultural Studies* 20 (1): 19–38.

Shilling, Chris. 1993. *The Body and Social Theory*. Sage.

Sidaway James, Yeoh Brenda, and Bunnell Tim. 2018. "Introduction to a Virtual Special Issue—Postcolonial and Post-tropical Geography." *Singapore Journal of Tropical Geography* 39 (3): 328–31.

Singer, Burton, and Carol D. Ryff. 2001. "Person-Centered Methods for Understanding Aging: The Integration of Numbers and Narratives." In *Handbook of Aging and the Social Sciences*, edited by Robert. H. Binstock and Linda. K. George. Academic.

Smit, Peter J., Michael Brady, Michael Carter, Ricardo Fernandes, Lance Lamore, Michael Meulbroek, Michel Ohayon, Tom Platteau, Peter Rehberg, Jurgen K. Rockstroh, and Marc Thompson. 2011. "HIV-Related Stigma within Communities of Gay Men: A Literature Review." *AIDS Care* 24 (3–4): 405–12.

Smith, Michael D., and Christian Grov. 2011. *In The Company of Men: Inside the Lives of Male Prostitutes*. Praeger, 2011.
Song, G., and Tracy Lee. 2012. "'New Man' and 'New Lad' with Chinese Characteristics? Cosmopolitanism, Cultural Hybridity and Men's Lifestyle Magazines in China." *Asian Studies Review* 36 (3): 345–67.
Song, Geng, and D. Hird. 2014. *Men and Masculinities in Contemporary China*. Brill.
Song, Jingyi. 2016. "Wives in Sham Marriages Hidden in the Shadows." *China Daily*, April 22. www.chinadaily.com.cn.
South China Morning Post. 2017. "How Gay Chinese Hide Their Relationships behind 'Sham Marriages.'" April 29. www.scmp.com.
Steier, Frederick.1991. "Introduction: Research as Self-Reflexivity, Self-Reflexivity as Social Process." In *Research and Reflexivity*, edited by F. Steier. Sage.
Swider, Sarah. 2015. *Building China: Informal Work and the New Precariat*. Cornell University Press.
Symons, Donald. 1979. *The Evolution of Human Sexuality*. Oxford University Press.
Tan, Chris K. 2014. "Rainbow Belt: Singapore's Gay Chinatown as a Lefebvrian Space." *Urban Studies* 52 (12): 2203–18.
———. 2016. "Gaydar: Using Skilled Vision to Spot Gay 'Bears' in Taipei." *Anthropological Quarterly* 89 (3): 841–64.
Tan, Chris K., and Jiayu Shi. 2021. "Virtually Girlfriends: 'Emergent Femininity' and the Women Who Buy Virtual Loving Services in China." *Information, Communication & Society* 24 (15): 2229–44.
Tan, Chris K., and Zhiwei Xu. 2020. "Virtually Boyfriends: The 'Social Factory' and Affective Labor of Male Virtual Lovers in China." *Information, Communication & Society* 23 (11): 555–69.
Tan, Eng Kiong. 2013. *Rethinking Chineseness: Translational Sinophone Identities in the Nanyang Literary World*. Cambria.
Tang, Lu, Cui Meadows, and Li Hongmei. 2019. "How Gay Men's Wives in China Practice Co-cultural Communication: Culture, Identity, and Sensemaking." *Journal of International and Intercultural Communication* 13 (1): 13–31.
Tang, Songyuan, Weiming Tang, Katherine Myers, Po Lin Chan, Zhongdan Chen, and Joseph. D. Tucker. 2016. "HIV and Syphilis among Men Who Have Sex with Men and Transgender Individuals in China: A Scoping Review." Special issue. *Lancet* 388 (574).
Taylor, Sanchez J. 2001. "Dollars Are a Girl's Best Friend? Female Tourists' Sexual Behaviour in the Caribbean." *Sociology* 35 (3): 749–64.
Threadcraft, Shatema. 2017. "North American Necropolitics and Gender: On #BlackLivesMatter and Black Femicide." *South Atlantic Quarterly* 116 (3): 553–79.
Tsai, Kellee S. 2007. *Capitalism without Democracy: The Private Sector in Contemporary China*. Cornell University Press.
Tsang, Eileen Y. 2014. *The New Middle Class in China, Consumption, Politics and The Market Economy*. Palgrave Macmillan.

———. 2017. "Neither 'Bad' nor 'Dirty': High-End Sex Work and Intimate Relationships in Urban China." *China Quarterly* 230 (June): 444–63.

———. 2018. "Finding Hope as a 'Tempting Girl' in China: Sex Work, Indentured Mobility, and Cosmopolitan Individuals." *Deviant Behavior* 39 (7): 896–909.

———. 2019. "Erotic Authenticity: Comparing Intimate Relationships between High-End Bars and Low-End Bars in China's Global Sex Industry." *Deviant Behavior* 40 (4): 461–475.

———. 2019a. *China's Commercial Sexscapes: Rethinking Intimacy, Masculinities and Criminal Justice in China's Commercial Sex Industry*. University of Toronto Press.

———. 2019b. "Being Bad to Feel Good: China's Migrant Men, Displaced Masculinity, and the Commercial Sex Industry." *Journal of Contemporary China* 29 (122) (2019): 221–37.

———. 2019c. "Real Men Get the Best Bar Girls: Performing Masculinities in China's Global Sex Industry." *Deviant Behavior* 40 (5) (2019): 559–73.

———. 2019d. "Selling Sex as an Edgework: Risk Taking and Thrills in China's Commercial Sex Industry." *International Journal of Offender Therapy and Comparative Criminology* 63 (8) (2019): 1306–29

———. 2020. "China's 'Money Boys' and HIV for the Greater Good: The Queer Body and Necropolitics." *American Journal of Biomedical Science* 7 (5): 421–22.

———. 2021a. "Transformative Emotional Labor, Cosmetic Surgery, and Masculinity: Rural/Urban Migration in China's Gay Commercial Sex Industry." *Singapore Journal of Tropical Geography* 42 (3) (2021): 469–83.

———. 2021b. "A 'Phoenix' Rising from the Ashes: China's Tongqi, Marriage Fraud, and Resistance." *British Journal of Sociology* 72 (3): 793–807.

Tsang, Eileen Y., John Lowe, Jeffrey S. Wilkinson, and Graham Scambler. 2018. "Peasant Sex Workers in Metropolitan China and the Pivotal Concept of Money: A Sociological Investigation." *Asian Journal of Social Science* 46 (3): 359–80.

Tsang, Eileen Y., Shan Qiao, Jeffrey S. Wilkinson, Freddy Lipeleke, and Xiaoming Li. 2019. "Multilayered Stigma and Vulnerabilities for HIV Infection and Transmission: A Qualitative Study on Male Sex Workers in Zimbabwe." *American Journal of Men's Health* 13:1–11.

Tsang, Eileen Y., Jeffrey S. Wilkinson, Jerf W. Yeung, Jacky C. Cheung, Raymond K. Chan, David Norton, and C. Y. Yeung. 2020. "Dead End of the Rainbow: How Environmental and Spatial Factors Create a Necropolis for Gay Sex Workers in China." *Deviant Behavior* 42 (8): 993–1007.

Vanwesenbeeck, Ine. 2013. "Prostitution Push and Pull: Male and Female Perspectives." *Journal of Sex Research* 50 (1): 11–16.

Wagner, Phillip E. 2016. "Picture Perfect Bodies: Visualizing Hegemonic Masculinities Produces for/by Male Fitness Spaces." *International Journal of Men's Health* 15 (3): 235–58.

Wang, Stephanie Y. 2017. *Gender, Dating, and Violence in Urban China*. Routledge, 2017.

———. 2019. "When Tongzhi Marry: Experiments of Cooperative Marriage between Lalas and Gay Men in Urban China." *Feminist Studies* 45 (1): 13–35.

---. 2020. "Live Streaming, Intimate Situations, and the Circulation of Same-Sex Affect: Monetizing Affective Encounters on Blued." *Sexualities* 23 (5–6): 934–50.
Wang, Yuanyuan, Amanda Wilson, Runsen Chen, Hu Zhishan, Ke Peng, and Xu Shicun. 2020. "Behind the Rainbow, 'Tongqi' Wives of Men Who Have Sex with Men in China: A Systematic Review." *Frontiers in Psychology* 10:2929.
Wang, Zheng. 2014. "The Chinese Dream: Concept and Context." *Journal of Chinese Political Science* 19:1–13.
Ward, Jane. 2015. *Not Gay: Sex between Straight White Men*. New York University Press.
Wei, Wei, and Siqing Cai. 2012. "Exploring a New Relationship Model and Lifestyle: A Study of the Partnership and Family Practice among Gay Couples in Chengdu." *Chinese Journal of Sociology* 32 (6): 57–85.
Wen, Hua. 2013. *Buying Beauty: Cosmetic Surgery in China*. Hong Kong University Press.
Wolkowitz, Carol, R. L. Cohen, Teeka Sanders, and Kate Hardy, eds. 2013. *Body/Sex/Work: Intimate, Embodied and Sexualised Labour*. Palgrave Macmillan.
Wood, Mitchell J. 2004. "The Gay Male Gaze: Body Image Disturbance and Gender Oppression among Gay Men." *Journal of Gay & Lesbian Social Services* 17 (2): 43–62.
World Health Organization. 2002. *World Report on Violence and Health*, 169–89.
Wright, Melissa W. 2011. "Necropolitics, Narcopolitics and Femicide: Gendered Violence on the Mexico–US Border." *Signs* 36 (3): 707–31.
Xie, Yu, and Xiaogang Wu. 2008. "Danwei Profitability and Earnings Inequality in Urban China." *China Quarterly* 19:558–81.
Yan, Yunxiang. 2003. *Private Life under Socialism: Love, Intimacy, and Family Change in a Chinese Village, 1949–1999*. Stanford University Press.
---. 2010. "The Chinese Path to Individualization." *British Journal of Sociology* 61 (3): 489–512.
Yang, Jie. 2010. "The Crisis of Masculinity: Class, Gender, and Kindly Power in Post-Mao China." *American Ethnologist* 37 (3): 550–62.
Yimei Zixun. 2021 *Zhongguo zaixian zhibo hangye niandu yanjiu baogao* [Live streaming in China]. 163.com, April. www.163.com/dy/article/G57R8DN00511A1Q1.html.
Zhang, B. C., Y. Li, X. F. Li, X. H. Li, P. H. Yu, and Z. Z. Yu. 2015. "The Health Status and Associated Factors of Women Having Regular Sexual Relationships with Men Who Have Sex with Men." *Chinese Journal of Human Sexuality* 24:119–23.
Zhao, Tianming, Liu Haixia, Gabriella Bulloch, Zhen Jiang, Zhaobing Cao, and Wu Zunyou. 2023. "The Influence of the COVID-19 Pandemic on Identifying HIV/AIDS Cases in China: An Interrupted Time Series Study." *Lancet Regional Health* 36 (100755): 1.
Zheng, Tiantian. 2008. "Complexity of Life and Resistance: Informal Networks of Rural Migrant Karaoke Bar Hostesses in Urban China's Sex Industry." *China: An International Journal* 6 (1): 69–95.
---. 2015. *Tongzhi Living Men Attracted to Men in Postsocialist China*. University of Minnesota Press.

Zheng, Weijun, Zhou Xudong, Chi Zhou, Wei Liu, Lu Li, and Therese Hesketh. 2011. "Detraditionalisation and Attitudes to Sex outside Marriage in China." *Culture, Health & Sexuality* 13 (5): 497–511.

Zhu, Jingshu. 2018. "'Unqueer' Kinship? Critical Reflections on 'Marriage Fraud' in Mainland China." *Sexualities* 21 (7): 1075–91.

INDEX

Acquired Immunodeficiency Syndrome (AIDS), 34, 101–2, 114–15, 145–46; cases and figures on, 163; healing from, 158; living with, 113; patients with, 34, 154; prevention methods for, 141
activists, LGBTQ+, 4
advocacy groups, LGBTQ+, 38
advocates: arrested, 4, 38; educational initiatives by, 33; LGBTQ+ community supported by, 36; police questioning, 38
aesthetic surgery, 60–61
affective labor, by migrants, 28, 54
agency (*jingjiren*), 197
Ai (emperor), 1
AIDS. *See* Acquired Immunodeficiency Syndrome
alcohol, drugs and, 168, 175, 177
architecture, in Tianjin, 12
"ass fucker specialists" (*caopi zhuanjia*), 45
at-risk population, high-risk behaviors by, 9

baoyang (full package services), 191
BDSM. *See* bondage, discipline, dominance and submission, sadomasochism
Beijing (China), 44, 51, 95, 119, 133, 162
bigfish. *See* clients
biopolitics, 10, 23, 28; bio-value and, 166; control and, 9, 150, 155, 158, 164–65; measures of, 9, 164–65, 199; modes of, 164; necropolitics and, 149, 165, 198–99; power and, 145
biopolitics surveillance, 9
birth-giving machine, 92

bisexual men, 159, 165
bisexuals, 1, 9, 50, 58, 95, 119–20
bishon (Japan's pretty boy), 57
black enemies (*heiwulei*), 2
bloodlines, 87, 104; extending, 79, 98, 117; inheritance and, 151. *See also* parents
blue-collar jobs, 55
Blued (app and website), 37, 47, 92, 131, 167
body awareness, 65
body capital, 61, 66
body image, 52–53
body issues, 64
body massages, 127
body shaming, 177
body shape, 194
body training, 56
body types, 63
bondage, discipline, dominance and submission, sadomasochism (BDSM), 85; clients seeking, 132; fantasy and, 122, 131; MSWs and, 58, 121, 132; sexually aggressive and dominating, 124
botox, 47, 52, 58–89, 123, 193
Bourdieu, Pierre, 55
bribes, 5, 69, 147, 150
bullying, 109, 169, 171, 178
'*bunfun paidui*' (Chem-fun parties), 175
bureaucracy, 166

cadres (government officers), 145, 147, 154–55
Caihong Jiayuan Xinghun Huzhu Jiaoyou Douban Xiaozu (The Rainbow Families Xinghun Mutual Help Friendship Douban Group), 93

Cambodia, 93
Cantonese, 43
caopi zhuanjia ("ass fucker specialists"), 45
Cartier, 123
Center for Disease Control (CDC), 31–32, 146, 152, 154, 162
Chanel, 123
Chaozhou (Guangdong, China), 137
cheap male prostitute (*pingya*), 178
Chem-fun parties (*'bunfun paidui'*), 175
Chengdu (Sichuan, China), 162, 194–95, 197
children who follow mother into re-marriage (*tuoyouping*), 100
China. *See* People's Republic of China
China dream, 165, 198, 200
Chinagayles.com (online mating website), 77, 93
China Wives of Gay Men Mutual Aid Studio (*Tongqi huyuan gongzuoshi*), 115
Chinese Communist Party, 144
Chinese opera, 12, 67, 167, 195
Chinese police, 5, 36, 38, 121, 193
Chongqing (Chinese direct-administered city), 44
cisgender, 2–3, 72
cities, 59, 71, 117, 144, 186; citizenship status in, 198; gay citizens in, 149, 201; gay communities accepted in, 18; gendered citizenship in, 165, 199; household registration system in, 115; large southern, 10; marginalized citizens in, 147, 155; Migration to, 25; model citizens in, 11; in North China, 102; precarious citizens in, 166; second-class citizenship in, 18, 149; traditional masculine Chinese citizenship and, 165. *See also specific cities*
citizenship, second-class, 18, 149
citizenship status, in cities, 198
clients (*bigfish*), 49–52, 64–65, 126–30, 142, 190–92; BDSM sought by, 132;

clubs protecting, 121; emotional abuse from, 19; female, 26–27, 36–37, 119–22, 134–36, 139–41; foreign, 132; HIV and, 154, 166; keeping, 58–60; male, 26–27, 36, 120–21; middle class, 61; non-Chinese, 46; old, 67
clubhouses, 30, 32, 181
clubs, 5, 49, 74–75, 123, 126; buying sex at, 130; clients protected by, 121; excitement and allure of, 13–14; full-time and "guest" workers at, 45–46; gay, 11, 125; sauna, 7; underground dance, 9. *See also* gay bars
coming out, 51; gay husbands and, 106; as MSWs, 152, 166; negative response to, 88–91; to parents or family, 66, 76, 78, 86, 105, 143, 151; positive experiences of, 90; Western narratives of, 18; to wives, 106, 124
commercial sex industry, 28, 71, 131, 191–92, 200–201; male-to-male, 20; urban gay, 27, 54, 63; workplace discrimination in, 186
companionship, 41, 47, 121–22, 134–36, 188
condom use, 139–41, 173
Confucianism, 18, 21, 57, 76–78, 87, 97, 98
connections (*guanxi*), 10, 28, 31, 42, 47, 50, 75, 120, 149; social bonds, 99; social cohesion, 173; social networks, 41, 181; social relationship, 19, 142; social unity, 35
Connell, Raewyn, 16, 53, 172–73
contract marriage. *See* nominal marriage (*xinghun*)
control, pleasure through, 122, 132–34, 135–39, 140
cooperative marriage, 75, 79
cosmetic products, 40, 56–61, 69, 122, 182, 197; botox, 47, 52, 58–89, 123, 193; whitening facial creams, 59
cosmetic surgery, 24, 27, 57, 79; aesthetic, 60, 61; on chins, 52, 59; on eyelids, 52, 59, 122, 193; face-slimming needle, 59,

193; invasive, 61; liposuction and, 122, 193; on noses, 46, 52, 58, 122, 193, 197; whitening needle, 59, 69. *See also* face-slimming needle
cosmopolitan identity, 21
cosmopolitanism, 20, 24, 52, 59–60, 62, 79, 176
cosmopolitan lifestyle, 52, 62
cosmopolitan look, 55
cosmopolitan luxury accouterments, 200
counseling, 111–13, 117, 146, 153; for emotional support, 121, 169, 172–73, 201; for personal support, 182; as safe space, 187, 201; services, 166, 169, 183, 187, 201
COVID-19, 26, 66, 162–63, 189, 191
cultural expectations, 85–88
Cultural Revolution, 2, 198

dagongzai (working-class man), 34, 55
Dalian rotation, 50
dating apps, 96, 130, 167–68, 175
dating sites, 62, 92
death worlds, 23, 148, 165–66, 198
"desiring China," 20, 80
destigmatization, 185, 200, 201
divorce, 94, 106–16, 143; cooperation during, 136–37; in-court, 99, 106, 108; laws, 36, 89, 100, 118; out-of-court, 78, 96, 106, 108–9; perceptions of, 104; stigma against, 106, 111; *tongqi* impacted by, 114–15
divorce agreements, 107
domestic violence, 3, 99–100, 118
Dongguan, in Guangdong (China), 29, 31
Douban (app), 93, 102
Douyin (version of TikTok), 190, 192–93
dress (*qipao*), 176
drug addiction, sex work in connection with, 28
drug dealers, 133, 151
drugs, 43, 140, 179; abuse of, 19, 35, 200; alcohol and, 168, 175, 177; buying, 168; carrying, 68; HIV treated with, 101; illicit, 3, 148; money for, 181; smuggling, 28; taking, 69, 137, 140, 150–52, 176; using, 149, 153, 155, 199; vaccines and, 146
Duneier, Mitch, 188
dushili nan (urban man with beauty), 60

ecommerce, 189–90, 192
economic mobility, sex work enabling, 72
edgework, 121, 192
efavirenz, 158
emigration, 49, 201
emotional abuse, 112, 114, 120, 129; from clients, 19; control through, 178; damage of, 186; emotional blackmail and, 84; risk and, 68
emotional labor, 25–26, 52–53, 62–68, 70, 201; intimacy through, 127; by MSWs, 27, 72; online sales industry and, 189; private emotions and, 54, 150, 179; sex work and, 71
Emperor Ai (Ancient China king), 1–2
England, 5–6, 104
entrepreneurs, 50, 79, 134
erotic capital, 21, 24, 56, 61
E-Smarts, 192

face (*mianzi*), losing, 81–83, 84, 85–87, 151
face-slimming needle (*shoumianzhen*), 59, 193
false marriage certificate, 96
fantasies of intimacy, 136
feiwu (scum), 152
female line managers, 51
female sexuality, 135
female sex workers (FSWs), 5, 20, 29, 46, 121–22, 171–73
femininity, 60, 79, 176, 179
feminism, 16, 122
fetishes, 45, 54, 85
filial piety, 21, 27, 36, 70, 74–78, 96–98; obligations and, 75, 88, 92, 117, 167; responsibility and, 87

financial exploitation, 179–80
fitness, MSWs emphasizing, 33, 56–57
floating populations (*liudong renkou*), 34
flower-like men (*huayang-nanzi*), 60
Foucault, Michel, 9, 172
Four Free One Care policy, 146
fraud marriages, 104–5, 116, 201–2
FSWs. *See* female sex workers
full package services (*baoyang*), 191

gangs, 2, 73, 108, 169, 183, 193
gay bars, 19, 39, 75, 131, 192, 201; culture of, 6–14; as gay spaces, 21, 56; high-end, 11–12, 15, 26–27, 31, 45, 176, 189, 193; in Tianjin, 6–11, 31, 44–46, 95; urban, 70
gay citizens, in cities, 149, 201
gay communities, 114, 162, 166, 194, 201; cities accepting, 18; cosmetic surgery in, 61; culture of, 1, 10, 21, 52; femininity accepted in, 60; lesbians in, 16, 96; as "living dead," 26; masculinity in, 54; men in, 11, 16, 77, 95, 96, 106; middle-class, 54–55, 156; migrants in, 18, 199; naked yoga practiced in, 63; NGOs helping, 33, 44; stigma toward, 10, 26, 117, 146; urban, 24, 53–56; in Western countries, 53; women in, 11, 16, 77, 95, 96, 106
gay culture, 21, 52–53
gay economy (pink-pound), 30, 47, 53
gay-friendly social media, government cracking down on, 9
gay husbands, coming out and, 106
gay marriage, 93, 114
gayness, 198
gay prostitution, 49
gay relationships, 106
gay rural migrants, 200–201
gays: historical relationship between China and, 1–5; lesbians marrying, 79, 87, 95, 106
gay sex workers, 2–3, 15, 66, 99, 144, 200

gender: equality, 16; heteronormativity and, 79, 172; hierarchy, 172; sexuality and, 3, 28, 97, 165
gender affirmation surgery, 170
gender and sexual movements, 18
gendered citizenship, in cities, 165, 199
gender identity, 11, 36, 170, 172, 184–85; gender nonconforming, 165, 169; nonbinary, 171; nonconforming, 37, 164; stigma and, 184. *See also* transgender people
gender order, and heteronormativity, 7
gender reassignment breast surgery, 193
geopolitical tensions, 17
girlfriend, renting of, 83–85
gogo boy (gay sex workers in Thailand), 66
golden leftover lady, 138
GONGOs. *See* government-owned nongovernmental organizations
government (China), 5, 162–63, 166–71, 183–88; calls and text messages monitored by, 43; gay-friendly social media cracked down on by, 9; LGBTQ+ communities decriminalized by, 2, 4; MSWs marginalized by, 19, 144–45, 152, 164; queer community marginalized by, 38, 147; stigma and, 152, 158
government-owned nongovernmental organizations (GONGOs), 31–32
Grindr (gay-oriented app), 47
Guangdong (China), 50, 137, 191
Guan Gong (warlord), 8
Guangzhou, Guangdong province (China), 50, 137, 191
guanxi. *See* connection
Gucci, 123

HAART. *See* Highly Active Anti-Retroviral Therapy
Haihe river, 12, 44
Hainan (China), 50

Harbin (Heilongjiang, China), 34
Haritaworn, Jin, 23, 147
health-care system (Chinese): doctors, 70, 95, 159–64; medical system and, 143–44, 156–57, 165; public, 3, 22, 73, 105, 114, 153, 163, 166, 170. *See also* HIV
hedonism, 142
hegemonic masculinity, 16, 53, 62, 154, 172; defined, 133; urban standards of maleness, 27, 54
Heilongjiang (China), 44, 49, 74, 89
heiwulei (black enemies), 2
Hermes, 123, 140
heteronormativity, 4, 10, 17, 83, 133, 149; compartmentalization and, 134; gender and, 79, 172; gender order and, 7; heterosexism and, 11, 169, 172; household registration system and, 200; non-, 2; reinforced, 114; resisting, 18; in society, 10, 199; values of, 1
heterosexism, heteronormativity and, 11, 169, 172
heterosexual: families, 24, 106; girls, 86, 93; hegemony, 165, 198; marriages, 17, 31, 75, 114; masculinity, 79; monogamous intimacy, 79; norms, 3, 199; populations, 10; top role, 13
heterosexuality, 1, 27, 37, 76, 105
heterosexual women married to gay men (*tongqi*), 2–5, 10, 36, 99–106, 109–19; high-risk behaviors and, 105; HIV and, 22; IPV reported by, 103; legal system disadvantaging, 112; lesbians and, 27; LGBTQ+ community and, 22; of MSWs, 10, 25–26, 32, 35; NGOs approached by, 115; stigma against, 104
high-end bar, 12, 26–27, 45, 176, 193
highest interest rate (*luodai*), 197
Highly Active Anti-Retroviral Therapy (HAART), 34, 145
high-risk behaviors, 37, 68, 146, 158, 161, 164, 198; by at-risk population, 9; heterosexual women married to gay men and, 105; HIV and, 105, 116, 144; public health and, 22
high-risk groups, 33, 201
HIV (human immunodeficiency virus), 3, 32, 40; carriers of, 9, 144, 148, 158, 164; clients and, 154, 166; contracting, 19, 22, 27 101, 105, 109, 114, 145, 150, 152, 154, 159–61, 199; data on, 152, 163; dealing with, 113; doctors for, 26, 30, 34, 43, 48, 144, 160–61; drugs treating, 101; as epidemic, 158; heterosexual women married to gay men and, 22; high-risk behaviors and, 105, 116, 144; history of, 166; HIV-negative, 148, 160; HIV-positive, 147, 155, 158–59, 164; living with, 22, 26, 28, 30, 34, 105, 144–50, 152–55, 158, 164–66; medicine for, 156, 158, 160; MSWs and, 171, 198; NGOs and, 152–53; as pandemic, 26; patients with, 31, 34, 43, 48, 102, 144, 146, 153, 159–62; potential vectors of, 113; research on, 135; transmission of, 33, 117, 172; treatment for, 101, 146, 150, 155–57; among TSWs, 30, 171. *See also* Acquired Immunodeficiency Syndrome
homonormativity, 10, 149, 199
homophobia, 11, 144, 169, 173, 199
homophobic families, patriarchy and, 18
homosexuality, 1, 9–10, 38
homowives, 3, 119
Hong Kong, 6, 10–11, 31–32, 40, 51, 56, 157
hormone therapy, 170
household registration system. *See hukou*
huayang-nanzi (flower-like men), 60
Hubei (China), 34
hukou (household registration system), 24, 103–4, 144; in cities, 115; heteronormativity and, 200; nonurban, 201; rural, 18, 145, 147–48, 155–56, 158, 162, 168, 200; urban, 28, 52, 145, 147–50, 156, 200–201
human immunodeficiency virus. *See* HIV

human rights, 22, 38, 104–5, 166, 171
human traffickers, 4, 19, 133
Hunan (China), 34
hypermasculinity, 62

iAround (app), 47
identity, 21. *See also* lesbian, gay, bisexual, transgender, and queer+ (LGBTQ+) identity
intersectionality, 10, 16, 26, 30, 60, 158
intimacy, through emotional labor, 127
intimate partner violence (IPV), 43; attacks of, 177, 178; domestic violence and, 3, 99–100, 118; female victims of, 172; financial exploitation, 179–80; heterosexual women married to gay men reporting, 103; hookups and, 130; in LGBTQ+ communities, 5; marital rape as, 100; physical abuse and, 19, 46, 120, 170; physical violence and, 100, 169, 171, 174; sexual assaults and, 37, 171, 174, 185–87; sexually aggressive, 124, 132; TSWs experiencing, 26, 28, 37, 167–69, 172–73; verbal assaults and, 171, 177–78
in vitro fertilization (IVF), 81, 92–96, 140
IPV. *See* intimate partner violence
IVF. *See* in vitro fertilization

Japan, 55, 57, 59–60, 66, 192
jiemei xiongdi zhiyuanzhe yizhan (Sister-Brother Voluntary Group), 115
Jilin (China), 34, 44, 49, 75
jingjiren (agency), 197
jishi (technicians), 3

karaoke, 14, 50
kinship systems, 23; LGBTQ+, 17; queer, 17, 114; values negotiated within, 79
Korea, 46, 55, 57, 59–60
Kuaishou (social media platform), 190, 192
kuer. *See* queers
Kuznetsova, Irina, 146–47

Laioning (China), 34, 44
lala. *See* lesbians
Lamivudine (HIV medicine), 158
laobaobei (old daddy), 70
laopo (wife), 70
laotie (loyal followers), 195
law enforcement, 3, 5, 42, 162. *See also* police
laws, Chinese, 107, 146, 171, 185; anti-LGBTQ+, 1; on divorce, 36, 89, 100, 118; men favored by, 89, 100
legal system, Chinese, 4, 99, 173, 185–86; advice on, 115; appeals to, 24; biases of, 2–3, 36; challenges with, 36; Chinese constitution and, 146; context for, 149; documents within, 133; framework of, 26, 185; heterosexual women married to gay men disadvantaged within, 112; legitimization of, 100; marginalization and, 187; protections from, 36; structures within, 104
lesbian, gay, bisexual, transgender, and queer+ (LGBTQ+): advocacy groups, 38; kinship systems, 17; nongovernmental organizations, 4, 35
lesbian, gay, bisexual, transgender, and queer+ (LGBTQ+) community, 3, 165, 187, 198–200; advocates supporting, 36; in China, 4–5, 9; discrimination against, 4, 31, 200; economic power of, 53; government decriminalizing, 2, 4; government marginalization of, 38, 147; groups within, 3, 184–85; heterosexual women married to gay men and, 22; IPV in, 5; issues within, 44; Mao targetting, 2; police interrogating, 36; queer community, 3, 15, 38, 56, 117, 147; stigma against, 31, 157; upper-middle-class, 11; during Zhou dynasty, 1. *See also* coming out; gay communities
lesbian, gay, bisexual, transgender, and queer+ (LGBTQ+) identity, 44–45, 96, 134, 147, 150; same-sex attraction and, 4,

88; same-sex eroticism and, 21; same-sex relationships and, 1–2, 5, 9, 11, 16, 19
lesbians (*lala*), 91–97, 158, 170, 198, 200; in gay communities, 16, 96; gays marrying, 79, 87, 95, 106; heterosexual women married to gay men and, 27; historical relationship between China and, 1–5; in marriages, 74, 76, 92, 96; MSWs marrying, 27, 35, 75, 77, 79, 91–97; rural to urban migration by, 18
LGBTQ+. *See* lesbian, gay, bisexual, transgender, and queer+ (LGBTQ+)
liposuction, and cosmetic surgery, 193
little boy slang (*xiaodi*), 3, 150
liubing (taking drugs), 140
liudong renkou (floating populations), 34
livestreaming, 28, 71, 189, 200; dancing during, 194–95; followers of, 190–91, 193–97; MSWs transitioning to, 192, 197, 198; programs on, 191; on Taobao, 96, 191, 193–96
livestreaming social media, 28, 71, 189–98, 200
"living dead," 23, 26, 113, 159, 165
London (England), 12
loveless marriage, 101, 104
low-quality (*lowsuzhi*), 149
loyal followers (*laotie*), 195
luodai (highest interest rate), 197
luxury, 12, 59–62, 71–72, 123, 140, 200–201

Malaysia, 63
maleness, urban standards of, 27, 54
male sex workers (MSWs), 97–102, 128–31, 134, 136–37, 189, 201; BDSM and, 58, 121, 132; coming out as, 152, 166; communities of, 21, 95; deaths of, 159; emotional labor by, 27, 72; female clients of, 120–22; fitness emphasized by, 33, 56–57; government marginalizing, 19, 144–45, 152, 164; heterosexual women married to gay men of, 10, 25–26, 32, 35; HIV and, 171, 198; industry entered by, 49, 60; lesbians married to, 27, 35, 75, 77, 79, 92; livestreaming transitioned to by, 192, 197, 198; migrants as, 18–21, 27, 34, 47, 53; necropolitics and, 10, 25–26; NGOs helping, 47, 61, 69; parents influencing, 83–84, 87–91; physical appearance optimized by, 193; police beating, 5; pricing of, 41; romantic attachments of, 133; rural, 61, 149, 155, 166; sexual identities of, 29–30; social death of, 199; sociologists focusing on, 3; stigma toward, 153, 158; in Tianjin, 31–32, 34, 85, 125, 128, 195; top, 126; urban, 147
mamasan (pimp), 13–14, 49, 75, 139, 141, 189
Mao Zedong, 1–6, 8, 78, 81, 153
marginalized citizens, 147, 155–58
marriage: contract, 75; dead-end, 126, 137; failed, 104; fraud, 104–5, 116, 201–2; gay, 93, 114; heterosexual, 17, 31, 75, 114; lesbians in, 74, 76, 92, 96; loveless, 101, 104; negotiating expectations, 83; nominal, 40, 43, 75, 77, 92, 93, 199; patrilineal, 87; pragmatic, 97; re-, 100; sham, 27, 104, 115, 117. *See also* heterosexual women married to gay men
marriage certificate, false, 96
marriage law, 26–27, 99, 107–8, 113, 118
marriage of convenience, 74–75, 85, 114–16; *lala* marriage to MSM, 91–97; for LGBTQ+, 198–201; for MSM, 27, 43, 74, 77–80; *tongqi* and, 103–6
masculinity, 71, 97, 198–99; bishonen, 57; in gay communities, 54; hegemonic, 16, 53, 62, 133, 154, 172; heterosexual, 79; hyper-, 62; metrosexuals performing, 66, 131; of queers, 24, 53–54; reclaiming, 66; rural, 79, 201; self-worth and, 52; soft, 25, 27, 54, 57, 60, 63; state-sanctioned notions of, 154; traditional *seonbi*, 57; urban, 52, 60; *wen*, 57; *wen-wu*, 60
Massachusetts, 170

228 | INDEX

masseuse, 47, 125
matrimonial agencies, 75
Mbembe, Achille, 9, 22, 115, 158, 164, 199
medical doctors, 70, 95, 159–64
medical transitioning, 37
mental illness, TSWs and, 184
men who have sex with men (MSMs), 153, 165; *lala* marriage to, 91–97; marriage of convenience and, 27, 43, 74, 77–80
methamphetamine (drug), 151
metrosexuals, 57, 60; masculinity performed by, 66, 131; metropolitan 25, 54–56, 62, 70
mianzi (face), 81–83, 84, 85, 151
middle class, 71
migrant journeys, 71, 201
migrants, 149–50, 164–65, 172, 191–92; affective labor by, 28, 54; in gay communities, 18, 199; gay rural, 200–201; literature focusing on female, 53; as MSWs, 18–21, 27, 34, 47, 53; sex work turned to by, 18, 24, 54; social death of, 146. *See also* rural migrants
migrant workers, 44, 115, 149
misgendering, 5, 17, 118
model citizens, in cities, 11
Momo (app), 47
money boy, 103, 124, 150
Mongolia, 34
MSMs. *See* men who have sex with men

naked yoga, 62–66
National Bureau of Statistics of China, 44
National People's Congress (NPC), 114
necropolitics, 9, 24, 114–15, 143; biopolitics and, 149, 165, 198–99; brutality of, 165; conditions of, 116, 149, 165, 199; discussion of, 147; environment and, 165; household registration system and, 148; 'living dead' and, 23, 26, 113, 159, 165; mechanisms of, 164; MSWs and, 10, 25–26; power of, 23, 27, 145, 148, 154, 158, 165; queers impacted by, 22–23, 103–4; queer studies and, 19–24; sexscapes and, 28; stigma and, 145
necropolitics of social death, 25–28, 104–5, 112, 155, 165–66; conceptualizing, 1–5, 19, 28; MSW and *tongqi* struggles in, 10, 25; overcoming, 64, 116; political rights and, 165–66; state-sanctioned stigma and, 145–48; stigma and marginalization in, 22, 198–99
neoliberalism, 16, 20–21, 24, 77–80, 149
"new Chinese self," 21
NGOs. *See* nongovernmental organizations
nominal marriage (*xinghun*), 40, 43, 75, 77, 92, 93. *See also* marriage of convenience
nonbinary gender identity, 4, 16, 169–71, 173, 186
nonconforming sexuality, 198
non-conformity, 3, 78
nongovernmental organizations (NGOs), 30, 34–37, 159, 161–66, 183, 187; directors of, 145; gay communities helped by, 33, 44; government-owned, 31–32; heterosexual women married to gay men approaching, 115; HIV and, 152–53; LGBTQ+, 4, 35; MSWs helped by, 47, 61, 69; transgender, 37, 183
non-heteronormative sexuality, 2
nonnormative sexuality, 7
nonurban *hukou*, 201

old daddy (*laobaobei*), 70
one-child policy, 85, 103–4
online sales industry, emotional labor and, 189

paida (big-dick), 69
Pakistan, 137
parental pressure, 80–83

parents: coming out to, 66, 76, 86, 88, 105, 143, 151; face of, 82; MSWs influenced by, 83–84, 87–91. *See also* filial piety
Paris, 12
patriarchy, 16, 87, 98, 140, 172; in communities, 17; homophobic families and, 18; norms of, 135; power structure of, 172; rules and, 97; in rural areas, 84–85, 99; tradition and, 99
patrilineal marriage, 87
People's Republic of China (PRC) (China), 29; contemporary, 19, 25–26; historical relationship between gays,, lesbians, and, 1–5; LGBTQ+ communities in, 4–5, 9; mainland, 2, 11, 17, 32, 77; National Bureau of Statistics of, 44; post-reform, 15, 31, 55, 61, 72, 75–79, 199; present-day, 2–3; SAPPRFT of, 184; sex work in, 2; urban, 18, 25, 34, 52–53, 60, 145, 149, 153, 156, 164–65, 200. *See also* cities; government; health-care system; *hukou*; laws, Chinese; legal system, Chinese
PEP. *See* post-exposure prophylaxis
performative marriage, 199
Phnom Penh (Cambodia), 93
photo elicitation, 42
photoshop, 62
physical abuse, IPV and, 19
pimp (*mamasan*), 13–14, 49, 75, 139, 141, 189
pingya (cheap male prostitute), 178
pink-pound, 53
plastic surgery, 55, 62, 73, 128, 197
pleasure, sex work and, 20
police: advocates questioned by, 38; gangs and, 193; LGBTQ+ community interrogated by, 36; MSWs beaten by, 5; sex work and, 121
post-exposure prophylaxis (PEP), 156–57, 159–61

post-reform China, 15, 31, 55, 61, 72, 75–79, 199; contemporary China, 19, 25–26; present-day China, 2–3
Prada, 123
pragmatic marriage, 97
PRC. *See* People's Republic of China
precarious citizens, 166
pre-exposure prophylaxis (PrEP), 145, 148, 154
pregnancy, unwanted, 141
prostitution, 2, 49–50, 70, 122
public health, and high-risk behaviors, 22
purchase of sex, 119–24, 134–36
Putonghua (language), 29, 43

qipao (dress), 176
QQ (app), 30, 38, 47, 110, 115
quality (*suzhi*), 24, 76
queer community, 3, 15, 38, 56, 117, 147
queer criminology, 28, 171–73, 185–86; stalking and extortion, 181–82. *See also* intimate partner violence
queer identity, 15, 19–20, 79, 201
queer kinship systems, 17, 114
queer men, 17, 71, 115, 138
queer movements, 38
queerness, 15–17, 21, 23
queers (*kuer*), 78–80, 93–98, 144, 155, 164–65; in LGBTQ+ communities, 3; masculinity of, 24, 53–54; necropolitics impacting, 22–23, 104–5; sex work decoupled from, 4
queer sexuality, 2
queer studies, 4, 16, 105; criminology and, 28, 171, 173, 185–86; necropolitics and, 19–24; research within, 17; Sinophone studies and, 15, 17, 78; theories within, 5, 15–19

The Rainbow Families Xinghun Mutual Help Friendship Douban Group (*Caihong Jiayuan Xinghun Huzhu Jiaoyou Douban Xiaozu*), 93

rhinoplasty, 122, 193
Rofel, Lisa, 20, 80
roleplay, 56, 138
Round, John, 146–47
rural *hukou*, 18, 145, 147–48, 155–56, 158, 162, 168, 200
rural migrants: cosmopolitanism emulated by, 24; destigmatizing gay, 200–201; patriarchy, 84–85, 99; rural to urban, 18, 27, 49, 54, 115, 149, 164

same-sex identity, Chinese, 20
SAPPRFT. *See* State Administration of Press, Publication, Radio, Film and Television
SARS virus, 157
sauna, 7, 30–32, 45–47, 50, 75, 119
Scambler, Graham, 148, 165
scum (*feiwu*), 152
search engines, 101–3, 122
second-class citizenship, 18, 149
self-help programs, 28, 64, 173, 187, 201–4
self-worth, masculinity and, 52
sex industry, 27, 49, 73, 131, 192–93; services offered by, 8, 37, 65, 69, 120–22, 127, 132, 135, 138; tourism and, 122; urban, 54, 56. *See also* commercial sex industry
sexscapes, 25, 28, 73, 121–22, 128, 171
sex trafficking, 2
sexual acts, 14
sexual appetite, 37, 135, 141
sexual assaults, on TSWs, 174
sexual behavior, 19, 30
sexual desires, 27, 78
sexual fulfillment, 37
sexual harassment, 185
sexual identities, of MSWs, 29–30
sexuality: female, 135; nonconforming, 198; non-heteronormative, 2; nonnormative, 7. *See also* lesbian, gay, bisexual, transgender, and queer+ (LGBTQ+); lesbians (*lala*); queers
sexually transmitted diseases (STD), 3, 18, 33, 50, 73, 103, 141, 201

sexually transmitted infections (STIs), 116, 171
sexual minorities, 18
sexual needs, 119, 134
sexual norms, 20, 79
sexual orientation, 22, 36, 104–5, 117–18, 155, 202–3
sexual pleasure, 27, 120, 138
sexual practices, 4, 17
sexual preferences, 30
sexual satisfaction, 140
sexual stamina, 33
sexual thrills, 27, 131, 141
sex work, 29–30, 125–26, 141–43, 148–50, 189–91, 200–201; as brief career, 28; in China, 2; drug addiction in connection with, 28; economic mobility enabled through, 72; emotional labor and, 71; migrants turning to, 18, 24, 54; pleasure and, 20; police and, 121; queers decoupled from, 4; regulations and penalties against, 41. *See also* clients; male sex workers; transgender sex workers
sex workers, gay, 2–3, 15, 66, 99, 144, 200
sham marriage, 27, 104, 115, 117
Shandong (China), 34, 84, 143
Shanghai, (China), 2, 66, 95, 123, 191, 193–94
shemale, 174, 179
Shenyang (Liaoning, China), 50, 108
Shi, Wei, 115, 149
shoumianzhen (face-slimming needle), 59, 193
Sina (Internet platform), 184–85
Sinophone, 15, 17
Sister-Brother Voluntary Group (*jiemei xiongdi zhiyuanzhe yizhan*), 115
sisterhood, 167–88
social death: of migrants, 146; of MSWs, 199. *See also* necropolitics of social death
social harmony, 201
social media: apps, 37, 63, 115, 169, 181, 196; government cracking down on

gay-friendly, 9; livestreaming, 28, 71, 189–98, 200; platforms, 53, 71, 103, 115, 181, 185, 189–92, 196; posts, 163; TikTok, 38, 181, 190–92; WeChat, 63, 115, 169, 181, 190–92, 196
social networks, 181–84
sociologists, MSWs focused on by, 3
soft masculinity, 25, 27, 54, 57, 60, 63
speed-dating forum, 75
stalking and extortion, 181–82
State Administration of Press, Publication, Radio, Film and Television (SAPPRFT), 184
stigma, 109, 116, 185, 199–201; collective, 9; disapproval and, 20; discrimination and, 31, 150; against divorce, 106, 111; effects of, 185; eliminating, 173; toward gay communities, 10, 26, 117, 146; gender identity and, 184; government and, 152, 158; against heterosexual women married to gay men, 104; against homosexuality, 38, 117, 198; internal, 148; against LGBTQ+ community, 31, 157; toward MSWs, 153, 158; multilayered, 144, 147, 150; necropolitics and, 145; pervasive, 164; professional, 169; social and societal, 2, 27, 30, 36, 105; tragedy and, 92
STIs. *See* sexually transmitted infections
street smarts, 192–93
sugar boy, 70, 125–28
sugar daddy, 41, 51, 58–59, 65–66, 123–24, 127–29
sugar momma, 136
Supreme People's Court (China), 99
surgery: aesthetic, 60–61; gender affirmation, 170; gender reassignment breast, 193; plastic, 55, 62, 73, 128, 197; transgender, 46–47. *See also* cosmetic surgery
suzhi (quality), 24, 76
sweetheart (*tianxin*), 136

taking drugs (*liubing*), 140
Taobao (online platform), 96, 191, 193–96
technicians (*jishi*), 3
Tianjin (China), 70, 194; architecture in, 12; gay bars in, 6–11, 31, 44–46, 95; MSWs in, 31–32, 34, 85, 125, 128, 195; transgender NGOs in, 37; TSWs in, 183
Tianjin Brokeback Mountain (*Tianjin Duanbeishan*), 45
tianxin (sweetheart), 136
Tianya (online forum), 74, 102
Tibet, 176
TikTok (social media platform), 38, 181, 190–92
tongqi. *See* heterosexual women married to gay men
Tongqi huyuan gongzuoshi (China Wives of Gay Men Mutual Aid Studio), 115
tongqiqun (tongqi group), 115
Tophot (livestreamer incubator), 193
tourism, sex industry and, 122
transgender communities, 178, 184
transgender issues, 77
transgender nongovernmental organizations, 37, 183
transgender people, 177–78, 181, 183, 186, 188, 198; struggle faced by, 118, 170; transphobia against, 169, 173; violence against, 172. *See also* transgender sex workers
transgender population, 171
transgender rights, 185
transgender sex workers (TSWs), 22, 37–38, 67; community of, 183; emotional support for, 172; experiences, 182, 188; freelance, 167; HIV among, 30, 171; IPV experienced by, 26, 28, 167–69, 172–73; mental illness and, 184; as precarious, 169; sexual assaults on, 174; sisterhood, 167–88; support and affirmation of, 183; in Tianjin, 183
transgender surgery, 46–47, 177
transphobia, 169, 173
trauma, 165, 173, 186, 188

Triumeq (antiretroviral drug), 155
TSWs. *See* transgender sex workers
tuoyouping (children who follow mother into re-marriage), 100
Turkey, 173
tycoon, 58, 120, 134, 136

unisex public washrooms, 194
United States, 63, 104, 148, 156–57, 173, 186
unwanted pregnancy, 141
urban areas, 5, 18, 201
urban attitudes and perceptions, 25, 53
urban gay consumers, 52
urban gay elites, 10–11
urban *hukou*, 28, 52, 145, 147–50, 156, 200–201
urban imaginaries, 201
urban lifestyle, 24, 55, 195
urban man with beauty (*dushili nan*), 60
urban queers, 54, 71, 73, 79
urban sex industry, 54, 56, 201
urban standards of maleness, 27, 54
urban *versus* rural binary, 24

vaccines, 146
vaginoplasty, 174, 177
values, Chinese, 7, 21, 31, 88, 97, 117
values, kinship systems negotiating, 79
Viagra pill (*waige*), 110, 141

waige (Viagra pill), 110, 141
Ward, Jane, 4, 17
webcam models, 20

WeChat (social media app), 63, 115, 169, 181, 190–92, 196
wedding, Chinese, 101
Weibo (social media platform), 103, 115, 181, 185, 190–92
Weidian (online shopping platform), 190, 192
wen masculinity, 57
Western countries, gay communities in, 53
Westernization, 2
whitening facial creams, 59
wife (*laopo*), 70
working-class man (*dagongzai*), 34, 55
workplace discrimination, in commercial sex industry, 186
Wuhan (Hubei, China), 162

xiaodi (little boy slang), 3, 150
Xiaohongshu (social media platform), 190, 192
Xi Jinping, 9, 16
xinghun (nominal marriage), 40, 43, 75, 77, 92, 93
Xinjiang (China), 176

Yunnan (China), 151
Zhejiang (China), 47, 58, 124
Zhihu (app), 102
Zhongguo Xingshi Hunyin Wang (Chinagayles.com), 77, 93
Zhou dynasty, LGBTQ+ communities during, 1
zidovudine, 158

ABOUT THE AUTHOR

EILEEN YUK-HA TSANG is Associate Professor in the Department of Social and Behavioural Sciences at the City University of Hong Kong. She is the author of several books about China, including *China's Commercial Sexscapes: Rethinking Intimacy, Masculinity, and Criminal Justice* (University of Toronto Press, 2019) and *Blending East and West: Understanding the Changing Chinese Society* (McGraw Hill, 2012). She received her PhD in sociology from the University of Birmingham.

Printed in the United States
by Baker & Taylor Publisher Services